Concentrations of some Commercially available Acids and Alkalies

	%	s.g.	Normality
HCl	25	1·127	7·7
	36–38	1·18	12
HNO_3	65	1·40	14
	70	1·42	16
	96	1·50	23
	100	1·52	24
H_2SO_4	25	1·36	6
	96–98	1·84	36
H_3PO_4	88–90	1·75	
	99	1·88	
NH_4OH	25	0·91	13·4
	30	0·896	16
	35	0·88	19·5

Solubility Products

	18°C	25°C	100°C
AgCl	1×10^{-11}	2×10^{-11}	$2·1 \times 10^{-11}$
$BaCO_3$	2×10^{-9}	8×10^{-9}	
$BaSO_4$	$0·9 \times 10^{-10}$	1×10^{-10}	$2·6 \times 10^{-10}$
$CaCO_3$	1×10^{-8}	6×10^{-8}	
CdS	5×10^{-29}		
FeS	$2·5 \times 10^{-19}$		
$PbSO_4$	1×10^{-8}		
ZnS		10^{-24}	

METHODS FOR CHEMICAL ANALYSIS
OF FRESH WATERS

Though this be madness, yet there is method in't.

Hamlet, II, ii (211)

IBP HANDBOOK No 8

Methods for Chemical Analysis of Fresh Waters

edited by

H. L. GOLTERMAN
Limnological Institute
Nieuwersluis
Netherlands

with the assistance of

R. S. CLYMO
Westfield College
London, N.W.3

Revised Third Printing

INTERNATIONAL BIOLOGICAL PROGRAMME
7 MARYLEBONE ROAD, LONDON NW1

BLACKWELL SCIENTIFIC PUBLICATIONS
OXFORD AND EDINBURGH

ISBN 0 632 05540 5

FIRST PUBLISHED 1969
REPRINTED 1970
REPRINTED 1971

Distributed in the U.S.A. by
F. A. DAVIS COMPANY, 1915 ARCH STREET,
PHILADELPHIA, PENNSYLVANIA

Printed and bound in Great Britain by
BELL AND BAIN LTD
GLASGOW

CONTENTS

FOREWORD

The International Biological Programme is a worldwide plan of co-ordinated research concerned with 'the biological basis of productivity and human welfare'. The handbook series of IBP is for volumes which are urgently needed by biologists around the world who are participating in the programme. Most of these handbooks, expected to number about a score when the series is complete, deal with methodology, and their purpose is to recommend the use of research methods which will give intercomparable results from any part of the world. Such methods are 'recommended' not 'standardised' or 'agreed', because the kind of science with which IBP is concerned includes many growing points, and methodology is evolving rapidly. The last thing that IBP would wish to do is, by standardisation, to discourage this process.

As concerns inland water ecosystems, the responsibility of section PF (Production Freshwater in IBP parlance), this is the second of four handbooks. It deals with the chemical ingredients which make biological production possible. Two others, which are still in preparation, are concerned with primary and secondary production respectively, and one, concerned with fish production, is already published (IBP Handbook no. 3, edited by W. E. Ricker).

For chemical methods, as with all other subjects in IBP for which handbooks have been found necessary, there was an international technical meeting; it was held in the Netherlands, Amsterdam and Nieuwersluis, from the 10th to the 16th October, 1966. About 50 scientists from 15 countries, reviewed the large existing literature on water analysis and the newest approaches to this rapidly growing and difficult field. The general results of this meeting and some of the papers contributed have been recorded in a handsome volume published in 1967 by the Royal Netherlands Academy of Sciences, under the title "Chemical Environment in the Aquatic Habitat, Proceedings of an IBP symposium held in Amsterdam and Nieuwersluis 10–16 October, 1966".

The subsequent critical assembly of recommended methods was a difficult and time consuming task. It involved problems of presentation rather different from other handbooks and, consequently, this volume in the series has a different format from its predecessors. The reason is that critical chemical methods generally have to be undertaken on the laboratory bench where it is desirable to have a substantial amount of description or data on each page, while for field work a pocket-sized book is more convenient.

Compared with section PF, the sister section of IBP which deals with marine ecosystems—section PM (Production Marine) is better provided with manuals on chemical methods. However, for the intermediate class of waters, which include estuaries and brackish lagoons, it is often more convenient to adapt methods which were originally devised for fresh water than sea water. Accordingly, at the request of section PM, there is an annex to this volume which has been prepared by Professor J. E. G. Raymont of Southampton University.

Our thanks must go to Dr. H. L. Golterman, Director of Hydrobiologisch Instituut, Nieuwersluis, and Dr. R. S. Clymo of Westfield College, London N.W.3. who devoted a great deal of their time to the final shaping of this volume. We thank

also a number of Dutch scientists, who extended hospitality to their foreign colla-
borators at the technical meeting, and the generous financial help and scientific
support given by the Royal Netherlands Academy of Sciences and the Organization
Z.W.O. (Nederlandse Organisatie voor Zuiver-Wetenschappelijk Onderzoek) is
likewise greatly appreciated.

E. B. WORTHINGTON
IBP Central Office,
7 Marylebone Road,
London, N.W.1.

September, 1968

POSTSCRIPT

The first printing of this book was sold out in little more than a year, which shows
that it filled a serious gap in the scientific literature. In this revised printing the book
has not been extensively revised but has been corrected in various respects.

Two other IBP handbooks on freshwater productivity which were mentioned in
the Foreword to the first printing have now been issued, one on fish production
(IBP Handbook No. 3, edited by W. E. Ricker) and one on primary production
(IBP Handbook No. 12, edited by R. A. Vollenweider). Another on secondary
production, edited by W. T. Edmondson, is now nearing completion, and a further
handbook on microbial production is in preparation.

The first printing contained an appendix of 9 pages entitled *A Preliminary
Report on Chemical Methods in Brackish Waters*, by J. E. G. Raymont. With the
aid of reprints of that appendix, Section PM (Productivity Marine) of IBP is
developing the problems of brackish waters. The appendix has therefore been
omitted from this revised printing.

February, 1970   E. B. WORTHINGTON

PREFACE

This manual is based on discussions during the IBP Technical Meeting *Chemical Environment in the Aquatic Habitat,* held in Amsterdam and Nieuwersluis, 10–16 October 1966. The participants are named on pp. 163–4. Methods of analysis for groups of compounds were considered by working groups, and the edited reports of the chairmen of these groups form the basis of the manual. The extent of changes made, for the sake of a unified style, varied considerably from one report to another. Responsibility for the final form is the editor's. The reports were written by:

N.J.Nicolson—Conductivity

C.S.Yentsch—pH, Redox-potential, Pigments

A.Rebsdorf—Alkalinity

C.J.Hogendijk—Ca^{2+}, Mg^{2+}, Na^+, K^+

J.Shapiro—Trace elements

S.Olsen

F.A.Armstrong $\Big\}$—Phosphorus

E.K.Duursma—Organic nitrogen, carbon and C.O.D.

H.A.C.Montgomery—Oxygen

A.F.Carlucci—Vitamins

J.E.Hobbie—B.O.D., Specific carbon compounds

D.Povoledo—Fluorescence

A.V.Holden—Chlorinated Hydrocarbons

Financial support for the Meeting was provided by the IBP and by the Netherlands Organization for Pure Scientific Research (ZWO).

The editor is grateful, for help with the manuscripts, to Mr D.J.Eagle, Dr J.R.Moed, Mrs J.C.Golterman and Mrs K.E.Clymo. He is also grateful to Mr H.van Tol, who drew the illustrations and particularly to Mrs G.H.Würtz for checking the references, and for her endless patience in preparing revised versions, final versions, revised final versions, and even ultimate versions of the manuscripts.

Finally the editor wishes to thank his wife, without whom the Technical Meeting would never have taken place.

During 1967 at a meeting in Paris of the IBP–PF committee the following resolution was moved:

'The IBP–PF committee having published a handbook on the chemistry of the aquatic environment recognizes the following difficulties which exist, arising from the suggestion to use the handbook in the work of the IBP:

(1) Some of the required urgent apparatus, literature and reagents are not available in many of the developing countries.

(2) It is essential that biologists without chemical training, but using chemical methods, must have a place for asking advice about chemical problems, or obtaining specific training in chemical methods.

(3) It is necessary that intercalibration is started in fresh water chemistry. This involves the checking of newly proposed methods, and comparing the results of already existing methods in different laboratories.

The IBP–PF committee proposes that the possibilities of establishing an international chemical centre should be explored, either by finding an international organization for support or by stimulating a national laboratory to accept responsibility as an international centre'.

The editor of this manual will try to fulfil this vacancy for the time being. Requests for advice and information may be sent to:
The Director of the Limnological Institute, Nieuwersluis, Netherlands and will, if necessary, be passed on to specialists.

The editor would be grateful for suggestions that may be of help for the production of a second edition.

Nieuwersluis. H.L.Golterman

PREFACE TO THE FIRST REPRINT

Some minor corrections and changes have been made to the original text. An additional method for chlorophyll has been added, and one of the methods for sulphate (§ 4.7.3) has been revised to make it simpler.

CHAPTER 1

INTRODUCTION

1.0 SCOPE AND LIMITATIONS OF THIS MANUAL

When separate workers or groups study a common scientific problem it seems to be desirable that they should use at least some methods in common, in order to allow direct comparisons of their results.

This manual of chemical methods is meant as a guide for research workers interested in those biological processes in fresh water, that lead, with inter-conversion of energy, to the production of organic material. The chemical environment is important for many of these processes and the methods in this manual may help to describe it. Interpretation of the results of chemical analyses is not considered here.

It is the editor's hope that sufficient detail and explanation have been included in the Manual to make at least the main part of it useful to those with little training in either chemistry or limnology. In particular chapter 9 contains mainly theoretical matter.

Many of the methods are intended for application only to filtered water. Some may also be used, with the modifications described, for particulate matter as well. A few (procedures § 7.5, § 7.6 and § 7.7) are intended for particulate matter only.

Further information about a number of the methods may be found in the Proceedings of the Symposium (Golterman and Clymo, 1967). A list of other works on chemistry and limnochemical methods is given in § 10.1 immediately preceding the bibliography § 10.2.

The methods given in this manual are not ideal, but the discussions during the Symposium seemed to show that those included here are amongst the best available at present. Whether or not to include a newly proposed method in this manual was often difficult to decide. As a rule, only those methods are included which have been tested in use, either by participants of the technical meeting or in limnological laboratories known to them.

The application of chemical methods of analysis to a system as delicately balanced as a sample of lake water, poses one main problem. The analyses are often made in a strongly acid or alkaline medium, which may change the state of the compound studied, especially if the original state is not the ionic state. The problem is serious in phosphate analysis, where easily hydrolysable compounds, colloids, or adsorbed phosphates, are converted to H_3PO_4 by the acid necessary for the determination. (See Olsen, 1967). The problem is less serious when titrating Cl^- with a silver containing titrant. The silver titration is, however, an example of a method which raises another problem. The method is normally considered specific, because we usually assume that interfering substances (for example I^-) are absent. The limno-chemist must be constantly aware that all methods of analysis may lead to such errors.

1

This manual, once more, is only a guide and the research worker must himself decide if this guide is suitable for his particular situation. The editor feels that there is a serious danger of the analyst assuming that, because a method appears in a manual, meaningful results will always be produced by following the directions in the manual.

There is a second danger. Methods are not ideal; improvements are necessary, and sometimes a completely new approach is desirable. The existence of a manual may counter such work, which remains important and necessary.

During the Symposium the problem of "availability" to algae of substances present in the water was discussed. There seems to be only one solution to the problem of the determination of this property; bioassay. The editor regrets that details of methods of bioassay will nevertheless not be found in this manual, though such methods will certainly become more important. Nor are details of methods included for substances (vitamins for example) which are normally present in very low concentration. For some bioassay procedures, however, references are given.

Many aquatic organisms, from algae to fish, produce substances that pass to the water and are capable of eliciting behavioural responses by other members of the same species or members of other species. This type of work can be done without complicated or expensive apparatus. An attack on such problems could pave the way for the elucidation of specific chemical control substances of profound economic value. (See Vallentyne, 1967).

The working conditions in limnological research vary from field work (some times in difficult and remote areas) to laboratory work in advanced institutions. Keeping this in mind this manual of methods is conceived on three levels of refinement of methods with differences in the necessary experience, exactitude and complexity of equipment or apparatus involved. Most determinations are therefore described—if possible—at three different levels, although the different levels are often variations on one theme.

1.1   LEVEL I

At Level I methods are described that can be used in the field or, more generally, in places where only primitive laboratory facilities are available. In the extreme case the limnologist arrives on foot at the lake with his laboratory in his rucksack. He can take with him some flasks, a calibrated pipette, some reagents, indicators and empty bottles. Until recent times he was interested mainly in such substances as oxygen, chloride, bicarbonate, and calcium, and he could determine these compounds with sufficient accuracy for his purposes. It may be in some cases, however, that the compounds he selected were dictated by the methods available rather than by the requirements of his problem.

In the study of productivity, however, other elements too are important. Amongst these are phosphorus, nitrogen and silicon, which are difficult to determine accurately. Titrimetric methods are usually unsuitable, and colorimetric methods are most often used.

Approximate results (accuracy perhaps $\pm$ 20%) can be obtained by matching the colour produced by the sample with the colour of two standard solutions, one of which is—by trial and error—of concentration just greater than the sample, and the other just less than the sample. Greater accuracy can be obtained by using comparators for this purpose—a well known instrument is the Lovibond comparator. This apparatus reduces the subjective element in the matching of colours, but still fits easily into the rucksack.

Still portable, but more cumbersome, is the battery operated colorimeter. A simple apparatus is made by Dr Lange (see § 10.3). The accuracy that can be obtained, is not, of course, equal to that obtainable with a spectrophotometer, but the instrument is nevertheless very useful for methods at level I.

Portable instruments are also available which enable measurements of pH and conductivity to be made in the field. These two measurements give some general idea of the type of water.

It should be remembered that interferences do occur in the level I methods— although the methods are usually simple. The danger is greater because level I methods are most often used on water samples of unknown character.

The results of all these field methods may lead to questions about the chemical changes during days or seasons. As soon as this happens the limnochemist realizes that he must now change to the methods of level II. The methods of level I are sufficient for a first crude description, but are inadequate for detailed chemical studies.

1.2 LEVEL II

At level II, methods are described that can be applied in a moderately well equipped laboratory. Most methods have as the final step a colorimetric or a volumetric determination. The user of the level II methods is supposed to have a basic know-ledge—both theoretical and practical— of analytic chemistry. In particular Beer's and Lambert's laws are supposed to be known. It is assumed that the user is able to carry out acid-base or $KMnO_4$ titrations with an accuracy of 0·2–0·3%.

Essential pieces of equipment are a colorimeter—or spectrophotometer— and a balance (accuracy $\pm$ 0·1 mg). A basic stock of borosilicate glassware is also essential. A detailed list of other apparatus is not given here because it depends largely on the substances to be estimated and the method to be used.

1.2.1 Use of colorimeters and spectrophotometers

A *colorimetric determination* involves matching of colours of solutions, although by the use of a calibration curve the two colours need not necessarily be compared directly. The colorimeter must be sufficiently sensitive to allow estimation of extinctions between 0·1 and about 0·65 to three significant figures. In this range the error is theoretically smallest (Kolthoff and Sandell, 1952). The colorimeter must have a stable zero and scale length. If $E = \infty$ is the extinction with no light reaching the photocell, and $E = 0·000$ is the extinction with the blank cell in position, then the stability must allow the sequence of readings: $E = \infty, E = 0·000$, E of sample, $E = 0·000$ and $E = \infty$ to be made without appreciable changes in zero or scale factor (i.e. in the points $E = \infty$ and $E = 0·000$). Spectrophotometers have a continuously adjustable wavelength. For most colorimetric methods a range from about 380 mμ to 750 or 800 mμ is suitable. The adjustment must be accurately reproducible and frequent standardization is essential. The wavelength at which the extinction is measured is often that of a peak (or the only peak) in the visible absorption spectrum. There is however no reason, in principle, why some other wavelength should not be used. This fact may be useful if the water contains natural coloured material which has a high extinction at the same wavelength as would usually be used for the analytic measurement.

It is desirable, in general, to use a part of the absorption spectrum in which the change of extinction with change of wavelength is small. If for some reason (as for example in some cases with the Si-determination) a part of the spectrum must be used where extinction changes rapidly with change of wavelength, then the reproducibility of wavelength selection in a spectrophotometer becomes very important. In such cases it may be preferable to use a colorimeter with a filter, because the wavelength characteristics of the filter depend mainly upon physical properties, whereas wavelength selection on a spectrophotometer is dependent on a mechanical linkage, and on the precision with which the wavelength adjustment can be read.

Use of a colorimeter in routine work has the additional advantage that operator errors, such as selecting a wavelength of 426 mμ instead of 462 mμ, are less likely.

The filters must be of narrow bandwidth, with good cut off properties. The extinction of light with a wavelength 15–25 mμ from that of maximum transmittance should not exceed 50% of the extinction at maximum transmittance.

The length of light path of optical cells (cuvettes) should, if possible, be such that the extinction of samples falls between 0·1 and 0·6. The statement "measure the extinction in suitable cells", which appears in many of the descriptions of methods, is intended to indicate that the cell path length should satisfy this criterion. Normally a set of 0·5 cm, 1 cm (or 2 cm), and 5 cm cells is sufficient. If two or more cells are used two types of error may be introduced. The first is due to unequal absorption of light by the glass of the cells. This will cause a constant difference in absorption between the cells, but is usually so small that it may be neglected. The second error is due to small differences in the dimensions of the cells, which affect the length of light path. These cause a constant difference in extinction, and may be corrected by introducing a cell constant, obtained by measuring the extinction of the same test solution in all cells. It is convenient to arrange that the cell with the lowest extinction contains the reagent blank, and to define all corrections as small positive numbers. The cell correction is then subtracted from the observed extinction. In many cases the cell corrections are relatively small and may be ignored.

1.2.2 'Blank' value for a colorimetric determination

It is essential to make at least one *reagent blank*. This is a sample of distilled water treated exactly as are the other samples. If the analysis is only performed occasionally, and not as a routine, it may be advisable to make at least two reagent blanks, since the information derived from them is used in the final calculation of all standard and sample extinction values. At least two reagent blanks should also be made if the extinction of the blank is known to be large compared to that of water, as is the case in determination of NH_3–N with Nessler's reagent.

If the reagent blank usually has a small extinction, relative to distilled water, a convenient procedure is to check that this extinction *is* small and then to make all other measurements relative to the reagent blank. Calculation of reagent blank corrections are thus avoided. If, however, the method is used infrequently, or the reagent blank has a large extinction relative to distilled water, it is preferable to measure all extinctions relative to a distilled water blank. Then calculate the mean reagent blank extinction and subtract this value from all other extinctions.

If the water sample itself, before treatment, absorbs light more strongly than distilled water at the wavelength at which extinction measurements are to be made, some error will be introduced in the final measurement. In many cases this absorbance is trivial compared with that due to the colour developed in the analytic reaction, and when high accuracy is not required the error can be ignored.

If the water sample does absorb appreciably in the spectral region to be measured (for example acid bog waters), or if high accuracy is required, two possible remedies may be tried.

First, it may be possible to destroy the natural colouring matter, without affecting the substance to be analysed (by heating with $(NH_4)_2S_2O_8$ for example).

Secondly, some form of correction may be made to the extinction measured after colour development. There is unfortunately no entirely satisfactory method of doing this. The simplest way is to measure the extinction of the untreated water sample, and subtract this value from the value after colour development, (after correction for the volume changes). In many cases however the added reagents alter the absorbance of the natural coloured compounds. Change of pH in particular frequently causes change in absorbance. A better correction may therefore be obtained by adding all reagents which affect the pH markedly, or, in difficult cases by using internal standards (see § 1.2.3).

The nearest to an ideal situation is that found in NO_2^- determination, where colour development depends on the order in which reagents are added. All reagents may therefore be added, but in a different order from that necessary to colour development.

1.2.3 Calibration of colorimetric methods

It is also essential—both at level I and II—to prepare *calibration curves using a range of standards* (containing known amounts of the substances to be analysed). If the analysis is made routinely, and the calibration curve is found to vary little from day to day, it may be sufficient to make a full calibration curve only infrequently. One or two check standards with each series of estimations may then be sufficient. Since the calibration information is used in every calculation, it is however unwise to skimp on standardization.

Calibration curves need not be linear, but it is much more convenient if they are, since results may then be calculated directly rather than by graphical comparison.

Two sorts of standards may be made. In both cases a known concentration (or known dilution from an arbitrary standard) of the substances to be analysed is treated in the same way as are the samples.

Ideally ALL *stages from the moment of sampling should be included*, but in many cases it may be established that the known amount of substances can be introduced just before the analytic reaction proper.

The first type of standard is made by dissolving the substance to be analysed in distilled water. This procedure may be suitable, but only if no residual interferences are present in the samples.

The second type of standard is made by dissolving the substance to be analysed in a sub-sample of the fresh water sample. This is referred to here as an *internal standard*. (This procedure is sometimes known as the method of standard addition. The name internal standard is sometimes used for a different procedure, particularly in flame photometry). In this case one expects, in the absence of interferences, to find that the concentration found from the extinction, in sample + standard is equal to the sum of the concentrations found in sample and standard when measured separately. If this expectation is not realised, then a series of internal standards must be made for each sample, and the results must be treated with caution, since there are in this case further possible difficulties if the internal standard curve is not linear. Only experience can teach the analyst if, when, and how often, this procedure is necessary.

In those cases where a series of samples are taken on different occasions from the same body of water and a calibration curve is made only infrequently, the standards should be made with the water sampled, and a separate calibration curve should be made for each body of water.

1.2.4 Volumetric determinations

For many *volumetric determinations* a good piston microburette is essential. It is preferable to have it attached to the reservoir of titrant, and with an automatic zero adjustment. Piston microburettes are commercially available with an accuracy of $\pm$ 0·001 ml of titrant. For precise work such accuracy is essential. As the concentrations of the compounds are often two or three orders of magnitude smaller than those familiar in classical analytical chemistry the addition of an indicator must often be avoided. Devices for electrometric end point determinations are therefore essential. A conductivity meter and pH meter of normal laboratory quality are suitable. For the pH determinations an accuracy of $\pm$ 0·02 pH units is usually sufficient, and allows one to perform acid-base titrations and all potentiometric determinations including "dead stop titrations" (see § 9.13). In many volumetric determinations, when the titrant is itself the primary standard, it is not necessary to use standard solutions of the substances to be determined, as the reactions involved are stoicheiometric. The use of standards is, however, useful for evaluating the techniques.

If more samples are entering the laboratory than can be analysed, the limnochemist should consider first, whether or not it is really necessary to analyse so many samples, and, if it is necessary, consider the possibilities of level III.

1.3 LEVEL III

1.3.1 Types of Level III methods

At this level two types of methods are described. First, methods are given for determinations which are not, at present, routine in most laboratories. These include specialized analyses for organic carbon and for some of the organic compounds. For these methods specialized equipment and considerable experience in, for example, microtechniques are necessary. Often it will take some time (from a few days to a few weeks) before the technique is mastered. Blanks and standards should be run, until the results are repeatable and blanks as low as the technique allows.

Secondly, methods are described which are essentially the same as those at level II, but with part of the analysis made by an automatic device. This can be either completely automatic or a semi-automatic titrator. As detailed instructions are always provided by the manufacturer, and advances in this field are rapid, this manual indicates only which methods can be automated and where published methods may be sought. A review of automatic methods is given by Lee (1967).

1.3.2 Limitations and scope of Level III methods

There are two generally accepted misunderstandings about automatic aids in analysis.

The first is that the chemist becomes redundant. Without proper chemical control automatic equipment will sooner or later begin to produce results of declining accuracy, while interferences in unknown water samples go unrecognised. The accuracy of properly functioning automatic equipment is generally the same as at level II, because the methods are generally the same. It may at best be greater because machines do not become tired, and have a smaller variability than human operators.

The second misunderstanding is that methods at level III are irrelevant to field work. It is quicker to make dissolved oxygen measurements with an oxygen electrode connected to a recorder (see § 8.1.3) than by Winkler titrations (see § 8.1.2). The increasing interest in this type of apparatus even in developing countries is encouraging.

1.3.3 Special problems of automatic devices
There are two main problems which arise with automatic devices.

The first is the cost of, and delay in, correction of faults. This may be particularly serious if no competent assistance is available in the laboratory, so that reliance has to be placed on the manufacturer or his agents.

The second problem is that it becomes all too easy to collect a mass of data, so that the reason for doing so is not considered. An automatic machine can easily become a Sorcerer's Apprentice; even worse the analyst may become a slave of the machine. These dangers are widely recognized, but perhaps too little considered.

1.3.4. Gas chromatography
In general an instrument is only described in this manual where there is a specific application of it. An exception must be made for gas-chromatography. In principle all volatile constituents can be determined with this instrument, and it is therefore potentially very important. At present commercially made models are of comparable expense to a good spectrophotometer.

The gases in the water sample (N_2, CO_2 and O_2, see § 8.3) are first removed from solution in a carrier gas. The gas sample is dried, and passed into the end of a long narrow column containing the stationary phase (a solid, or a non volatile liquid supported on an inert solid). Carrier gas is passed through the column. The sample gases become partitioned between moving and stationary phases to differing degrees, and therefore travel along the column at different rates. The gases are detected and amounts measured, as they emerge from the column.

Only small water samples (ca. 10 ml) are needed, and several gases may be determined on each sample.

Gas chromatography has furthermore been used for organic C and N compounds (Povoledo 1967) and for chlorinated hydrocarbons (see § 7.10). Detailed description of gas chromatography (and of many more of the methods outlined in this manual) will be found in Jones (1960).

1.4 NOTES COMMON TO ALL METHODS

1.4.1. Reagents and chemicals
In many cases the quantities, containers, times and temperatures specified in this manual are not critical. It is however advisable to check that any alteration in the methods has not destroyed their precision, accuracy or validity. In general the number of significant places quoted indicates the precision required. Thus 4 N means about 4 N (± 0.1), while 0·100 N means that a solution must be prepared as accurately as possible, i.e. with a precision better than 0·5 %. If a dilution to 100·0, 250, or 1000 ml is specified a volumetric flask should be used. If 0·25 or 1·0 litre or a concentration in per cent is specified a calibrated cylinder may be used.

In all cases *Mixing* must be done *carefully*.

Many of the reagents specified in the methods must be of high purity. For high purity the different makers use different names, such as "Proanalyse", "Analytical grade", "Analar", "Baker Analyzed" etc. In the manual these are described as "Analytical Reagent Grade", abbreviated to A.R. They must, if used as a standard, generally be dried at 105°C for 1 hour to remove traces of water. The fact that the composition of the impurities is known enables one to calculate how much of the compound to be analysed will be introduced in the blank. This degree of purity (and expense) is not always necessary. The cheaper "laboratory grade" or "purissimum" may often be suitable.

The most important reagent is H_2O. In this manual H_2O means distilled water collected in a container not releasing substances to the water. In some cases it is necessary to redistill the water, e.g. for the NH_3 determination. If a second distillation is carried out the purpose for which this H_2O is to be used must be considered. To remove the last traces of NH_3, for example, the second distillation is made after adding H_2SO_4 to the first distillate. The use of ion exchangers alone has often been reported but many of the organic compounds present in tapwater are not then removed. Ion exchangers may indeed add organic substances to the water.

An ion exchanger used before or after distillation may be an improvement, but is not always necessary. As there are so many makes of ion exchangers and the editor has heard of more and more difficulties caused by the organic material in the eluate no specific exchanger is recommended here.

In limnochemistry there is a second function for ion exchangers. In theory it is feasible to go to a lake with an anion exchanger in the right pocket and a cation exchanger in the left one and to return to the laboratory with cations and anions from a large volume of water separately concentrated. With suitable elution a 10 or 100 fold concentration is obtainable. As the absorption and elution will induce changes of the chemical state there are problems to be solved yet, but the idea is attractive, particularly for the phosphorus problem.

The editor does not dare to recommend this procedure yet but hopes to stimulate research in this direction.

It is useful to check the quality of the H_2O by measuring the conductance. If this increases in the course of time the distillation apparatus probably needs cleaning. The amount of organic substances is not usually indicated by conductivity measurements: a low conductance does not necessarily mean that there is little organic material in the water.

It is useful to have a stock of the following solutions: (Unless indicated otherwise "dilution" means dilute with H_2O).

HCl, 12 N
(i.e. s.g. = 1·18 or 37%).

HCl, 4 N
Dilute 12 N HCl (s.g. = 1·18) (0·33 litre → 1·0 litre).

HCl, 1 N
Dilute 4 N HCl (0·25 litre → 1 litre).

H_2SO_4, 36 N
(i.e. s.g. = 1·84 or 96–98%).

H_2SO_4, (1+1), about 20 N
Add 500 ml of H_2SO_4 (A.R., s.g. 1·84) cautiously, with stirring, and slowly, to 500 ml of H_2O.

Warning: Never add H_2O to H_2SO_4

H₂SO₄, 4 N
Dilute 20 N H_2SO_4 (0·2 litre → 1 litre).

HCl or H₂SO₄, 0·100 N
Standardize against 0·100 N NaOH.

NaOH, 10 N
Dissolve 400 g of NaOH in 500 ml of H_2O and dilute to 1 litre.

NaOH, 0·100 N
Standardize against oxalic acid.

Oxalic acid, 0·100 N
Dissolve 6·300 g of $(COOH)_2.2H_2O$ in H_2O and dilute to 1000 ml (small crystals of the hydrate are stable between 5% and 95% relative humidity). This solution remains usable for months if kept in a refrigerator, and is the ideal primary standard for both acid-base and oxidimetric titrations.

K₂Cr₂O₇, 0·100 N
Dissolve 4·903 g of $K_2Cr_2O_7$ (A.R., dry for 2 hours at 105°C) in H_2O and dilute to 1000 ml.

Na₂ EDTA, 0·100 M
Dissolve 37·22 g of Na_2EDTA (A.R., dried at 80° C) in H_2O and dilute to 1000 ml. (The H_2O should contain no polyvalent cations; use either freshly distilled H_2O, or H_2O stored in polythene or borosilicate glass containers.)

The use of commercially available standardized solutions is strongly recommended, as the saving in time is considerable. Some independent check must, of course, be kept.

1.4.2 Expression of results
The *results of an analysis* are perhaps best expressed in meq/l if the compound analysed contributes significantly to the ionic balance. In the other cases mg/l or —to avoid too many zeros—μg/l are more commonly used.

The concentrations refer to the elements concerned but, if confusion is possible, an indication of their compounds or fractions is also given. For example, 10 μg/l of PO_4–P means 10 μg of phosphorus is present as o-phosphate per litre of sample. 10 μg/l of NO_2–N means 10 μg of nitrogen is present as nitrite per litre of sample.

Supposing that all major ions have been determined, the calculation of an ionic balance (see 4.10), followed by comparison of the conductance calculated from this balance with the observed conductance gives a good check of the overall accuracy obtained.

1.4.3. Glassware
Clean all glassware with hot chromic acid (dissolve 100 g of $K_2Cr_2O_7$ in 1 litre of H_2O and add 1 litre of H_2SO_4) or allow it to stand overnight. Rinse carefully with H_2O.

1.4.4. Accuracy, precision and sensitivity
The terms accuracy, precision and sensitivity are defined here. The terms are used with the same meaning in the rest of manual.

There is no general agreement about the definition of these terms. Precision is a measure of the dispersion about the mean of many (at least 10) samples. The smaller the dispersion, the greater the precision. A small dispersion (for example 2%) should strictly be reported as a precision of 98%, but the almost universal usage is to report, precision 2%.

The accuracy is the difference between the mean from the samples and the true value. As with precision, the common use is to call a small numerical value of accuracy a "high" accuracy. Accuracy is a measure of the bias of the method. It is important to realize that high precision may be combined with low accuracy, just as in rifle shooting it is possible to get close grouping of shots but some way from the centre of the target.

The most useful definitions of dispersion are those involving the standard deviation (or the standard error of the mean), because a lot is known about the mathematical properties of these quantities. Limnologists have not, however, generally felt much need for statistical aids in chemical work, because the dispersion of chemical methods is usually only a few percent of the mean values. A statistical text should be consulted for further information if need be.

For some of the methods in this manual, the precision is shown as a standard deviation for about 10 samples. For others the figure given is a much more vague quantity; half the maximum deviation from the mean commonly observed in a group of 10 samples. It is probably rather greater than the standard deviation.

In all cases the quoted precision for a method should be taken only as a rough guide.

The dispersion of estimates may vary with mean value, and usually varies with time (due to correlated changes in personal and physical factors). The analyst should therefore determine the standard deviation for a particular method in the conditions in which it will be used.

If the dispersion of measurements is small, it may be possible to improve accuracy by direct calibration with known amounts of the substance to be determined. In most volumetric determinations precision is determined by the precision of end point detection.

The sensitivity is defined here as the lowest concentration that gives a value three times the value of the blank. The useful range of application for the colorimetric determinations extends from an extinction of 0·1 (using 5 cm cells) up to an extinction of 0·6 (using an 0·5 cm cell). If a calibration curve is straight up to a certain concentration, and becomes nonlinear beyond, this concentration will often be the upper limit of the useful range. The upper limit will in most cases set no serious problems as the sample can always be diluted beforehand. (For an exception see the Si-determination). One of the factors setting the lower limit to the range of application in a volumetric determination is the volume of titrant that can be determined with a precision of 1–2%, and depends therefore on the burette used. With piston microburettes as little as 0·1 ml can be determined with this accuracy. The other factor affecting the lower limit is the degree to which the solution can be diluted. This is generally 0·01–0·02 N, but in some cases 0·001 N can be used.

In some methods the range of application is indicated; in other cases it is the same as the range of the calibration curve and indicated as such.

1.5 TIME AND PLACE OF SAMPLING

No manual can hope to give comprehensive directions about the place of sampling. If the aim is to characterize a lake as a whole then a single analysis may be sufficient, but a single *sample* will not often be so, unless the lake is known to be homogeneous.

Three or more samples from different places may give some indication whether the lake is homogeneous or not. If the lake stratifies the number of samples to be taken must be greater and will depend on the problem studied.

When the thermocline moves (either up- or downwards) depth and time of the sampling must be chosen with great care. If a lake shows a change of concentration of one or more compounds with depth a "mixed sample" may be compounded to represent the lake as a whole. The lake is then thought of as divided into layers, and a sample is taken in each layer. Aliquots of the samples are then mixed in proportion to the volume of the layers.

Even fewer directions can be given about the time and frequency of sampling. The frequency depends on the rapidity of the changes in the concentrations. The time of day must also be taken into account. During a sunny day the pH may rise —especially in poorly buffered waters—due to uptake of CO_2 by plants in the water, and the phosphorus concentration for example may decrease. It may be useful therefore to sample a given lake at a fixed time, preferably in the first half of the morning.

Time of sampling, temperature and weather conditions should always be noted.

CHAPTER 2

SAMPLE TAKING AND STORAGE

2.0 INTRODUCTORY

There are two main aspects to the problem of sampling. First, as it is usually impossible to analyse the whole of a body of water, samples are taken which are considered representative of the whole volume. When and where to sample in order to achieve this aim is considered briefly in § 1.5. The second aspect of sampling is the transfer of the water from the original place to another where the chemical analysis is to be made. In a few cases, for example measurement of O_2 concentration by an electrode system suspended over the side of a boat, the problems are minimal, because the water is never removed. In most cases however the sample must be collected, and then transferred to the laboratory in a container. With some exceptions, there will usually be less adsorption on, less diffusion through, or less contamination from, borosilicate glass than plastics or metal.

The aim must be to collect the sample from a known position, and to transfer it to the laboratory with a minimum of change in chemical composition. It is useless to make a highly accurate analysis of an inaccurately collected sample. The importance of this aspect of sampling is roughly inversely proportional to the concentration of the substance to be analysed; Na^+ and Ca^{2+} usually present few problems, Mo and vitamins far more. Changes in samples are mostly attributable to reaction on the surfaces of the container, or to metabolic activity, or to change of temperature. These changes may be minimized but no one method of sample treatment between collection and analysis is suitable for all analyses. The analyses to be made must therefore be known before the sample is collected. There follow general notes on this aspect of sampling. The methods for a particular compound should be consulted for any further specific sampling requirements.

Samplers and containers should always be cleaned carefully before use to avoid contamination of the samples.

2.1 SAMPLING DEVICES

Sampling disturbs any existing stratification. To reduce this error the apparatus must be as small as possible. Thus the Ruttner sampler (vide infra) is less suitable for temperature determination than the thermistor thermometer. The material of which the sampling container is made should be selected with the analyses which are to be made in mind. Three types of sampler are commonly used in limnology.

Ruttner and Kemmerer samplers
Both consist of a tube of 1–3 litres volume, with a hinged lid at each end of the tube. The tube is of polymethylmethacrylate (= Plexiglass = Perspex) in the Ruttner sampler, and of copper in the Kemmerer sampler. The two lids can be caused to

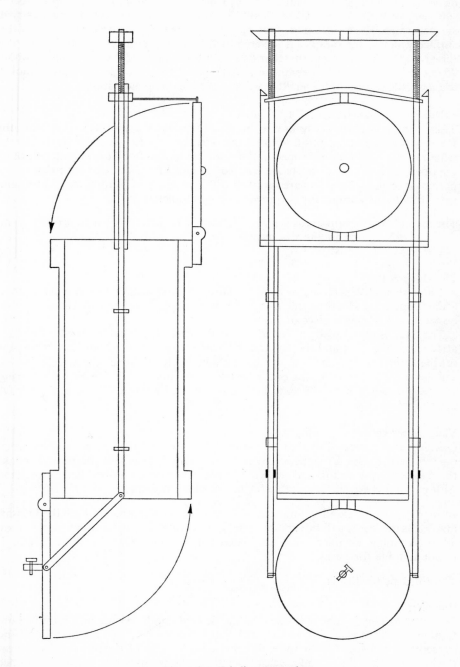

Figure 2.1. Friedinger sampler.

close by a messenger (a weight allowed to slide down the supporting cable). As the sampler, with the tube held vertically, is lowered into the lake it first fills with surface water. The positioning of the open lids prevents the complete removal of this surface water as the sampler is lowered further. If deeper layers are to be sampled the apparatus must be alternately raised and lowered a number of times by about 25 cm about the depth to be sampled. This is clearly undesirable, but these samplers are nevertheless useful for shallow waters that are completely mixed.

Friedinger sampler (see fig. 2.1)
This sampler is particularly useful for sampling deeper layers. It differs from the Ruttner sampler in the positioning of the open lids. These are held parallel to the length of the sampler when open and do not hinder the free flow of water through the open tube. All inside parts are completely metal free, and may be either transparent or opaque. Samplers are supplied with a capacity of $3\frac{1}{2}$ litres and 5 litres and with or without a frame for two reversing thermometers.

The second type of apparatus is a closed, gas filled, glass flask which is opened and subsequently closed in the desired position.
   The simplest one is:

The Dussart flask (see fig. 2.2)
A 1 litre glass flask is closed by a rubber stopper fitted with two narrow bore tubes, a short one (*a*) and a long one (*b*), joined by a single U-tube. This U-tube is connected to a cable by a piece of string.
   The flask is attached by a thread round the neck to the cable. A 1 kg weight is attached to the flask and the apparatus lowered to the desired position, where the sewing-thread is broken by a jerk on the cable. This removes the U-tube, which enables the water to enter the bottle by the longer tube, while the air (or nitrogen) escapes through the shorter one. This flask can be used to collect samples for O_2 determinations.

Valås water collector (see fig. 2.3)
Opening and closing of the bottles is effected by two successive jerks on the cable; the first jerk causes a magnetic device to open the bottle, and the second breaks the magnetic connection and seals the bottle. The bottle can be filled beforehand with gas and is especially suitable for bacteriological work.

In many cases the small volume (maximum 1 litre per sample) of both the Dussart and Valås devices is a disadvantage. The flasks cannot be used in water deeper than 40 m. A simple sampler using evacuated flasks is described by Watt (1966). It is not suitable for gases.

The third possibility is:

Pumping
A rubber or plastic tube is lowered to the desired depth. By use of a pump a continuous stream of water is obtained with which the sample flasks are first rinsed and subsequently filled. If O_2 is to be determined the outlet of the tube is placed near the bottom of the flasks and at least three times the volume of the flasks is pumped through. To ensure that a horizontal sample is taken two plates (diameter 10 cm)

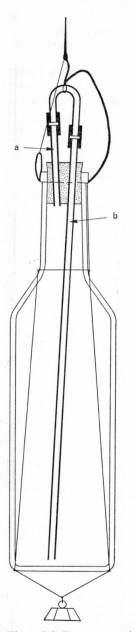

Figure 2.2. Dussart sampler.

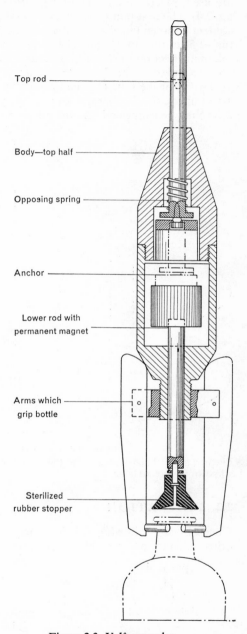

Top rod

Body—top half

Opposing spring

Anchor

Lower rod with
permanent magnet

Arms which
grip bottle

Sterilized
rubber stopper

Figure 2.3. Valås sampler.

are used, placed in a horizontal position a few centimeters above each other (see fig. 2.4). The best pumps are finger pumps or peristaltic pumps, in which there is no contact between metal and water and the pumping rate is constant. A simple device (fig. 2.5) is that of Damas (1954). The advantages of pumping are that it has a minimal effect on the stratification and that large samples may be obtained. Pumps are particularly suitable for taking a mixed "mean" sample from stratified layers as the end of the tube may be lowered by regular steps. If the layers to be sampled are of unequal volume, samples of varying volume must be collected. The collecting flask may be calibrated for this purpose in advance.

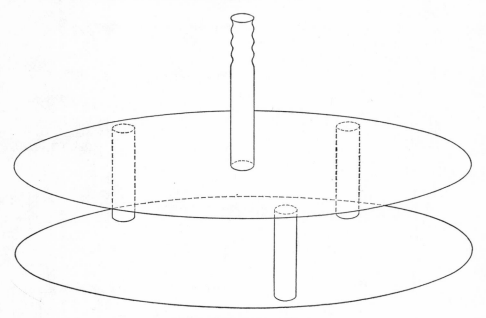

Figure 2.4. Lower end of tube of pump sampler.
The two parallel plates ensure that the stream of water in the tube is drawn predominantly from a known horizontal layer.

2.2 FILTRATION

Generally the following fractions may be recognized in a water sample (though other schemes are possible).

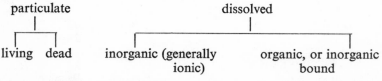

During storage, interconversion of fractions can occur, so that, although separation of all these fractions is in most cases difficult, an early step in storage should be the separation of particulate from dissolved matter. Except when gases, pH or the carbonate system are to be analysed, this may be done by filtration under pressure or vacuum through a membrane filter with $0.5\ \mu$ pores.

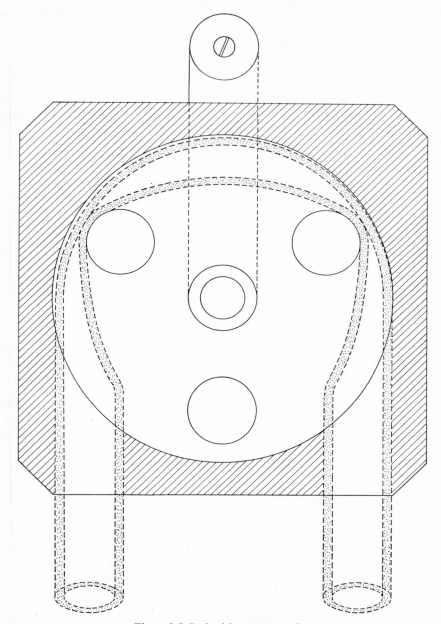

Figure 2.5. Peristaltic pump sampler.

C

The definition of particulate matter, in terms of size, must be arbitrary (see Olsen, 1967). The boundary at about 0.5μ is convenient, and it does seem to be generally agreed that this coincides approximately with a change in the character of the material. The rate of filtration is nearly always inversely proportional to the amount of sample which has passed through the filter, because particulate matter gradually blocks the pores. The area of the filter must be chosen so that a sufficient volume of sample may be filtered before the rate of filtration becomes very slow. Glass fibre filters give a greater filtration rate; the deposit is, however, more easily collected from membrane filters. Unfortunately the latter release a considerable quantity of N-, P-, and organic compounds to the filtrate. If the release of N- or P-compounds to the water by filters of the same batch is reproducible then a correction can be applied (equal to the amount found in an analysis of a filtered sample of H_2O equal in volume to that of the fresh water samples). In such cases filters should be washed before use with 250 ml of H_2O. This prewash should remove much of the contaminants, and thus reduce the size of the correction. Glass fibre filters can be heated to 500–600°C, or may be boiled in strong oxidising agents to remove organic carbon (see § 7.1). In batches of Whatman glass fibre filters we could detect considerable amounts of phosphate. Gelman filters proved to be nearly phosphate free. The porosity is 2–3μ. This is normally sufficient to remove algae, but not bacteria. Silver filters of different pore size (0.2–5.0μ) are now available (Flotronics). They are expensive and have not yet been much used.

If the laboratory cannot be reached quickly then filtration must be carried out in the field using a pressure filtration device and a bicycle pump or a small cylinder of compressed N_2.

The separation of living from dead particulate matter is much more difficult. For some water samples fractional centrifugation can be used, for example, if the dead particles are small humic complexes. Microscopic examination during the separation is then essential.

The separation between "inorganic" and "bound" dissolved substances can only be achieved during the analyses by chemical methods. (In most cases the "inorganic" fraction is estimated, and then the "bound" fraction found by difference from the total after wet oxidation. Details are discussed in the appropriate chapters, but the problem must be reconsidered for each body of water).

2.3 PRESERVATION

If the samples cannot be analysed within a few hours of filtration then some form of preservative treatment must be given to prevent, or at least minimize, changes in the sample. Zobell and Brown (1944) have studied the action of different preservatives on samples of marine waters; Åberg and Rodhe (1942) proposed 0.5% $CHCl_3$ or 0.5 ml bromine-water/100 ml sample as preservatives for fresh water samples.

Another method is to acidify with H_2SO_4 or HCl to pH = 1–2. This method has the advantage that it prevents precipitation of iron (and other metals), but the disadvantage that it may easily cause changes in the state of ions in solution.

A third method is to freeze the filtered samples in polyethylene bottles. These may then be stored for a long time. Before analysis the samples must be thawed completely and thoroughly mixed. Particular care must be taken if silicates are to be analysed (see § 5.9).

It is seldom enough to store only one sample; in most cases both an acid and a neutral sample must be stored. Borosilicate glass is preferable to plastic as many plastics adsorb phosphorus compounds and allow ammonia to escape.

2.4 SCHEME OF STORAGE

The following scheme of treatments is suggested.

Bottle	Determination	Sample volume	Sample container	Preservative
A	*O_2	100–125 ml	glass	if necessary, 0·5 ml Br_2 water (see Alsterberg modification) or carbonate (see Bruhn's modification)
B	carbonate-system (pH, rH, CO_2, HCO_3^-, CO_3^{2-}) SO_4^{2-}, Cl^-, NO_3^-, silicate	500 ml	glass or thick plastic; no contact with air, dark.	2·5 ml $CHCl_3$ (only for storage longer than 24 hours).
B/C	*Org.–P (dissolved) and PO_4–P	as for B, but if Fe precipitates; as C.	as for B, but if Fe precipitates; as C.	as for B, but if Fe precipitates; as C.
C	All other (Nitrogen system except NO_3^-, major and minor elements, organic C, total P).	500–1000 ml	glass	5 ml 4 N H_2SO_4

* See analysis section for other details.
For many compounds (e.g. vitamins, gases etc.) separate samples are necessary.

It is extremely important to clean the sampler and storage container, completely as extremely small concentrations must often be measured.

Detailed instructions about sampling and storage for specific compounds are to be found in the following paragraphs: 4.8.2, 5.4.1, 5.5.1, 5.7, 6.0.1, 7.1, 7.1.2, 7.3.

DETERMINATION OF CONDUCTIVITY, pH, REDOX POTENTIAL, ALKALINITY, TOTAL CO₂, AND ACIDITY

For theoretical considerations see chapter 9.

3.1 CONDUCTIVITY

Introduction

Specific conductance (= conductivity) is a measure of the ability of a conductor to convey an electric current. In the case of water it is related to the concentration of ions present and to the temperature at which the measurement is made. Specific conductance is the inverse of the specific resistance, and is generally reported as mho/cm. The conductivity of most fresh waters is so low that it is usual to report the results as micromho/cm (μmho/cm), or, loosely, as μmho.

Results are conventionally reported at 20° or at 25°C. Conductivity gives no indication of the nature of the substances in solution, but any increase or decrease in concentration will be reflected in a corresponding increase or decrease in conductivity.

Apparatus for the measurement of conductivity is sold by many makers. The instruments all consist of two distinct parts.

(*a*) A conductivity cell containing a pair of rigidly mounted electrodes (usually made of Pt, with a coating of Pt-black). The cell constant, which has to be determined experimentally before the instrument is used, depends on the area of the electrodes and their relative position.

(*b*) An instrument for measuring the electrical conductance (or resistance) between the electrodes of the cell.

Most instruments consist of a (low voltage) alternating current generator feeding a Wheatstone bridge network, of which the cell forms one arm.

Battery operated apparatus may be useful for field measurements of changes in time, or to detect chemoclines (changes of concentration with depth).

LEVEL I

3.1.1 With field apparatus

Apparatus

For measurement of conductivity in the field, apparatus specially designed for this purpose must usually be used. The most important requirements are portability and independence of mains electricity.

Clean the Pt-electrodes with chromic-sulphuric acid if necessary. Platinize by immersing the electrodes in a solution of 1 g of chloroplatinic acid ($H_2PtCl_6 . 6H_2O$) and 10–20 mg of $Pb(CH_3COO)_2$ in 100 ml of H_2O. Alternatively use 0·3 g of $PtCl_4 + 10$–20 mg $Pb(CH_3COO)_2$ in 100 ml of 0·025 N HCl. Connect both conductivity electrodes to the negative terminal of a 1·5 V cell. Connect the positive side to a Pt-wire dipped into the solution. Continue the electrolysis until both electrodes are coated; only a small quantity of gas should be evolved (corresponding to a current density of about 10 mA/cm^2). Keep the solution for later use. Conductivity cells containing electrodes of impervious carbon are available and are particularly suitable for monitoring and field studies. (For example Electronic Switchgear, § 10.3). A thermometer covering the range $-5°$ to 30°C is also necessary.

Procedure

Rinse the cell well with the sample to be measured, finally filling the cell. Measure the conductance (or resistance) of the sample in accordance with the instructions supplied by the manufacturer, noting the temperature of the water.

Calculation

If the instrument is calibrated in conductance units, multiply directly by the cell constant (see level II; § 3.1.2). If the instrument is calibrated in resistance units, multiply by the reciprocal of the cell constant to obtain resistivity in ohm centimetre.

Then specific conductance (in μmho/cm) $= 10^6$/resistivity (in ohm/cm)

If the conductivity was measured at a temperature other than 25°C, it may be corrected to 25°C, by use of a factor obtained from table 3.1.

Table 3.1. Factors for converting specific conductance of water to values at 25°C (based on 0·01 M KCl and 0·01 M NaNO$_3$ solutions).

°C	factor	°C	factor	°C	factor
32	0·89	22	1·06	12	1·30
31	0·90	21	1·08	11	1·33
30	0·92	20	1·10	10	1·36
29	0·93	19	1·12	9	1·39
28	0·95	18	1·14	8	1·42
27	0·97	17	1·16	7	1·46
26	0·98	16	1·19	6	1·50
25	1·00	15	1·21	5	1·54
24	1·02	14	1·24	4	1·58
23	1·04	13	1·27	3	1·62

LEVEL II

3.1.2 With laboratory apparatus

Apparatus

There are several satisfactory commercial models. Essentially the apparatus is a waterbath, with racks in which tubes containing samples and standards may be kept at a known constant temperature. Large borosilicate test tubes are convenient for holding the samples. It is essential that the diameter of the test tube be at least twice the diameter of the cell. Soda glass tubes are unsuitable for soft water samples because appreciable changes in conductivity may result from solution or exchange of ions from the glass.

Reagents:

KCl, 0·0100 M.

Dissolve 0·7456 g of KCl (A.R., dry) in freshly boiled H_2O with a conductivity not greater than 2 μmho/cm, and make up to 1000 ml. Store in a glass stoppered borosilicate bottle. This standard is satisfactory for most samples when using a cell with a constant between 1 and 2. Stronger or weaker standards may be needed; see procedure and Table 3.2. When preparing very dilute standards it is essential to use freshly prepared conductivity water.

Procedure

The water should, if possible, be maintained at 25°C, although any controlled temperature between 15° and 30°C may be used, as the conductance of the KCl standard will vary with temperature to nearly the same extent as that of the samples. The conductivity cell should be stored in H_2O at the temperature of the waterbath. Place four tubes of standard KCl solution (see Table 3.2) in the waterbath. Place two tubes of each sample to be measured in the waterbath, and allow 30 minutes for thermal equilibrium to be established. A KCl solution should be chosen with a conductance value differing by a factor of less than 5 from that of the samples (see Wilcox, 1950).

Table 3.2. Specific conductances of KCl solutions at 25°C.

Concentration M	Specific conductance μmho/cm
0·0001	14·94
0·0005	73·90
0·001	147·0
0·005	717·8
0·01	1413·0
0·02	2767
0·05	6668
0·1	12900
0·2	24820

Rinse the conductivity cell, in turn with the contents of three of the tubes of KCl solution, measure the conductance (or resistance R_{KCl}) of the fourth solution and record the results.

Next rinse the cell with one tube of the first water sample, ensuring that the rinsing is thorough, and measure the conductance (or resistance R_S) of the solution in the second tube. Proceed in the same way with the other samples.

Calculation

The cell constant C is equal to the product of the measured resistance, in ohms, of the standard KCl solution (R_{KCl}) and the specific conductance, in mho/cm, of this standard solution. For example

$$C = R_{KCl} \times 0·001413$$

if 0·01 M KCl at 25°C is used.

The specific conductance (mho/cm) of the water sample at 25°C is equal to the cell constant, C, divided by the resistance, in ohms, of the sample R_S, measured at 25°C.

Specific conductance $= \dfrac{C}{R_{\mathrm{S}}} \times 10^6 \ \mu\text{mho/cm}$.

The amount of dissolved ionic matter in mg/1 in a sample may be estimated approximately by multiplying the specific conductance by an empirical factor, varying from 0·55 to 0·9. A similar estimate in meq/1 may be made by multiplying the conductance in micromhos by 0·01 (see § 9.1).

3.2 pH

pH may be measured by a colorimetric method (using indicators) or by an electrical method. The colorimetric method, requires a smaller capital expenditure on equipment, but is less convenient and needs more time for a determination than the electrical method. If more than a very few measurements are to be made the colorimetric method will probably be more expensive when all costs are considered.

A colorimetric measurement may also need even more correction for temperature effects than does an electrical measurement. The types of water in which colorimetric measurements can be made are also more limited than those to which the electrical method can be applied.

There may, however, be local circumstances which force the limnologist to use the colorimetric method, and for this reason some details are given here.

LEVEL I

3.2.1 Colorimetric; with Double Wedge Comparator (*not suitable for waters with low buffer capacity, nor for coloured waters*).

Reagents

A Buffer solutions—*suitable for colorimetric determinations of pH.*

A₁ Acetate buffer (Walpole, 1914)

CH_3COONa, 0·20 M
Dissolve 27·2 g of $CH_3COONa.3H_2O$ in H_2O and dilute to 1000 ml.

CH_3COOH, 0·20 M
Dilute 12 ml glacial CH_3COOH to 1 litre with H_2O.
Standardize against NaOH, with phenolphthalein as indicator, and dilute to 0·20 M.

Range of pH values which may be obtained by mixing CH_3COONa and CH_3COOH solutions.

pH at 18°C	0·2 M CH_3COONa ml	0·2 M CH_3COOH ml
3·6	0·75	9·25
3·8	1·20	8·80
4·0	1·80	8·20
4·2	2·65	7·35
4·4	3·70	6·30
4·6	4·90	5·10
4·8	5·90	4·10
5·0	7·00	3·00
5·2	7·90	2·10
5·4	8·60	1·40
5·6	9·10	0·90
5·8	9·40	0·60

A$_2$　Phosphate buffer after Sørensen (Gomori, 1955)

Na$_2$HPO$_4$, 0·2 M

Dissolve either 35·6 g of Na$_2$HPO$_4$.2H$_2$O or 71·6 g of Na$_2$HPO$_4$.12H$_2$O in H$_2$O and dilute to 1000 ml.

NaH$_2$PO$_4$, 0·2 M

Dissolve either 27·6 g of NaH$_2$PO$_4$.H$_2$O or 31·2 g of NaH$_2$PO$_4$.2H$_2$O in H$_2$O and dilute to 1000 ml.

Range of pH values which may be obtained by mixing these phosphate solutions.

pH	0·2 M Na$_2$HPO$_4$ (ml)	0·2 M NaH$_2$PO$_4$ (ml)	H$_2$O (ml)
5·8	8·0	92·0	100
6·0	12·3	87·7	100
6·2	18·5	81·5	100
6·4	26·5	73·5	100
6·6	37·5	62·5	100
6·8	49·0	51·0	100
7·0	61·0	39·0	100
7·2	72·0	28·0	100
7·4	81·0	19·0	100
7·6	87·0	13·0	100
7·8	91·5	8·5	100
8·0	94·7	5·3	100

A$_3$　Borate buffer (Holmes, 1943)

Na$_2$B$_4$O$_7$, 0·05 M

Dissolve 19·1 g of Na$_2$B$_4$O$_7$.10H$_2$O in H$_2$O and dilute to 1000 ml.
(Borax may lose water of crystallization and should therefore be kept in a stoppered bottle).

H$_3$BO$_3$, 0·2 M

Dissolve 12·4 g of H$_3$BO$_3$ in H$_2$O and dilute to 1000 ml.

Range of pH values which may be obtained by mixing Na$_2$B$_4$O$_7$ and H$_3$BO$_3$ solutions.

pH	0·05 M Na$_2$B$_4$O$_7$ (ml)	0·2 M H$_3$BO$_3$ (ml)
7·4	1·0	9·0
7·6	1·5	8·5
7·8	2·0	8·0
8·0	3·0	7·0
8·2	3·5	6·5
8·4	4·5	5·5
8·7	6·0	4·0
9·0	8·0	2·0

B　Buffer solutions—*suitable as standards for calibration of pH meters.*

K hydrogenphthalate, 0·05 M

Dissolve 10·2 g of K hydrogen phthalate in H$_2$O and dilute to 1000 ml.

Phosphate buffer, 0·05 M

Dissolve 3·40 g of KH$_2$PO$_4$ and 4·45 g of Na$_2$HPO$_4$.2H$_2$O in H$_2$O and dilute to 1000 ml. This solution is 0·025 M in H$_2$PO$_4^-$ and in HPO$_4^{2-}$.

Borax buffer, 0·01 M

Dissolve 3·81 g of $Na_2B_4O_7 . 10H_2O$ in H_2O and dilute to 1000 ml.

pH of buffer solutions B at various temperatures.

Temperature °C	Phthalate	Phosphate	Borate
0	4·01	6·98	9·46
5	4·00	6·95	9·39
10	4·00	6·92	9·33
15	4·00	6·90	9·27
20	4·00	6·88	9·22
25	4·01	6·86	9·18
30	4·01	6·85	9·14

C   Indicators

Dissolve 40 mg of the appropriate indicator in about 100 ml of H_2O or alcohol. Adjust the pH (with dilute strong acid or alkali) to near the middle of the range.

Suitable indicators, with the range of pH which each covers, are shown below.

Indicator	pH range
Thymol Blue	1·2–2·8
Bromophenol Blue	3·0–4·6
Methyl Orange	3·1–4·4
Methyl Red	4·4–6·0
Bromocresol Purple	5·2–6·8
Bromothymol Blue	6·0–7·6
*Neutral Red	6·8–8·0
Cresol Red	7·2–8·8
Thymol Blue	8·0–9·6
*Phenolphthalein	8·0–9·8

* Soluble in alcohol, but not in H_2O.

Principle

The pH of the solution can be measured in the field by measuring the colour of an indicator (see § 9·4) with the Double Wedge Comparator, or with the Lovibond or Hellige Comparators. In both cases the colour of the added indicator is compared with the colour of the same indicator in a solution of known pH. In the first case the "mixed" colour is prepared optically, in the other case by using buffer solutions with a known pH, or by using coloured glasses.

The Hellige or Lovibond colour discs and comparators are more convenient to use than the La Motte comparator block with standard buffers. The light attachment of the Hellige comparator increases the accuracy of the colour matching considerably. Neither of these comparators permits the accuracy that may be attained with the double wedge comparator.

Apparatus and procedure

The double wedge comparator consists of a rectangular glass cell with a glass partition running diagonally across, thus dividing it into two wedge-shaped cells. One compartment is filled with an acid solution containing 0·5 ml of 0·04% indicator per 10 ml of solution, while the other compartment is filled with an alkaline solution with the same concentration of indicator. The cell is then closed with a lid to prevent evaporation and the absorption of CO_2 from the air. Viewing the cell laterally, at one end the acid colour only of the indicator is observed, while at the other end the alkaline colour only is seen. In between are all the intermediate mixtures of the two colours.

The cell should be calibrated colorimetrically at 20°C with standard buffer solutions which have been checked with the glass electrode, and a scale prepared on the side graduated into divisions of 0·02 pH units.

For a determination, mix the unknown sample with a 0·04% indicator solution in the proportion of 0·5 ml of indicator per 10 ml of solution. Transfer the solution to the small cell which slides along on top of the double wedge comparator. The construction of this cell is such that its internal width is the same as the sum of the internal widths of the two wedges at any one position. This ensures the same thickness of solution and the same intensity of indicator colour in the two cells. After the colour of the unknown in the sliding cell has been matched with some portion of the double wedge, the pH is read directly from the scale. See note (e) (§ 3.2.4) and § 9.5 for the effect of temperature.

3.2.2   Colorimetric with the Hellige or Lovibond Comparator
For principle and reagents, see § 3.2.1.
Rinse one of the graduated 10 ml test tubes with sample and then fill to the mark. Mix 0·5 ml of 0·04% indicator with the solution. Place the tube in the compartment of the comparator nearest the source of light. Compare with the various coloured glasses of the standard colour disc or with the standard buffer solutions. The individual glasses differ by 0·2 pH units. By careful interpolation, an accuracy of ±0·05 pH units can be attained by this method. See note (e) (§ 3.2.4) and § 9.5 for the effects of temperature.

3.2.3.   With a battery operated field pH meter
Battery operated pH meters may be bought. As instructions are given by the manufacturer no procedure is detailed here. See § 9.5 for the effects of temperature.

The following points should be noted.
The accuracy in normal use is probably ± 0·1 of a pH unit, but can be improved by checking against buffers of a known pH value close to that of the sample.
It is particularly important with portable pH meters to check that the scale factor is correct. This may be done by standardising with one buffer solution and then checking that the correct reading is obtained (without further adjustment of the controls) on a second buffer solution with pH 2–3 units different from the first.

When the apparatus is not in daily use batteries which are not leakproof are best removed. The apparatus must be kept absolutely dry.

LEVEL II

3.2.4.   With a Laboratory pH meter
Very many types of pH meters are commercially available. For most limnological work an ordinary laboratory pH meter with an accuracy of ± 0·02 pH units will be sufficient. Only the investigator can decide when greater accuracy is needed. The cost will, however, increase more rapidly than the accuracy.

Two electrodes are necessary with the apparatus; a glass electrode (see § 9.9) and a calomel electrode. Combined "glass calomel" electrodes can be obtained.
See § 9.5 for the effects of temperature.
The following notes are intended to supplement the makers instructions.

Notes

(a)   Soak new or dried out glass electrodes for several hours in 0·01 N HCl.

(b)   Contact between the sample and KCl solution of the salt bridge is established by a small porous fibre, sintered glass disc, or ceramic disc sealed into the lower tip of the KCl holder. The KCl holder should be open to the atmosphere and the KCl solution level should be kept above the sample solution level, so that there is a very slow flow of KCl into the samples.
The KCl solution in the bridge should not be allowed to dry out nor to become unsaturated. It is usual to keep some crystals of KCl in the solution to ensure saturation.

(c)   Make sure that air bubbles are not trapped in the ends of either electrode, or in the salt bridge.

(d)   If possible arrange the tip of the glass electrode slightly above the tip of the reference electrode to minimise danger of breakage.

(e)   Changes in temperature and unnecessary contact of the water samples with air should be avoided while making readings. (In some circumstances it may be useful to measure the pH both at the in situ temperature and at room temperature (20°C) though in most circumstances a difference of less than 0·1 pH unit will be found). Avoid contact of the sample with air during storage by filling the bottles completely when sampling. For theoretical aspects see § 9.5.

(f)   "Drifting" of the pH reading may occur if the glass electrode bulb is insufficiently cleaned between samples. Sometimes cleaning with cotton wool soaked in detergent may be necessary. Before measuring poorly buffered samples it is essential to rinse the electrodes with the sample. The pH of unbuffered samples may drift due to absorbtion of CO_2 from the air or to alkali leached from the glass.

(g)   Sudden and large changes of reading may be produced due to static electrical charges accumulated on clothes worn by the operator. Difficulties from this cause may be reduced by using a special screened glass electrode, or by placing an earthed metal shield round the electrodes.

(h)   When not in use the glass electrodes should be immersed in water (or 0·01 N HCl). The electrodes should be kept clean. If the calomel electrode is to be stored for an extended period the protecting cap should be replaced on the end.

(i)   When making measurements on samples of pH 9·5 or higher, readings should be corrected for alkali-ion error according to the correction sheet supplied with the meter. It is better to use a special glass electrode designed for this type of work.

(j)   The response of old glass electrodes may become slow. They may be reactivated by dipping in a 20% solution of NH_4HF_2 for a few minutes followed by dipping in 12 N HCl (s.g. = 1·19). The accuracy of such reactivated electrodes must be checked carefully.

LEVEL III

3.2.5.   With a pH meter
pH measurements can easily be automated and carried out continuously with a recording device.

3.3.   MEASUREMENT OF OXIDATION-REDUCTION POTENTIAL

Most pH meters are designed so that they may be used to measure small potential differences directly.

Samples must be taken with the same precautions as for pH. Connect a Pt-electrode to the indicator electrode terminal of the pH meter and switch the range to "millivolts". The polarity may be wrong, in which case move the switch to "−millivolts". Most scales read from 0 to 1300 or 1400 millivolts. The zero adjuster and temperature compensator are often automatically disconnected from the circuit when the switch is in the millivolt positions.

Using suitable electrodes, for example platinum and calomel, the above procedure can be used to determine oxidation-reduction potentials or to make oxidation-reduction titrations.

It is often difficult to obtain reproducible results. Platinum electrodes may be cleaned either by heating in H_2SO_4 $(1+1)$, and leaving to stand in H_2SO_4 $(1+1)$ overnight, or by heating to red heat in a gas flame. Calibration of electrodes in absolute terms is very difficult, though relative measurements are fairly simple. (See § 9.11 and Effenberger, 1967).

The continuous measurement of the redox potential has also been described by Effenberger (1967).

For interpretation of redox potentials the pH must be known (see § 9.11).

3.4 DETERMINATION OF TOTAL AND PHENOLPHTHALEIN ALKALINITY

LEVEL I

3.4.1. Indicator method

Principle

See § 9.7 for further detail.

The amount of $CO_3{}^{2-} + OH^-$ is determined by titration with acid to pH $\simeq 8\cdot3$, the end point being detected with phenolphthalein.

The amount of $HCO_3{}^-$ is determined by further titration with acid to an end point pH between $4\cdot2$ and $5\cdot4$, with methyl orange or mixed indicator as end point indicator.

There are at least 4 quantities commonly reported:

Quantity	Symbol	Compounds	End point pH
1. Phenolphthalein alkalinity	PA	$OH^- + CO_3{}^{2-}$	$\simeq 8\cdot3$
2. Total alkalinity	TA	$OH^- + CO_3{}^{2-} + HCO_3{}^-$	$4\cdot2$ to $5\cdot4$
3. Carbonate alkalinity	CA	$CO_3{}^{2-} + HCO_3{}^-$	
4. Total CO_2	TC	$CO_3{}^{2-} + HCO_3{}^- + CO_2$	

CA and TC may be found by calculation from TA, the pH and conductivity of the original water sample.

The exact end point pH of the TA titration depends on the amount of CO_2 in solution and is therefore related to TC. For precise work therefore the complete titration curve should be obtained potentiometrically. If indicators must be used, an approximate value of TA is first found. From this an approximate value of TC can be obtained and then a value very close to the true TA end point may be calculated. The titration is taken to this pH as end point.

Total CO_2(TC) may also be measured directly (see § 3.5). It should be noted that $H_3SiO_4{}^-$, $H_2BO_3{}^-$, $NH_4{}^+$, HS^- and some organic anions will be included in the TA estimate. So will colloidal and suspended $CaCO_3$.

Reagents:

A H_2SO_4 or HCl, 0·100 N or 0·050 N. See § 1.4.1.

The concentration to which the standard acid should be diluted depends on the size of the burette and on the order of magnitude of the alkalinity to be determined.

B Phenolphthalein indicator

Dissolve 0·5 g of phenolphthalein in 50 ml of 95% ethanol, and add 50 ml of water. Add a dilute (e.g. 0·05 N) CO_2-free NaOH solution dropwise, until the solution turns faintly pink.

C Mixed indicator

Dissolve 0·02 g of methyl red and 0·08 g of bromcresol green in about 100 ml of 95% ethanol. This indicator is suitable over the pH range 4·6–5·2. It is advisable to prepare buffer solutions, (see § 3.2.1.) to which are added indicator in the same amount as in an alkalinity titration. These provide standard end points.

D Methyl orange indicator, 0·05%

Dissolve 0·05 g of methyl orange in about 100 ml of water. This indicator is suitable for equivalence points below pH 4·6. Just as for the mixed indicator, it is advisable to prepare a buffer solution to provide standard end points.

E Buffer solution pH 8·3

59·4 ml of 0·05 M $Na_2B_4O_7$ + 40·6 ml of 0·1 N HCl. See § 3.2.1, solution A_3, and § 1.4.1.

Table 3.3. Factors (β) for calculating carbonate alkalinity (CA) from total alkalinity (TA), and from pH and conductivity of the original water sample.

The factor (β), is related to [OH$^-$], (see § 9.8) and CA = TA $- 0·01\beta$. The units are meq/l.

pH_{20}	Conductivity (μmho/cm)		
	0–40	40–300	300–550
8·8	0	0	0
8·9	1	1	1
9·0	1	1	1
9·1	1	1	1
9·2	1	1	1
9·3	1	1	1
9·4	2	2	2
9·5	2	2	2
9·6	3	3	3
9·7	4	4	4
9·8	4	5	5
9·9	6	6	6
10·0	7	7	7
10·1	9	9	9
10·2	11	11	12
10·3	14	14	15
10·4	17	18	19

Chapter 3

Table 3.4. Factors δ for calculating total CO_2 (TC) from carbonate alkalinity (CA), and from pH and conductivity of the original water sample.

$$TC = CA \times \delta$$

The units are meq/l. CA may be obtained from table 3.3.

pH$_{20}$	Conductivity (μmho/cm)						
	0–10	10–40	40–110	110–200	200–315	315–430	430–550
6·4	1·96	1·93	1·93	1·90	1·89	1·88	1·86
6·5	1·76	1·74	1·74	1·72	1·71	1·70	1·69
6·6	1·60	1·59	1·59	1·57	1·56	1·55	1·55
6·7	1·48	1·46	1·46	1·45	1·45	1·44	1·43
6·8	1·38	1·37	1·37	1·36	1·35	1·35	1·34
6·9	1·30	1·29	1·29	1·29	1·28	1·28	1·27
7·0	1·24	1·23	1·23	1·23	1·22	1·22	1·22
7·1	1·19	1·19	1·18	1·18	1·18	1·17	1·17
7·2	1·15	1·15	1·15	1·14	1·14	1·14	1·14
7·3	1·12	1·12	1·12	1·11	1·11	1·11	1·11
7·4	1·09	1·09	1·09	1·09	1·09	1·09	1·09
7·5	1·07	1·07	1·07	1·07	1·07	1·07	1·07
7·6	1·06	1·06	1·06	1·06	1·05	1·05	1·05
7·7	1·05	1·05	1·04	1·04	1·04	1·04	1·04
7·8	1·04	1·04	1·03	1·03	1·03	1·03	1·03
7·9	1·03	1·03	1·03	1·03	1·02	1·02	1·02
8·0	1·02	1·02	1·02	1·02	1·02	1·02	1·02
8·1	1·01	1·01	1·01	1·02	1·01	1·01	1·01
8·2	1·01	1·01	1·01	1·01	1·01	1·01	1·01
8·3	1·00	1·00	1·00	1·00	1·00	1·00	1·00
8·4	1·00	1·00	1·00	1·00	1·00	1·00	1·00
8·5	1·00	·99	·99	·99	·99	·99	·99
8·6	·99	·99	·99	·99	·99	·99	·98
8·7	·99	·98	·98	·98	·98	·98	·98
8·8	·98	·98	·98	·97	·97	·97	·97
8·9	·97	·97	·97	·97	·97	·96	·96
9·0	·96	·96	·96	·96	·96	·95	·95
9·1	·95	·95	·95	·95	·94	·94	·94
9·2	·94	·94	·94	·93	·93	·93	·93
9·3	·93	·93	·92	·92	·92	·91	·91
9·4	·91	·91	·91	·90	·90	·90	·89
9·5	·90	·89	·89	·88	·88	·87	·87
9·6	·88	·87	·87	·86	·85	·85	·85
9·7	·85	·85	·84	·84	·83	·83	·82
9·8	·83	·82	·82	·81	·80	·80	·79
9·9	·80	·79	·79	·78	·77	·77	·76
10·0	·77	·76	·76	·75	·75	·74	·74
10·1	·74	·74	·73	·72	·72	·71	·71
10·2	·72	·71	·70	·70	·69	·69	·68
10·3	·69	·68	·68	·67	·66	·66	·65
10·4	·66	·65	·65	·64	·64	·63	·63

Table 3.5. End point pH values, at 20°C, for the total alkalinity (TA) titration.

Total CO_2 (TC) may be found from tables 3.3 and 3.4.

Total CO_2 mMol/l	End point pH	Total CO_2 mMol/l	End point pH
0·05	5·36	1·2	4·65
0·08	5·25	1·5	4·61
0·10	5·20	2·0	4·54
0·15	5·11	2·5	4·49
0·2	5·05	3·0	4·46
0·3	4·96	4·0	4·39
0·4	4·90	5·0	4·34
0·5	4·85	6·0	4·30
0·6	4·81	7·0	4·27
0·8	4·74	8·0	4·24
1·0	4·69	10·0	4·19

Procedure

Mix 100 ml of sample with 2 drops of phenolphthalein indicator (B) in a conical titration beaker. If the solution remains colourless the PA = 0, and the total alkalinity is determined as described below. If the solution turns red, determine the PA by titrating with standard acid until the colour practically disappears. The very faint colour at the end point is best estimated by comparing with a standard end point in pH = 8·3 buffer (E).

Determine the TA by continued titration to the second equivalence point, after the addition of 3 drops per 100 ml of sample of either the mixed indicator or methyl orange.

For more precise work read the burette when the first slight tendency to change colour appears. With this approximate value of the TA, and with the initial pH and conductivity of the water, the approximate value of total CO_2 may be found from table 3.3 and 3.4. This value for total CO_2 may then be used in table 3.5 to give the calculated end point pH for the TA titration. This calculated end point pH differs insignificantly from the true end point pH.

Add 3 drops of mixed indicator or methyl orange to 100 ml buffer with the same pH as the calculated end point and continue the titration until the same colour is observed in the sample as in the buffer. Loss of CO_2 must be minimized.

Notes

All reagents should be low in CO_2. This is particularly the case when determining low alkalinities. Removal of dissolved CO_2 from the dilution water may be done in two ways: (1) Reduce the pressure for 10–15 minutes with a water jet pump, or (2) boil for 10–15 minutes and subsequently cool. Reabsorption of CO_2 from the air may be prevented by a soda lime tube.

Calculation

$$TA \text{ (meq/l)} = \frac{(ml \times \text{Normality}) \text{ of titrant} \times 1000}{ml \text{ sample}}$$

Total CO_2 (mMol/l) $= CA \times \delta = (TA - 0 \cdot 01\beta) \times \delta$

(see tables 3.3 and 3.4).

Precision and accuracy

The precision is estimated at 2% at TA 1 meq/l and 2–10% at TA between 1 and 0·1 meq/l. Below 0·1 meq/l the method is probably unreliable, unless the end point is made sharper by bubbling CO_2-free gas through the solution during the titration. This can best be carried out by putting the sample into a sintered glass filter 15–40 μ mean pore size (e.g. Jena G3) and passing N_2 from below through the filter. Add the sample after the N_2-stream has started and after the filter is wetted. Rinse the sample away with H_2O while the N_2 is still passing through. Calculation of the end point is not appropriate.

LEVEL II

Conductometric or potentiometric titration

Principle

The titration is carried out as described for level I, but a pH meter is used to locate the end point. For dilute solutions a conductivity meter is used.

3.4.2. Potentiometric

Procedure

Pipette a suitable volume of sample (e.g. 100 ml) into a conical titration beaker placed on a magnetic stirrer. Lower a glass and a calomel electrode, and the capillary tip of a (micro) burette into the sample. Take care that the stirrer cannot damage the electrodes.

For precise work construct a titration curve by plotting the pH values, against the volume of the titrant added, continuing well beyond the end point.

In routine determinations a more rapid method may be used. Take the first end point at pH = 8·3, corresponding to the PA. TA is determined by continuing the titration to the second end point. When the second end point is nearly reached (pH = 5·0–5·5) read the burette. With this approximate value of the alkalinity and the initial pH and conductivity of the water, follow through tables 3.3, 3.4 and 3.5 (as described in the indicator method, § 3.4.1) to obtain the calculated end point pH. This calculated end point differs insignificantly from the true end point pH. Continue the titration to the calculated end point pH. Use the final reading of the burette for the calculation of the exact TA and total CO_2. Loss of CO_2 must be minimized.

Notes and calculation

See § 3.4.1.

Precision and accuracy

The precision and accuracy are estimated at 1% or better at TA > 1 meq/l and at 1–5% at TA < 1 meq/l. Total CO_2 is most accurately calculated in comparatively soft waters and in waters where the pH lies between 7·0 and 9·2, but an absolute condition is that the pH is measured accurately. The error in % of the total CO_2 arising from an error in the pH measurement of 0·1 pH-unit is:

pH	6·4	7·4	8·4	9·4	10·4
% error in total CO_2	10·8	2·0	0·5	2·6	5·2

For unfamiliar waters it is recommended that the calculation method be checked by some independent method involving the liberation of CO_2, subsequent absorption of the CO_2 in another solvent, and measurement of CO_2 in the second solvent.

Interferences

Precipitation may occur during storage if the sample is supersaturated with $CaCO_3$. This will affect the alkalinity determination. In such cases the alkalinity titration should be performed as soon as possible after sampling.

3.4.3. Conductometric

Procedure

For waters of low alkalinity the same procedure as § 3.4.2 can be used with a conductivity meter as end point detector instead of a pH meter.

Most devices for conductivity measurements can be used, as it is sufficient to determine relative units. Meters with a titration attachment are preferable. A cell constant of $1\cdot0$ cm^{-1} is suitable. The Pt-electrode should be covered by Pt-black (see § 3.1.1).

Frequencies of 60 cycle/sec up to 1000 cycle/sec and a voltage of 10–15 V are suitable for the analysis.

Readings should be plotted against ml of titrant as described in § 9.1 and § 9.7, fig. 9.2B.

LEVEL III

3.4.4. Potentiometric titration

The same method as in level II is used but with a pH meter with recorder connected to a motor-driven piston burette or automatic titrator. As the pH of the end point depends on the water to be titrated the recording type of apparatus is preferable to the pre-set end point type.

3.5 DETERMINATION OF TOTAL CO$_2$

LEVEL II

Principle

Free CO_2 and CO_3^{2-} are both converted to HCO_3^-; free CO_2 by titration with (carbonate-free) NaOH; CO_3^{2-} by titration with HCl. Both titrations have end point pH $= 8\cdot3$. The HCO_3^- concentration is then determined with HCl.

Reagents

A HCl $0\cdot1$ N or $0\cdot05$ N See § 3.4.1.

B NaOH $0\cdot1$ N or $0\cdot05$ N, carbonate free

Dissolve 50 g of NaOH (A.R.) in 50 ml of H_2O in a Pyrex flask. Filter this concentrated caustic solution through a sintered glass filter (excluding air) to remove the Na_2CO_3. The strong carbonate-free NaOH solution can be kept in thick walled polythene or polypropylene bottles, (the solution is about 19 N).

D

Dilute with CO_2-free (boiled) H_2O to the desired strength. Exclude air.
Standardize against standard acid.

If the standard solutions are transferred quickly to a burette, contamination by
CO_2 may be disregarded. The burette must be protected by a soda lime tube. It is,
however, recommended that burettes connected directly to stock bottles should be
used.

NaOH is tested for carbonate by mixing 20 ml with 1 ml of 0·5 N $BaCl_2$ out of
contact with air. No turbidity should appear.

3.5.1

Procedure

Add several drops of phenolphthalein indicator (§ 3.4.1) to 100 ml of the sample.
Then titrate with 0·05 N NaOH until the solution has a faint pink colour. If the
solution turns pink when the indicator is added, titrate with 0·05 N HCl instead.
Then add the mixed indicator (see § 3.4.1, solution C) and titrate with 0·05 N HCl
solution. The end point may be sharpened by bubbling N_2 through the liquid to
remove CO_2 (see § 3.4.1, precision and accuracy).

Interferences

The estimation of bicarbonate in waters heavily contaminated with organic
matter or in distinctly saline waters is best done by distilling off the CO_2 from an
acidified sample, and estimating the amount of this CO_2. This may be conveniently
done in a Warburg apparatus, or gas analysis apparatus.

3.5.2

Same as 3.5.1, but with potentiometric end point (see § 3.4.2 or § 3.4.4).

3.5.3

Gas chromatographic. See § 8.3 or § 8.4.

Calculation

$$CO_2 \text{ meq/l} = \frac{\text{ml titrant (between both end points)} \times \text{normality of acid} \times 1000}{\text{ml sample}}$$

1 meq/l CO_2 = 44 mg/l CO_2 = 12 mg/l C.

3.6 ACIDITY

Follow one of the procedures for alkalinity (3.4) with indicator (C) of § 7.1.4, but
use 0·01 N $Ba(OH)_2$ in place of 0·01 N HCl. See § 7.1.4 for precautions to be
observed. The $Ba(OH)_2$ should be diluted 5 times.

CHAPTER 4

DETERMINATION OF MAJOR ELEMENTS*

CALCIUM, MAGNESIUM, SODIUM, POTASSIUM, IRON, CHLORIDE, SULPHATE, HYDROGEN SULPHIDE, CARBONATE AND BICARBONATE

4.1 CALCIUM

LEVELS I AND II

4.1.1. Colorimetric

Principle

Calcium forms a coloured complex with glyoxalbis-(2-hydroxyanil) = di-(o-hydroxyphenylimino)ethane (Kerr, 1960).

Reagents

A₁ Standard Ca²⁺ solution, 400 μg/ml

Dissolve 1·000 g of $CaCO_3$ (dry, A.R.) in 25 ml of 1 N-HCl and dilute to 1000 ml with H_2O.

A₂ Standard Ca²⁺ solution, 4 μg/ml

Dilute 5·0 ml of this stock solution to 500 ml to give a solution containing 4 μg/ml of Ca^{2+}.

B Buffer solution, pH = 12·6

Dissolve 10 g of NaOH and 10 g of $Na_2B_4O_7$ in 1 litre of H_2O.

C Glyoxalbis-(2-hydroxyanil), 0·5 % in methanol

This substance may be either purchased or prepared thus:

  Dissolve 4·4 g of freshly sublimed o-aminophenol in 1 litre of H_2O at 80°C; add 3·5 ml of glyoxal solution (30 % w/w); maintain the temperature at 80°C for 30 minutes, cool, and allow to stand for 12 hours in a refrigerator. Filter off the precipitate, wash with water, and recrystallize from methanol.

Dissolve 0·5 g of glyoxalbis-(2-hydroxyanil) in about 100 ml of methanol.

D Ethanol-n-butanol solvent mixture

Mix equal volumes of ethanol and n-butanol.

Procedure

Put 20·0 ml of sample containing not more than 80 μg of Ca^{2+} (or an aliquot diluted to 20·0 ml) into a large test tube. Add in succession 2·0 ml of buffer (B), 1·0 ml of glyoxalbis-(2-hydroxyanil) reagent (C) and 20·0 ml of solvent mixture (D), mixing after each addition. Measure the extinction of the reagent blank, standards and samples in suitable cells at a wavelength as close as possible to 520 mμ. The measurement should be made not less than 25 minutes after mixing. The colour is stable for at least 35 minutes after this. Prepare a calibration curve covering the range 0–80 μg/sample or 0–4 mg/l of Ca^{2+}(= 0–0·2 meq/l).

---

* MAJOR ELEMENTS is a term of convenience. Included are most of the ions commonly present as about 1 % or more of the total ions.

Interferences

According to Kerr (1960), up to 50 ppm of Mg^{2+} and Al^{3+} do not interfere; Ba^{2+} and Sr^{2+} do interfere above 4 ppm. Fe^{2+} has no effect if precipitation is prevented by adding cyanide. SO_4^{2-}, Cl^-, and NO^- are without effect up to 500 ppm. Cu^{2+} above about 0·1 ppm appears to delay colour formation but this interference can be suppressed by adding a few drops of a 2% solution of sodium diethyldithiocarbamate before adding the reagents.

Sensitivity

0·1 mg/l.

Precision and accuracy

Estimated at 5%.

4.2 MAGNESIUM

LEVEL I

4.2.1. Colorimetric

Principle

Magnesium forms a coloured complex with the dye Brilliant Yellow (Tarras, 1948).

Reagents

A Standard Mg^{2+} solution, 1 mg/ml
Dissolve 10·135 g $MgSO_4.7H_2O$ in H_2O and dilute to 1000 ml; 1 ml of this solution contains 1 mg of Mg^{2+}.

B H_2SO_4, 0·1 N
Add 5 ml of H_2SO_4 (1+1) to 1 litre of H_2O.

C NaOH, 5 N
Dilute 10 N NaOH (0·5 litre → 1·0 litre) (see § 1.4.1).

D $Ca^{2+}-Al^{3+}$ solution
Dissolve 1·5 g of $Al_2(SO_4)_3.18 H_2O$ in 500 ml of H_2O. Add 30 g of $CaCO_3$ and 40 ml of HNO_3 (s.g. 1·42), taking care to avoid excessive effervescence. Make up to 1 litre.

E Brilliant Yellow solution
Dissolve 10 mg of Brilliant Yellow (B.D.H.) in 0·1 litre of H_2O. Prepare a fresh solution every 2 or 3 days.

F Starch solution 2%
Dissolve 1 g of soluble starch in 50 ml of H_2O. Heat to aid solution.

Procedure

Put 50·0 ml of sample containing not more than 0·1 mg of Mg^{2+} (or an aliquot diluted to 50·0 ml) into a 100 ml volumetric flask. Add in succession 1 ml of 0·1 N H_2SO_4 (B), 1 ml of $Ca^{2+}-Al^{3+}$ solution (D), 5 ml of starch solution (F) and 4 ml of NaOH (C). Rinse the neck of the flask with H_2O and add 10 ml reagent solution (E). Mix well and make up to 100 ml with H_2O. Measure the extinction of the reagent blank, standards and samples in suitable cells at a wavelength as close as possible to 540 mμ after 15 to 20 minutes. Prepare a calibration curve using known amounts of Mg^{2+} covering the range 1·0–10·0 mg/1 (1 meq Mg^{2+} = 12·15 mg). The calibration curve is not linear.

Interferences

Normally interference would be expected from varying concentrations of Ca^{2+} and Al^{3+} in the sample, but these variations are largely avoided by the addition of the relatively large quantities of these elements.

Precision, accuracy and sensitivity

Precision and accuracy are unknown. The sensitivity is about 0·5 mg/l.

4.3   CALCIUM AND MAGNESIUM

LEVEL II

Volumetric with EDTA

Principle

METHOD 4.3.1

EDTA[1] is added to a solution of Ca_2^+ and Calcon.[2] The last two form a pink coloured complex. As EDTA forms a stronger complex with Ca^{2+} than does Calcon the solution changes from pink to the blue colour of Calcon itself. Mg^{2+} is first precipitated by adding NaOH, so that Ca^{2+} alone is determined. The total of Ca^{2+} plus Mg^{2+} is determined according to the same principle in a second sample with Eriochrome Black T[3] at pH = 10.

METHOD 4.3.2

The same principle as in method 1, but with glyoxalbis-(2-hydroxyanil) as indicator, again at pH = 12·6. After the Ca^{2+} determination, acid is added to dissolve the Mg precipitate and to destroy the indicator. Mg^{2+} is then determined according to method 1.

4.3.1.   With Calcon and Eriochrome Black T

Reagents

A   Na$_2$ EDTA, 0·01 M[1]

Dilute 0·100 M Na$_2$EDTA (see § 1.4.1) (100 ml → 1000 ml). 1 ml is equivalent to 0·4 mg of Ca^{2+}. The solution may be stored in Pyrex glass vessels or in thick walled polythene bottles, through which evaporation is negligible.

B $Ca^{2+}+Mg^{2+}$ solution

Mix 25·0 ml of standard Ca^{2+} solution A$_1$ of § 4.1.1 and 10·0 ml of standard Mg solution of § 4.2.1 and dilute to 1000 ml; 1 ml of this solution contains 10 μg of Ca^{2+} and 10 μg of Mg^{2+}.

---

[1] Na$_2$EDTA = disodium dihydrogen ethylenediaminetetra-acetate. As one mol of EDTA forms a complex with one mol of both bivalent and trivalent ions, concentrations are here expressed as mol/l.

[2] Calcon = Solochrome Dark Blue = Eriochrome Blue Black R = Colour index No. 202.

[3] Eriochrome Black T = Solochrome Black T = Colour index 203. (Probably better, but difficult to obtain is Solochrome Black 6B = Eriochrome Blue-Black B = Colour index No. 201).

C_1 Borax-buffer for $Ca^{2+} + Mg^{2+}$

Dissolve 8 g of $Na_2B_4O_7.10H_2O$ in 160 ml of H_2O. Add to this solution 2 g of $NaOH + 1$ g of $Na_2S.9H_2O$ previously dissolved together in 20 ml of H_2O, and dilute the mixed solutions to 200 ml.

C_2 Dilute C_1 10 times with H_2O directly before use.

D NaOH, 0·1 N

Dissolve 4 g of NaOH in 1 litre of H_2O.

E HCl, 1 N (see § 1.4.1)

F_1 Calcon indicator*

Grind together 0·20 g of powdered Calcon and 100 g of solid NaCl (A.R.) and keep in a stoppered bottle. Keep dry.

F_2 "Glyoxal" indicator solution

Dissolve 0·03 g of glyoxalbis-(2-hydroxyanil) = di-(o-hydroxyphenylimino)ethane in about 100 ml of methanol.

G Eriochrome Black T indicator*

Grind together 0·4 g of Eriochrome Black T and 100 g of solid NaCl (A.R.) and keep in a stoppered bottle. Keep dry.

Procedure

Calcium

Prepare a standard end point. Put 40·0 ml of the $Ca^{2+} + Mg^{2+}$ solution (B) in a 100 ml flask, add 5 ml of 0·1 N NaOH (D) and 100–200 mg of indicator mixture (F_1) (a "constant spoonful"). From a 2 or 5 ml microburette run in slowly 1·00 ml of EDTA solution (A). The pink colour will change to blue, which is the end point colour. Repeat the procedure with the unknown sample adding the EDTA solution slowly until the colour matches that of the standard end point.

Calcium plus Magnesium

Prepare a standard end point. Put 40·0 ml of the $Ca^{2+} + Mg^{2+}$ solution (B) in a 100 ml flask, add 1 ml of diluted buffer solution (C_2) and about 100 mg of Erio-chrome Black T indicator (G) (a "constant spoonful"). Heat at 70°C and run in slowly 2·645 ml of EDTA solution (A) from a piston microburette; the wine-red colour changes to blue. (The total of 2·645 ml is made up of 1·000 ml equivalent to the $Ca^{2+} + 1·645$ ml equivalent to the Mg^{2+}). Mix an aliquot of the sample, containing not more than 0·4 mg of Ca^{2+} and not more than 0·4 mg of Mg^{2+} with 1 ml of the diluted buffer (C_2) in a 100 ml flask. (If the water contains more than 0·3 meq/l HCO_3^- add first an equivalent amount of dilute HCl, and boil to remove the CO_2. This prevents $CaCO_3$ precipitation). Add the same amount of indicator (G) and titrate at 70°C as described above to the colour of the standard end point.

---

* See footnotes, p. 37.

Interferences

Relatively high concentrations of Mn^{2+} lead to an unsatisfactory end point. A remedy is described by Cheng, Melsted and Bray (1953).

Note

If Mg^{2+} is present in much smaller concentrations than Ca^{2+} the EDTA difference method is relatively inaccurate. In these cases more accurate results for Mg^{2+} will be obtained with the colorimetric method § 4.2.1 or method § 4.3.2.

4.3.2. With glyoxalbis-(2-hydroxyanil) and Eriochrome Black T

Reagents See § 4.3.1

Procedure

Calcium

Prepare a standard Ca^{2+} end point as in § 4.3.1, but with 3 ml indicator F_2; the colour will change from orange red to lemon yellow.
Titrate an aliquot of the sample, containing not more than 0·4 mg of Ca^{2+}, in the same way.

Magnesium

After the calcium titration, acidify the same samples with 1 N HCl (E) to pH 4·0. This destroys the colour of the "glyoxal indicator", and dissolves the $Mg(OH)_2$. Then add 1 ml of buffer solution (C_2) and indicator Eriochrome Black T (G). Determine the end points using a standard end point as described in method § 4.3.1.

Interferences

Al^{3+} interferes in the Mg^{2+} determination when 1 mg/l or more is present.

LEVELS II AND III

4.3.3. Calcium and Magnesium, potentiometric

Principle

Ca^{2+} is titrated potentiometrically with EDTA solution using a Hg–Hg EDTA indicator electrode and a calomel reference electrode. The titration is carried out at a pH = 12 at which Mg^{2+} precipitates. After acidification (to dissolve the $Mg(OH)_2$) and subsequent adjustment of the pH to 10·0, the Mg^{2+} can be titrated.

Apparatus

Recording potentiometric titrator, with J-type Hg-electrode (see figure 4.1), glass and calomel electrodes.

Reagents

A EDTA solution, 0·025 M

Dilute 0·100 M Na_2EDTA (see § 1.4.1) (250 ml → 1000 ml).

B NaOH, 10 N (see § 1.4.1)

C HCl, 1 N (see § 1.4.1)

D Diethylamine buffer (pH = 11·5)

Dissolve 5 g of diethylamine and 1 g of NH_4Cl in about 100 ml of H_2O.

E Hg-EDTA solution, 0·002 M (highly poisonous)

Prepare 0·025 M $Hg(NO_3)_2$ by dissolving 0·850 g $Hg(NO_3)_2 \cdot H_2O$ in 100 ml H_2O. Mix equal volumes of this solution and of 0·025 M EDTA (A).

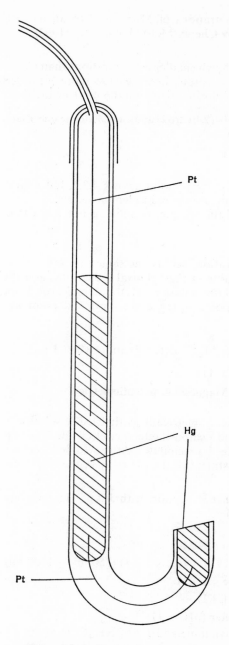

Figure 4.1. J type mercury electrode.

Before use dilute 20 ml of this mixture to 250 ml with H_2O.

Procedure

Put 50 ml of the sample containing not more than 1·0 mg of Ca^{2+} and 1·0 mg of Mg^{2+}, (or an aliquot diluted to 50 ml) in a 100 ml beaker with a slight excess of HCl and boil to remove the CO_2. (The samples used for determining alkalinity, procedure § 3.4.2, can be used if no coloured indicators have been added). If the volume is too small to cover the electrodes, add H_2O, which has been acidified with 5 ml 0·1 N HCl per litre and boiled to remove CO_2. Add 0·4 ml of the Hg–EDTA solution (E), adjust to pH = 12 with NaOH (B) and titrate with EDTA solution (A) from a suitable microburette to a point beyond the end point of the Ca^{2+} titration.

Adjust the pH to 4·0 with HCl (C) and leave until the $Mg(OH)_2$ is dissolved (about 1 minute). Add diethylamine buffer (D) sufficient to make the pH = 10·9 and continue the titration with EDTA to the end point. Prepare a standard end point with solution (B) of § 4.3.1.

Interferences

Fe^{2+}, when more than 10 mg/l is present must be masked with o-phenanthroline. When more than 28 mg/l is present it must be removed.

Cu^{2+}, Mn^{2+}, and Zn^{2+} at concentrations up to 10 mg/l do not interfere.

LEVEL II AND III

4.3.4. Calcium and Magnesium, by atomic absorption flame spectrophotometry

Principle

Measurement of the light absorption by Ca^{2+} and Mg^{2+} when these elements are excited in a flame. Light is provided by a hollow cathode lamp, the cathode containing Ca^{2+} or Mg^{2+}.

Instruments suitable for limnological work are now commercially available, though they are expensive. Cheaper instruments may not be sufficiently sensitive. The method is dependant on the nature and characteristics of the flame, so no specific details can be given here. The manufacturer's instructions should be followed.

There are more interference problems than used to be thought. For example, it is usually necessary in measuring Ca^{2+} to suppress interference by adding excess of La^{3+}. Details are usually supplied by the manufacturer.

As a check, internal standards (in the sense described on p. 5 of this book) should be run frequently.

Further information may be found in Fassel (1965), Herrmann (1965), Walsh (1965), Elwell and Gidley (1966), Reynolds and Aldous (1969).

4.4 SODIUM AND POTASSIUM

LEVEL II

4.4.1. Flame emission spectrophotometry

Principle

Measurement of the light emitted by Na^+ and K^+ when these elements are excited in a flame.

(K: 769 mμ; Na: 589 mμ).

Procedure

Follow the instructions provided by the manufacturer. The samples must be free of solids.

Prepare a calibration curve. This is often appreciably non-linear. In the case of determination of Na^+, dilute the sample until the Na^+ content is lower than 5 mg/l.

Interferences

The nature and extent of interferences depend very much on the characteristics of the flame, and hence on the particular instrument used. Internal standards should therefore be used.

No detailed guidance can therefore be given, but it may be noted that in some cases mutual interference of Na^+ and K^+ may be serious. In this case make a K^+ calibration curve using K^+ solutions containing the same concentration of Na^+ as is present in the sample and reciprocally for Na^+. Anion interferences (particularly PO_4^{3-} and SO_4^{2-}) may also be troublesome.

Note

Collect and store samples in polyethylene or polypropylene bottles only.

4.5 IRON

ALL LEVELS (See also § 6.4.)

4.5.1. Colorimetric with o-phenanthroline

Principle

Iron after reduction to Fe^{2+} reacts with o-phenanthroline to form a red compound (see e.g. O'Connor et al., 1965, Nicolson, 1966). Total iron can be estimated after digestion and reduction.

Reagents

A   Standard Fe^{2+} and Fe^{3+} solutions. See § 6.4

B_1 H_2SO_4 [1+1]

See § 1.4.1. Use iron free grade.

B_2 H_2SO_4, 0·01 N

Dilute B_1 2000 times (0·5 ml → 1 litre).

C NH_4OH, 4 N

Dilute NH_4OH (s.g. = 0·91) (0·3 litre → 1·0 litre).

D $NH_2OH.HCl$, 1·0%

Dissolve 1·0 g of $NH_2OH.HCl$ in about 100 ml of 0·01 N H_2SO_4 (B_2). If necessary, to remove iron, see § 6.4, reagent (F).

E   o-Phenanthroline solution, 0·5%

Dissolve 0·5 g of o-phenanthroline in about 100 ml of 0·01 N H_2SO_4 (B_2).

Procedure

Fe^{2+} (*in ionic form*)

Add 1 ml of reagents (B_2) and (E) to 25 ml of sample. The pH should now be between 2 and 3. Measure the extinction of the reagent blank, standards and samples in suitable cells at a wavelength between 490 and 510 mμ and follow the change of the extinction with time. If only ionic Fe^{2+} is present, the maximum is reached in 30 minutes, but if other forms of Fe are present they may also react, but more slowly, and the extinction will continue to increase for some hours. Whether or not it is practicable to estimate the amount of Fe^{2+} will depend on the occurrence either of the maximum after about 30 minutes, or of a distinct break in the curve of extinction against time.

Make a calibration curve covering the range of 50 μg–5 mg/l of Fe.

$Fe^{3+} + Fe^{2+}$ (*in ionic form*)

Add 1 ml of reagents (D) and (E) to 25 ml of sample. Then proceed as for Fe^{2+}. Follow again the change of extinction with time.

Total Fe

Digest 25 ml, or a measured larger volume, of sample with 2–4 ml H_2SO_4 (B_1) and, if the destruction of the colour takes too long a time, with $(NH_4)_2S_2O_8$. Add 10 ml of H_2O and wait until all Fe is dissolved. (A rusty circle on the glass will sometimes take 24 hours to dissolve.) Adjust the pH to 2–3 with NH_4OH (C) and adjust the volume to 50 ml. Add 1 ml of reagents (D) and (E) to 25 ml and proceed as for Fe^{2+}.

Interferences

Other complex forming substances such as phosphate and humic acids keep the iron from forming the iron-phenanthroline complex. The colour will develop slowly in such cases; (ionic Fe^{2+} takes about 30 min.) The samples can, however, easily be left overnight. In some waters acidification to pH = 2 to 2·5 is sufficient to render the Fe reactive. Boiling the sample will help, but will reduce Fe^{3+} to Fe^{2+}. All acids, including the reagents (D) and (E), may convert complex iron to the ionic state.

Self colour of the water sample may be allowed for by measuring the extinction of a sample blank, made from sample + 1 ml solution (B_2) + 1 ml solution (D).

Precision, accuracy, sensitivity

The precision is estimated at 1–2%. The accuracy depends on the interfering substances. The sensitivity is 10–50 μg/l of Fe, depending on the colour of the water. For a method with greater sensitivity see § 6.4.

4.6 CHLORIDE

LEVEL I

4.6.1. Volumetric; with indicator

Principle

The chloride is titrated with $Hg(NO_3)_2$ at a pH of 3·1. (Bromphenol blue). $HgCl_2$ is formed which is slightly dissociated. At the end point the excess Hg^{2+} produces a violet colour with diphenylcarbazone.

Reagents

A Standard NaCl, 0·0100 N

Dissolve 5·845 g of NaCl (dry A.R.) in H_2O, and make up to 1000 ml. Dilute by 10 times (100 ml → 1000 ml).

B   Hg(NO$_3$)$_2$, 0·02 N (highly poisonous)

Dissolve 3·4 g of Hg(NO$_3$)$_2$.H$_2$O in 800 ml of H$_2$O to which 20 ml of 2 N HNO$_3$ has been added. Dilute to 1000 ml. Standardize against NaCl as described in the procedure.

C   HNO$_3$, 0·2 N

Dilute 13 ml of HNO$_3$ (A.R., s.g. = 1·42) to 1 litre.

D   Diphenylcarbazone-bromphenol blue mixed indicator solution

Dissolve 0·5 g of diphenylcarbazone and 0·05 g of bromphenol blue in about 100 ml of 95% ethyl alcohol or methylated spirit. The solution is stable if kept in a brown bottle.

Procedure

Mix 100 ml of sample containing not more than 10 mg of Cl$^-$, (or an aliquot diluted to 100 ml) with 10 drops (0·5 ml) of indicator solution D. (If more than 10 mg/l SO$_3$$^{2-}$ is present add 3 drops (0·15 ml) of H$_2$O$_2$). Add 0·2 N HNO$_3$ (C) dropwise until the solution becomes yellow (pH = 3·6). Add 5 drops (0·25 ml) more of 0·2 N HNO$_3$.

Titrate with Hg(NO$_3$)$_2$ (B) to the point where the first tinge of blue-purple appears which does not disappear on shaking. Prior warning that the end point is near is given when the colour changes to orange.

Prepare a blank to identify the end point colour.

Interferences

I$^-$, Br$^-$, CNS$^-$ and CN$^-$ are measured as equivalents of Cl$^-$. The ions CrO$_4$$^{2-}$, Fe^{3+}, Mn^{2+}, Zn^{2+}, and Cu^{2+} react with the diphenylcarbazone and must be removed if present in concentrations greater than 10 mg/l.

Calculations

$$Cl^- \text{ meq/l} = \frac{(\text{ml} \times \text{Normality}) \text{ of B} \times 1000}{\text{ml sample}}$$

$$Cl^- \text{ mg/l} = Cl^- \text{ meq/l} \times 35·46.$$

Precision and accuracy

The precision is estimated at:

0·05 mg per sample for Cl$^-$ from 0 to 5 mg.

0·1 mg per sample for Cl$^-$ from 5 to 10 mg

LEVEL II

4.6.2.   Volumetric; with indicator

Principle

To the chloride is added an excess of AgNO$_3$ in *acid* solution, in order to prevent the co-precipitation of the Ag-salts of CO$_3$$^{2-}$, PO$_4$$^{3-}$, SiO$_3$$^{2-}$ etc. (Such precipitation is a disadvantage of Mohr's method). Without removing the AgCl, the excess Ag$^+$ is titrated with CNS$^-$ in the presence of Fe^{3+} and nitrobenzene. (Volhard's method).

Reagents

A   Standard NaCl, 0·0100 N (see § 4.6.1)

B   AgNO$_3$, 0·1 N

Dissolve 8·5 g of AgNO$_3$ (dry, A.R.) in H$_2$O and dilute to 500 ml. Standardize against NaCl as described in the procedure below.

C   HNO$_3$, 1+1

Mix equal volumes of HNO$_3$ (s.g. = 1·42) and H$_2$O. Boil until colourless and store in a glass stoppered brown bottle.

D   Fe$_2$(SO$_4$)$_3$, 25%

Dissolve 25 g of NH$_4$Fe(SO$_4$)$_2$.12H$_2$O in about 100 ml of H$_2$O to which 5 drops (0·25 ml) of HNO$_3$ (C) have been added.

E   KCNS, 0·02 N

Dissolve 2 g of KCNS in 1 litre of H$_2$O. Standardize against AgNO$_3$ as described in the procedure below.

F   Nitrobenzene, pure (POISONOUS)

Procedure

Mix 100 ml of the sample containing not more than 35 mg Cl$^-$, (or an aliquot diluted to 100 ml) with 5 ml HNO$_3$ (C). Add AgNO$_3$ (B) from a burette, mixing vigorously, to the approximate end point. This may be recognized as the point when no precipitation near the AgNO$_3$ drops occurs. Add about 2 ml more (= excess) of AgNO$_3$, and record the volume of AgNO$_3$ added. Add 3 ml of nitrobenzene (F) and 1 ml of Fe$_2$(SO$_4$)$_3$ solution (D). Shake vigorously and titrate the excess Ag$^+$, after the coagulation of the precipitate, with standardized KCNS (E). At the end point a permanent reddish colour appears, which does not fade in 1 minute of intensive shaking.

For the standardization of the KCNS (E) use 100 ml of H$_2$O + 10·0 ml of AgNO$_3$ (B).

Interferences

I$^-$, Br$^-$ and S^{2-} are measured as equivalents of Cl$^-$.

Calculation

$$Cl^- \text{ meq} = Ag^+ \text{ meq} - CNS^- \text{ meq}$$
$$Cl^- \text{ meq/l} = \frac{[(ml \times Normality) \text{ of B} - (ml \times Normality) \text{ of E}] \times 1000}{ml \text{ sample}}$$
$$Cl^- \text{ mg/l} = Cl^- \text{ meq/l} \times 35·46$$

Precision and accuracy

Both are limited by the accuracy of the end point detection, which is better than 0·2 ml, or 0·1 mg Cl$^-$. To obtain higher precision the AgNO$_3$ may be added from a pipette. This means however that the concentration of Cl$^-$ must be known approximately before starting.

Note

The use of the commercially available standardized solutions of AgNO$_3$ and KCNS is strongly recommended.

LEVEL II

4.6.3. Potentiometric titration

Principle

The change of an Ag-electrode potential with the Ag^+ concentration in the solution, is of the same nature as the change of the potential of the glass electrode with H^+ concentration—see § 9.7 and § 9.9. The Ag-electrode can therefore be used to follow the course of the titration with Ag^+.

Reagents

A_1 $AgNO_3$, 0·1 N. See § 4.6.2
A_2 $AgNO_3$, 0·02 N
Dilute A_1 5 times.

B HNO_3, 1+1. See § 4.6.2.

Apparatus

Silver rod indicator electrodes and reference electrodes, made of either calomel or silver-silver chloride, may be bought. (As Cl^- diffuses from calomel electrodes into the sample, the electrode must be placed in a second flask connected to the titration flask by an NH_4NO_3 or KNO_3 agar bridge. Alternatively $HgSO_4$ electrodes can be used.) A normal pH meter can be used.

Procedure

Mix 100 ml of sample, containing not more than 35 mg of Cl^- (if using 0·1 N $AgNO_3$) or not more than 7 mg of Cl^- (if using 0·02 N $AgNO_3$) (or an aliquot diluted to about 100 ml) with 10 drops (0·5 ml) of HNO_3 (B). Add $AgNO_3$ from a burette, at first in relatively large portions (e.g. 1/5, 2/5, 3/5 and 4/5 of the expected quantity) but approaching the equivalence point in smaller quantities, depending on the precision required. Continue beyond the equivalence point in larger steps again. Record the potential difference at each point.

Interferences

Br^-, I^- and S^{2-} are measured as equivalents of Cl^-.

Calculation

Plot potential difference E, versus ml $AgNO_3$ used, and if necessary

$$\frac{\Delta E}{\Delta V} \quad \text{and} \quad \frac{\Delta^2 E}{\Delta V^2}$$

versus ml $AgNO_3$ used. The last curve gives the greatest precision.

Precision and accuracy

These depend on the apparatus used and the quantity of Cl^- present. The accuracy can be 0·2 % if a microburette is used.

Sensitivity

The sensitivity is about 1–2 mg/l of Cl^-. In this range and below use the method of § 4.6.4.

4.6.4. Conductometric titration for low Cl^- concentrations

Principle

See § 9.1 and fig. 9.2B.

Reagents

As for § 4.6.3.

Apparatus

A normal conductivity meter can be used. Meters with a titration attachment are preferable for accurate work.

Procedure

As for § 4.6.3, but also record the conductance well beyond the end point. Note that if the curve before the equivalence point is nearly horizontal, then the precision of the conductometric titration depends mostly on the points beyond the equivalence point. Points around the end point are of no use.

Interferences

As for § 4.3.3.

Calculation

Plot the conductance versus ml $AgNO_3$. The equivalence point is given by the point of intersection of the two lines

$$Cl^- \text{ meq/l} = \frac{(\text{ml} \times \text{Normality}) \text{ of A} \times 1000}{\text{ml sample}}$$

$$Cl^- \text{ mg/l} = Cl^- \text{ meq/l} \times 35 \cdot 46.$$

Precision and accuracy

As for § 4.6.3.

LEVEL III

4.6.5. Potentiometric

The same as in level II, but with an automatic recorder and motorburette or an automatic titrator. The procedure § 4.6.3 can easily be automated.

4.7 SULPHATE

LEVEL I

4.7.1. Turbidimetric

Principle

SO_4^{2-} is precipitated with Ba^{2+} in an acid solution. It is assumed that it is possible to obtain $BaSO_4$ crystals of uniform size. (Glycerol–ethanol solution is added as a stabilizer). Light extinction is measured with a (battery operated) colorimeter (or turbidimeter). Any wavelength between 380 and 420 mμ, or white light can be used.

Reagents

A   Standard H_2SO_4, $0 \cdot 0200$ N ($= 961$ mg/1 SO_4^{2-}).

Dilute $0 \cdot 100$ N H_2SO_4 (see § 1.4.1), ($50 \cdot 0$ ml → 250 ml).

B   NaCl–HCl solution

Dissolve 240 g of NaCl in 900 ml of H_2O. Add 20 ml of HCl (A.R., s.g. = 1.19) and dilute to 1 litre.

C BaCl$_2$.2H$_2$O dry, 20–30 mesh crystals.

D Glycerol–alcohol solution
Mix 1 volume of glycerol with two volumes of ethanol.

Procedure
Mix 50·0 ml of filtered sample containing not more than 10 mg/1 SO$_4^{2-}$ (or an aliquot diluted to 50·0 ml) with 10·0 ml each of solution (B) and (D). Measure the extinction against a H$_2$O blank in a colorimeter at any wavelength between 380 mμ and 420 mμ, or in a turbidimeter with white light.
   Add 0·15 g of BaCl$_2$ (a "constant spoonful") and place on a magnetic stirrer for 30 minutes, or shake constantly and in a repeatable manner for 5 minutes exactly. Measure the extinction after 30 minutes. The extinction due to SO$_4^{2-}$ is obtained by difference.

Calibration and calculation
Prepare a calibration curve in the range of 0·02–0·2 meq/1 SO$_4^{2-}$ or 1–10 mg/1 SO$_4^{2-}$ using dilutions of H$_2$SO$_4$ (A). It is desirable to make this calibration curve with the lake water itself.
1 meq SO$_4^{2-}$ = 48·05 mg SO$_4^{2-}$ = 16·0 mg SO$_4$–S.

Interferences and errors
In highly acidified fresh water, SO$_4^{2-}$ is the only ion which forms a precipitate with Ba^{2+}. Coloured and suspended compounds interfere, while organic compounds may alter the crystal size.

Precision and accuracy
   The precision will be about 10%, but under favourable conditions (e.g. dilution of the sample) it may be better. The use of monochromatic light and a magnetic stirrer improves the precision. The use of internal standards will improve the accuracy.

LEVEL I

4.7.2. By calculation (from the conductivity)
The sulphate concentration can sometimes be calculated from the conductivity of the sample and the concentrations of NO$_3^-$ and Cl$^-$. See Mackereth (1955).

LEVEL II

4.7.3. Complexometric (Tentative)

Principle
An accurately measured (excess) amount of Ba^{2+} is added to the sample. BaSO$_4$ precipitates, and the remaining Ba^{2+} is back-titrated with Na$_2$–EDTA; see § 4.3. Interference may occur from Ca^{2+} or Mg^{2+}. If SO$_4^{2-}$, and Ca^{2+} plus Mg^{2+} is present in high concentration, the cations are best removed by sorption on a cation exchange resin. The effluent SO$_4^{2-}$ may then be determined. If the concentration of Ca^{2+} plus Mg^{2+} is high relative to that of SO$_4^{2-}$, then it may be better to separate the cations and anions with an anion exchange resin. This retains the SO$_4^{2-}$, which is subsequently eluted and estimated. An additional advantage of this method is that the SO$_4^{2-}$ may be concentrated from a large sample volume.
   Organic compounds, which may also interfere, are partly destroyed by boiling the eluate (from the anion exchange resin) with HClO$_4$.

The anion exchanger method is given here in detail; the cation exchanger method only in outline.

Reagents

A₁ Na₂EDTA solution, 0·050 M*

A₂ Na₂EDTA solution, 0·020 M
Dilute 0·1 M of Na₂EDTA (see § 1.4.1).
(A₁ 50.0 ml → 100·0 ml; A₂ 50·0 ml → 250 ml)
(See note on H₂O on page 9, § 1.4.1.)

B Mg–Na₂EDTA solution, 0·25 M
Dissolve 98·5 g of Mg–Na₂EDTA in 1 litre of H_2O.

C HCl, 1 N
Dilute 4 N HCl (see § 1.4.1) (0·25 litre → 1 litre).

D HClO₄, 60%

E NaOH, 1 N
Dilute 10 N NaOH (see § 1.4.1).

F NH₄OH, 2·5 N
Dilute NH₄OH 25% × 5 (0·2 → 1 litre).

G₁ BaCl₂ solution, 0·01 M

G₂ BaCl₂ solution, 0·05 M
Dissolve 2·5 g (G₁) or 12·5 g (G₂) of BaCl₂.2H₂O in 1 litre of H_2O.
Standardize against the EDTA solution as described in the procedure below.

H₁ Buffer solution
See Ca^{2+} plus Mg^{2+} determination, § 4.3.1, solution C₁.

H₂ Buffer solution
See Ca^{2+} plus Mg^{2+} determination, § 4.3.3, solution C₂.

I Eriochrome Black T indicator (solid)
See § 4.3.1.

J KCN solution, 0·1% (highly poisonous)
Dissolve 0·1 g of KCN in 100 ml of H_2O. Keep in a brown glass bottle.
Dispense from a dropping bottle.

L Amberlite I.R.A. 68 anion exchange resin column in $HCO_3{}^-$ form
Details of resin column packing and management are given in most books dealing with ion exchange. The most important point is to prevent the prepared column getting air into it. This may be done by taking a capillary tube from the outlet of the resin bed to just above the top of the resin bed.

Prepare a column, about 1–2 cm diameter with a resin bed about 20 cm deep. To do this, close the outlet and pour in a slurry of resin and H_2O. The resin will settle to form a bed without air bubbles.

---

* See footnotes on p. 37.

E

The resin must be converted to the HCO_3^- form by passing through it about 100 ml of H_2O saturated with CO_2 (bubble CO_2 for about half an hour). The bed may be used repeatedly, but should be regenerated to the HCO_3^- form before each determination.

K   Methyl orange, 0·05% (see § 3.4.1).

Procedure 1

Titrate a 50 ml filtered subsample with HCl (C) to the methyl orange (K) end point. To a second filtered subsample add the same amount of HCl (C), and then an accurately measured (excess) amount of $BaCl_2$ (G_1).

Boil for 1 minute and cool to room temperature. Titrate the excess of Ba^{2+} (plus Ca^{2+} and Mg^{2+}) as described for the Ca^{2+} plus Mg^{2+} determination (§ 4.3.1 or § 4.3.3).

Interferences and errors

In the acidified fresh water sample SO_4^{2-} are the only ions that precipitate with Ba^{2+}. The concentrations of Ca^{2+} and Mg^{2+} can, however, be so high that the estimation becomes unreliable. Humic substances, and/or iron also affect the result. Ion-exchangers can be used to overcome interferences from these causes. Ca^{2+} and Mg^{2+} can be removed by passing 100 ml of the sample over a strong cation-exchanger in H^+ form (washed free of acid with H_2O), and discarding the first 25 ml of eluate. The following 50 ml may be used as the acidified sample in § 4.7.3 procedure.

Calculation

mM SO_4^{2-} = mM $(Ca^{2+}+Mg^{2+})+$mM $Ba^{2+}-$mM EDTA
1 mM SO_4^{2-} = 32 mg SO_4-S = 96·1 mg SO_4^{2-}
mM $(Ca^{2+}+Mg^{2+})$ is found in ml EDTA (see § 4.3.1 or § 4.3.3).
mM Ba^{2+} follows from the standardization.
When ion exchangers are used:

$$mM\ (Ca^{2+}+Mg^{2+}) = 0.$$

Ca^{2+} plus Mg^{2+} may be removed by procedure 2, which increases the SO_4^{2-} concentration if samples larger than 100 ml are used.

Procedure 2

Pass a suitable sized sample (usually between 100 to 500 ml) over the anion-exchanger in the HCO_3^- form. The flow rate should be about 1 ml per 10–20 sec. Elute with 100 ml of 2·5 N NH_4OH (F). Boil in 250 ml covered beakers with 2–5 drops (0·1–0·2ml) of 1 N NaOH (E) till the NH_3 has been removed. Use anti-bumping glass rods. Acidify with $HClO_4$ (D) till the pH = 1·5–2·0. Heat to boiling and add slowly exactly 4 ml of $BaCl_2$ (G_2) from a piston microburette. Boil for 10 min. Cool and adjust the pH to 9 with 2·5 N NH_4OH (F). Add from a dropping bottle 5 drops of KCN (J), 4 ml of Mg EDTA (B) and buffer solution (H_2) to pH = 10. Add about 50 mg of the indicator (I) and titrate at once with 0·050 M Na_2EDTA (A_1). Just before the end point, add more indicator if need be. Titrate from red till there is no further change in the blue colour. Make a blank using H_2O instead of the sample.

Calculation

$$mM\ SO_4{}^{2-} = [(ml\ of\ A_1)_{blank} - (ml\ of\ A_1)_{sample}] \times Molarity\ of\ A_1$$

Note:

If sufficient $SO_4{}^{2-}$ is present procedure 4.7.4 may be tried after the acidification with $HClO_4$. In this case, use as little NaOH as possible.

LEVEL II

4.7.4. Potentiometric (Tentative). (Only for $SO_4{}^{2-}$ exceeding 50 mg/l)

Principle

Pb^{2+} forms a precipitate with $SO_2{}^{2-}$. Ethanol is added to reduce the solubility of the $PbSO_4$. When all the $SO_4{}^-$ ions are precipitated Pb^{2+} will precipitate ferrocyanide (added to the sample) as lead-ferrocyanide, causing a sharp change in potential of the indicator electrode. Pt and Ag-electrodes are used.

Reagents

A H_2SO_4, 0·0200 N (See § 4.7.1).

B $Pb(NO_3)_2$, 0·025 N

Dissolve 4·14 g of $Pb(NO_3)_2$ in 1 litre of H_2O.
Standardize against 0·0200 N $SO_4{}^{2-}$ as described in § 4.7.4, procedure.

C $K_4Fe(CN)_6$ solution, 0·005 M

Dissolve 0·21 g of $K_4Fe(CN)_6.3H_2O$ (A.R.) in about 100 ml of H_2O.

D $K_3Fe(CN)_6$ solution, 0·1 M

Dissolve 33 g of $K_3Fe(CN)_6$ (A.R.) in 1 litre of H_2O.

Procedure

Put 25·0 ml of slightly acidified sample into a 100 ml titration flask fitted with a Pt-electrode (0·5 mm diameter), (as reference electrode) and a Ag-electrode (3–4 mm rod). Add an equal volume of 96% ethanol, 0·1 ml of solution (C) and 1·0 ml of solution (D). Stir with a magnetic stirrer, and add from a 5 ml microburette the $Pb(NO_3)_2$ (B) in portions of 1 ml at first, and then in portions of 0·1 ml when the end point is near.

Interferences

Phosphate and Ca^{2+} may interfere if present in high concentrations.

Precision and accuracy

Unknown.

Calculations

$$Plot\ \frac{\Delta E}{\Delta V}\ \ or\ \ \frac{\Delta^2 E}{\Delta V^2}\ against\ volume\ as\ described\ in\ \S\ 9.12.$$

$$SO_4{}^{2-}\ meq/l = \frac{(ml \times Normality)\ of\ B \times 1000}{ml\ of\ sample}$$

$$SO_4{}^{2-}\ mg/l = meq/l\ SO_4{}^{2-} \times 48·05.$$

4.8 TOTAL AND DISSOLVED HYDROGEN SULPHIDE

LEVEL I

4.8.1. Titrimetric

Principle

The S^{2-} is precipitated with $CdCl_2$ in the same type of bottle as used for the Winkler method of O_2 determination (see § 8.1). When the precipitate has settled the supernatant is removed and the CdS is dissolved in an acid iodine solution. The excess iodine is titrated with $S_2O_3^{2-}$

$$H_2S + I_2 \rightarrow S + 2H^+ + 2I^-$$

Reagents

A   HCl, 4 N (See § 1.4.1).

B   Na$_2$S$_2$O$_3$ solution, 0·025 N (See § 8.1.2).

C   CdCl$_2$, 2 % (See § 4.8.2).

D   Iodine solution, 0·025 N

Dissolve 20 g of KI in 50 ml of H_2O and add 3·17 g of I_2. After the iodine has dissolved, dilute to 1 litre and standardize against standardized $Na_2S_2O_3$ with starch as indicator. (see § 8.1.2.).

Procedure

Completely fill a glass stoppered bottle with the water sample in the field, following the procedure described in § 8.1.2. The volume of the bottle should be about 110 ml, and should be known. Add 1 ml $CdCl_2$ solution (C). Take the sample to the laboratory and allow to stand for 24 or 48 hours. Decant the supernatant (for example with a pipette connected to a vacuum pump). Dissolve the precipitate in an exactly known small volume of iodine solution (D) and 5 ml HCl (A). Titrate the excess iodine with standardized $S_2O_3^{2-}$ as described in procedure § 8.1.2.

Interferences

If much organic matter is present the precipitate should be collected on a membrane filter and washed with H_2O.

Calculation

$$H_2S \text{ meq/l} = \frac{I_2 \text{ meq} - S_2O_3^{2-} \text{ meq}}{\text{ml sample} - 1 \text{ ml}} \times 1000$$

$$1 \text{ meq } H_2S = 17 \text{ mg of } H_2S = 16 \text{ mg of S.}$$

Precision and accuracy

The precision and the accuracy are estimated at 5–10 % and depend on the care with which the different steps are carried out.

LEVEL II

4.8.2. Colorimetric

Principle

H_2S and N,N-dimethyl-p-phenylenediamine (I) (=p-amino dimethylaniline) are converted to methylene blue (II) in the presence of $FeCl_3$ and in suitable physical conditions.

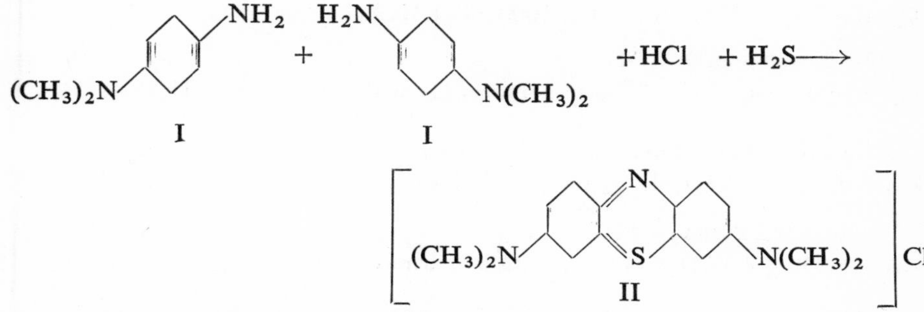

A distinction between dissolved and total H_2S can be made by using a filtered and an unfiltered sample.

Storage

If necessary the S^{2-} in a sample can be stored as a precipitate by adding 2 ml of solutions (C) or (F) per litre of sample (for total sulphide) or of filtrate (for dissolved sulphide). Each precipitate must then be transferred quantitatively into a 100 ml volumetric flask.

Reagents

A_1 Standard Na_2S solution

Rinse quickly with H_2O about 0·6 g of large crystals of $Na_2S.9H_2O$. Discard the washings. Dissolve the washed crystals in about 500 ml of recently boiled H_2O which has cooled out of contact with the air. Fill the container completely (to exclude gas bubbles), stopper, and mix.

Mix 200 ml of H_2O with 50·0 ml 0·025 N iodine solution (§ 4.8.1), 25 ml of 0·1 N HCl, and 20·0 ml of solution (A_1). Titrate the excess iodine with thiosulphate (see § 8.1.2). 2·5 ml of iodine solution is equivalent to 1·00 mg of S^{2-}.

A_2 Diluted Na_2S standard

Dilute an aliquot of solution (A_1) containing 10·0 mg of S^{2-} to 500 ml with O_2-free H_2O. Stopper at once and mix (A_2). Avoid contact with air.

Both solutions are extremely unstable and must be used immediately.

B Stock solution of N, N-dimethyl-p-phenylenediamine

Add 50 ml of H_2SO_4 (A.R.) (s.g. 1·84) to 30 ml of H_2O, and cool. Dissolve in this solution 20 g of the redistilled amine or 27 g of the amine sulphate. Stir and make up to about 100 ml with H_2O.

B_1 Test solution, 0·5%

Mix 25 ml of the stock solution (B) with 975 ml H_2SO_4 (1+1).

B$_2$ Test solution, 0·2%
Mix 10 ml of the stock solution (B) with 990 ml H$_2$SO$_4$ (1+1).
Do not use solutions B$_1$ and B$_2$ which have been mixed for more than 24 hours.

C   CdCl$_2$ solution, 2%
Dissolve 20 g of CdCl$_2$ in 1 litre of H$_2$O.

D$_1$ FeCl$_3$ solution, 0·1 M
Dissolve 27 g of FeCl$_3$.6H$_2$O in 1000 ml of HCl (1+1).

D$_2$ FeCl$_3$ solution, 0·02 M
Dilute before use one volume of solution D$_1$ with 4 volumes of H$_2$O.

E   (NH$_4$)$_2$HPO$_4$ solution, 3 M
Dissolve 400 g (NH$_4$)$_2$HPO$_4$ in 800 ml H$_2$O.

F   Zn acetate solution, 1 M
Dissolve 240 g Zn(CH$_3$COO)$_2$.2H$_2$O in 1 litre of H$_2$O.

Procedure
Put 90·0 ml of sample or the CdS or ZnS precipitates into a 100 ml volumetric
flask, and add 5 ml (B$_1$) or (B$_2$) (neither more than 24 hours old). Use (B$_1$) if 0·2 to
20 mg/l S^{2-} and (B$_2$) if 0·05 to 5 mg/l S^{2-} is expected. Mix well and add 1 ml of
freshly diluted FeCl$_3$ solution (D$_2$) with gentle shaking. Dilute to 100 ml. Measure
the extinction of reagent blank, standards and samples in suitable cells at a wavelength as close as possible to 745 mμ after not less than 15 minutes but not more
than 2 hours.
    If a separation between dissolved and particulate S^{2-} is required the filtration must
be carried out with exclusion of O$_2$, for example under N$_2$. If vacuum filtration is
to be used the sample must be made strongly alkaline beforehand, to prevent loss
of H$_2$S.
    The yellow colour of the iron may be destroyed by adding a few ml of solution (E).

Calibration and calculation
Make a calibration curve covering the range 0·05 to 20 mg S^{2-}.

1 meq H$_2$S = 17 mg H$_2$S = 16 mg H$_2$S—S.

Interferences
Organic sulphides do not interfere.
    Strong reducing agents prevent the formation of the colour. High S^{2-} concen-
trations (above several hundred mg/l) may inhibit the reaction. Dilute in this case.
SO$_3{}^{2-}$ does not interfere up to 10 mg/l.
    Aeration of samples and standard solutions leads to oxidation and volatilization
and must therefore be avoided.

Precision and accuracy
The standard deviation is unknown. The accuracy is about 10% and depends
mainly on the accuracy of the standard curve.
    The method is sensitive to 0·005 mg/l S^{2-}.

4.9 CARBONATE AND BICARBONATE

Determination of CO_3^{2-} and HCO_3^- is described in chapter 1. (In those cases where H^+ or OH^- are important, they may be estimated from the pH.)

4.10 CALCULATION OF IONIC BALANCE AND CONDUCTANCE

LEVEL II

If all major elements are estimated, an ionic balance may be calculated. The sum of all positive ions (in meq/l) should equal the sum of all negative ions (in meq/l). Furthermore comparison of the conductance calculated from this balance with the observed conductance gives a good check of the overall accuracy obtained.

For calculation of the ionic balance the *total alkalinity* (expressed in meq/l) as determined in procedures § 3.4.2, § 3.4.3 or § 3.4.4 may be used.

For calculation of the conductance it is important to know what part of the total alkalinity is caused by HCO_3^-, CO_3^{2-} and organic acids.

In an ionic balance there is usually a difference of 2% (favourable conditions) to 5%, due to analytical errors, even if all the sort of ions have been analysed. A larger imbalance may indicate the presence of unsuspected ions in unusual quantities. A smaller difference may be due to compensating errors. The ions normally contributing much to the ionic balance are mentioned in this chapter. In certain types of water other cations form a significant proportion of the whole. Such a case may be that of NH_4^+ in anaerobic waters. (The anions of weak acids are estimated in the alkalinity-titration, see § 3.4 and § 9.7).

To calculate the conductance it is necessary to add the contributions of the different ions. These are found by multiplying the ionic conductance per meq/l (Table 4.1) by the meq/l found.

Table 4.1. Equivalent conductance of major ions in micromho/cm at 18° and 25°C.

	18°C	25°C		18°C	25°C
OH^-	172	192	H^+	314	350
HCO_3^-		44·5	$\frac{1}{2}Ca^{2+}$	51	60·0
$\frac{1}{2}CO_3^{2-}$		69·3	$\frac{1}{2}Mg^{2+}$		53·0
Cl^-	65·5	76·4	K^+	64·6	74
NO_3^-	62	71·5	Na^+	43·5	50·5
$\frac{1}{2}SO_4^{2-}$	68	80·0	NH_4^+	64·5	74
			Fe^{2+}		54

There are discrepancies of 1% to 5% in different reported values for these "constants".

The best results ($\pm 5\%$) are obtained if the water sample is diluted with H_2O (by trial and error) until the conductance is about 100 (± 20) μmho/cm. The dilution factor must be known. The conductance of the dilution H_2O should not be greater than 2 micromhos/cm and the contribution from this source should be subtracted from the measured conductance.

CHAPTER 5

DETERMINATION OF MINOR* ELEMENTS

NITROGEN, PHOSPHORUS AND SILICON COMPOUNDS

NITROGEN COMPOUNDS

5.1 AMMONIA, NITRATE AND NITRITE

Note

Special attention should be given to ensure that no NH_3 from the environment is taken up during these analyses, particularly by the H_2SO_4. For example, smoking should be prevented in the laboratory. Ammonia bottles should not be kept or opened in the laboratory.

LEVEL II

Colorimetric

5.1.1. Ammonia

5.1.2. Nitrate

Principle

NH_4^+ reacts with K_2HgI_4 in strongly alkaline conditions to form a brown coloured substance. In nearly all fresh waters interfering substances are present which make a steam distillation of the NH_3 obligatory. This distillation can also be used to concentrate the NH_3.

NO_3^- (and NO_2^-) are completely reduced to NH_3 by Devarda's alloy under strongly alkaline conditions and may then be determined as NH_3. The NO_3^- and NO_2^- determination may be made later on the same sample as was used for NH_3 determination.

Apparatus

There are a number of satisfactory designs of apparatus for distilling off NH_3. That described here is a modified Parnas–Wagner still (see fig. 5.1). Simpler apparatus can also be used, but will not usually allow the determination of NH_3, the reduction of NO_3^- and the determination of organic nitrogen in one sample.

Reagents

H_2O

If the H_2O contains traces of NH_3, redistill the H_2O with a small quantity of H_2SO_4 added. Deionized H_2O may also be used. Care should be taken if this method of purification is used because there are commercially available ion exchangers which produce H_2O with a very low conductivity (practically no ions) but which release organic substances into the water which interfere with the NH_3 determination.

---

* MINOR refers to concentrations, not to biological importance.

A₁ (NH₄)₂SO₄ **standard solution, 200 µg/ml of NH₃–N.**

Dissolve 0·9433 g of $(NH_4)_2SO_4$ (A.R., dried in a desiccator) in 1000 ml of H_2O. This solution contains 200 $\mu g/ml$ of NH_3–N. Standardize with procedure § 5.2.2.

A₂ (NH₄)₂ SO₄ **standard solution, 2 µg/ml of NH₃–N**

Dilute solution A_1 100 times. Solution A_2 contains 2 $\mu g/ml$ of NH_3–N.

B KNO₃ **standard solution, 2 µg/ml of NO₃–N**

Dissolve 0·3611 g of KNO_3 (A.R. dried at 105°C) in 250 ml of H_2O. Dilute an aliquot 100 times (10·0 ml → 1000 ml). This diluted solution contains 2 $\mu g/ml$ of NO_3–N.

C H₂SO₄, 0·04 N

Add 2 ml of H_2SO_4 (1+1) (A.R.) (see § 1.4.1) to 1 litre of H_2O.

D NaOH, 5 N

Dilute 10 N NaOH (see § 1.4.1).

E Na₂B₄O₇.10 H₂O (saturated solution)

Add 4 g of $Na_2B_4O_7.10H_2O$ (A.R.) to 100 ml of H_2O. Heat until all crystals are dissolved and store at room temperature. A small amount of precipitate will appear.

F Nessler's reagent.

F₁

Dissolve 25 g of HgI_2 (red) and 20 g of KI in 500 ml of H_2O.

F₂

Dissolve 100 g of NaOH in 500 ml of H_2O. These reagents can be stored for several months in air-tight bottles. Glass stoppered bottles are not suitable.
Mix 1 vol. F_1 + 1 vol. F_2, and keep in a refrigerator.

G Devarda's alloy (A.R.)

Commercially available. If blanks are high due to the Devarda's alloy it must be purified by heating for one hour at 120–150°C in an open dish.

Procedure

5.1.1. Ammonia

Put a 50 ml volumetric flask below the condenser outlet of the distillation apparatus if 50–500 μg of NH_3–N is expected. Use a 25 ml volumetric flask if only 5–100 μg of NH_3–N is expected.

Close tap C. Put the sample in the distillation apparatus through the funnel and tap A. Add 1 ml of buffer solution (E). Close tap A immediately. The outlet of the condenser dips just into 2·5 ml of 0·04 N H_2SO_4 (C) in the volumetric flask. Close tap B and pass steam through the apparatus until 40 ml (or 20 ml if the smaller flask is used) of distillate has been collected. Lower the volumetric flask and collect a few more mls of distillate. If NO_3 is to be determined subsequently (§ 5.1.2), leave the sample in the still by opening tap B and then shutting off the steam supply. If the sample is no longer required however it may be removed by simply shutting off the steam supply. The sample will suck back into the outer container and may be

removed by opening tap **B**. Make the distillate up to volume and mix. Take 20 ml
of the distillate, (or an aliquot containing not more than 100 μg of NH$_3$–N and
diluted to 20 ml), in a tube 20 cm × 3 cm and add 1·00 ml of Nessler's reagent (F)
very slowly, while swirling. Cover with, for example, a watch glass.

Run a blank (using twice distilled H$_2$O) before and after each series of samples,
and standards covering the range 10 to 100 μg of NH$_3$–N. The same curve should
fit standards both before and after distillation. Measure the extinction of the
reagent blank, standards and samples, against water, in suitable cells using any
wavelength between 380 and 430 mμ. Reagent blanks in one series should not differ
more than 5%. Daily variations may be two or three times as much.

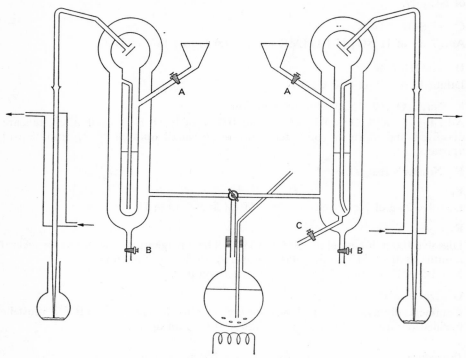

Figure 5.1. Modified Parnas–Wagner distillation apparatus.

5.1.2. Nitrate (and nitrite)

Add about 0·2 g of Devarda's alloy (G) to the sample—after NH$_3$ has been
removed by distillation—and then add slowly 5 ml of 5 N NaOH. Put a volumetric
flask containing H$_2$SO$_4$ (C) below the condenser outlet (as described for NH$_3$–N
determination). Close tap **A**. Leave tap **B** open and pass steam through the outer
container (but not through the sample) for 10 minutes. The sample is thus heated
and H$_2$ gas is generated. Because the condenser outlet is narrow, pressure inside the
apparatus increases, and sample may be forced over into the outer steam jacket. To
prevent this happening the tap **B** may have to be closed partly, but not so much
as to force steam through the sample. During this procedure the NO$_2^-$ and NO$_3^-$
are reduced to NH$_3$, which is later distilled off by completely closing tap **B**.

Determine the NH_3 as described above.

Calibrate against the NH_3 standard curve, and use KNO_3 to check that reduction is stoicheiometric. The sample can be recovered through tap C for determination of organic nitrogen compounds (§ 5.5.1).

Calculation

The amount of the NO_2^- is determined according to procedure § 5.4 and must be subtracted to give the amount of NO_3^-.

Note

Blanks and samples containing Nessler's reagent and the stock of the mixed reagent itself must be exposed to the air as little as possible. With the mixed reagent, blanks are higher but the colour of the samples is more stable than with reagent mixed just before use.

Interferences

In polluted water (e.g. water polluted by sewage, water from fish ponds etc.) nitrogen compounds may occur which hydrolyse during the distillation procedure § 5.1.1 or § 5.1.2.

If these compounds are present they will hydrolyse in part during the first distillation step (2), but some may hydrolyse slowly, and NH_3 will be found in a subsequent distillate (3). Consider this NH_3 (3) to be organically bound and estimate the inorganic NH_3 in the first distillate by subtracting the NH_3 in distillate (3) from that in distillate (2).

Alternatively, try the tentative procedure § 5.2.3.

When compounds which hydrolyse during the reduction step are present, add to the main procedure a distillation step using 5 N NaOH, before the reduction step takes place. Collect this distillate. Then add Devarda's alloy to the sample (carefully), and measure the NH_3 in both distillates. Alternatively, try the tentative procedure § 5.3.1.

The following scheme should deal with these situations.

Determination of NH_3–N
(1) Add 1 ml of borax to the sample and
(2) collect distillate; analyse for NH_3 and
(3) collect in the meanwhile another distillate and analyse for NH_3
(4) If NH_3 is present hydrolysable products are present, GO BACK TO step 3 (continue distillation).
    If no NH_3 is present GO ON TO step 5

Determination of NO_3–N + NO_2–N
(5) Add 10 ml of NaOH to the sample in the still
(6) Collect distillate, analyse for NH_3
(7) If NH_3 is present, decomposable products are present, GO BACK TO step 6 (continue distillation)
    If no NH_3 is present, GO ON TO step 8
(8) Add Devarda's alloy
(9) Collect distillate; analyse for NH_3

Calculations
(A) If the answer to (4) is **NO** on the first pass: Total NH_3 is given by (2) above
(B) If the answer to (4) is **YES** on the first pass: Total NH_3 is given approximately by $(2)-(3)_{1st}$
    Hydrolyseable NH_3 is given approximately by $2 \times (3)_{1st} + (3)_{2nd} + (3)_{3rd} + (3)_{nth}$
(C) If the answer to (7) is **NO** on the first pass: $NO_3^- + NO_2^-$ is given by (9)
(D) If the answer to (7) is **YES** on the first pass: Decomposable –N is given by $(6)_{1st} + (6)_{2nd} + (6)_{3rd} + (6)_{nth}$ and $NO_3^- + NO_2^-$ is again given by (9).

After the "reduction" distillation, and before another sample is introduced, the Devarda's alloy must be removed carefully from the still. This is laborious, and can be avoided if two apparatuses can be used; one for $NH_3 + NO_2^- + NO_3^-$, and the other for NH_3 alone. This is suitable only if NH_3 and $NO_3^- + NO_2^-$ are present in approximately equal amounts.

AMMONIA

LEVEL I

5.2.1. Colorimetric (tentative)

Principle

As for level II but using a simple colorimeter or Hellige comparator without a preceding distillation.

This method is rarely suitable, owing to the variety of types of interfering agents, (e.g. organic matter, precipitation of Ca^{2+}, natural colour of the water).
Precipitation of salts of Ca and Mg can be prevented in some cases by adding an equivalent amount of EDTA

Reagents

See level II, § 5.1.1.

Procedure

Dissolve about 50 mg of Na_2 EDTA (see § 4.3.1) in 25 ml of sample. Add dropwise 1 ml of Nessler's reagent (F).
Measure the extinction according to the directions given in level II, but using a simple colorimeter.

LEVEL II

5.2.2. Volumetric (tentative)

Principle

When much NH_3 is present (or is formed by the reduction of NO_3^- or by destruction of organic nitrogen) the determination can be carried out by titration with HCl. The distillate is first collected in saturated H_3BO_3 solution. H_3BO_3 is so weak an acid that it does not interfere with the acidimetric titration.

Reagents

A   HCl, 0·0100 N
Dilute 0·100 N HCl (see § 1.4.1) (25·0 ml → 250 ml).

B   Saturated H_3BO_3 + mixed indicator
Dissolve 40 g of H_3BO_3 in 1 litre of H_2O and add 5 ml of a mixed solution of bromcresol green (0·5 %) and methyl red (0·1 %) in 95 % ethanol. Adjust the pH with HCl until the bluish colour turns faint pink.

Procedure

The distillation of the NH_3 present in the sample, is carried out as described in procedure § 5.1.1, but 2 ml of H_3BO_3 (B) is used in the volumetric flask instead of

H_2SO_4. Titrate with 0·01 N HCl (A) from a microburette until the bluish colour changes back to pink (= α ml). Run a blank using NH_3-free H_2O instead of the sample and titrate until the same colour as the sample (= β ml).

Calculation

$$\text{N mg per sample} = (\alpha - \beta) \text{ ml} \times 0·01 \times 14$$

and

$$\text{N mg/l} = \frac{(\alpha - \beta) \text{ ml} \times 0·01 \times 1000 \times 14}{\text{ml sample}}$$

Note

The titration method can only be used when sufficient NH_3–N is present to neutralize about 1 ml of 0·01 N HCl i.e. 0·14 mg of N or 2·8 mg/1 N (using 50 ml samples). In most cases the titration cannot therefore be used for fresh water, but is suitable for samples of particulate organic nitrogen (after filtration and destruction, see § 5.5.2) and to check the NH_3 – N standard solution (A_1 procedure § 5.1.1) after distillation.

LEVEL II

5.2.3. Colorimetric (tentative)

Principle

Ammonia and bis-pyrazolone are converted to rubazoic acid in the presence of chloramine T at pH about 6. Rubazoic acid is pink violet in an aqueous solution, and can be extracted into the less polar organic solvents as the yellow undissociated acid. (See Procházková, 1964).

Bis-pyrazolone is:

3,3′-dimethyl-5,5′-dioxo-1,1′-diphenyl-(4,4′-bi-2-pyrazoline).

Rubazoic acid is:

3-methyl-4-(3-methyl-5-oxo-1-phenylpyrazonyliden-4-amino)-5-oxo-1-phenyl-2-pyrazoline.

Reagents

A $(NH_4)_2SO_4$ standard solution, 200 µg/ml of NH_3–N (See § 5.1.1).

B HCl, 0·5 N

Dilute 4 N HCl (§ 1.4.1) 8 times.

C Citrate-phosphate buffer, pH = 5.8

Dissolve 8·30 g of citric acid [(COOH)CH_2C(OH)(COOH)CH_2COOH . H_2O] and 21·5 g of Na_2HPO_4 . $2H_2O$ in H_2O, and dilute to 1 litre. Add several drops of CCl_4 as preservative.

D Bis-pyrazolone solution

Dissolve 0·2 g of bis-pyrazolone in 120 ml of 0·5 N Na_2CO_3 at about 90°C and cool to room temperature before use. This solution is usable for up to 3 days if kept in dark bottles containing as little air as possible. The bottles should be kept in a refrigerator. When kept under nitrogen at 0°C it shows no change in reactivity for at least 10 days.

E   Mono-pyrazolone solution, 0·25%
Dissolve 0·25 g of mono-pyrazolone in 100 ml of hot H_2O. Cool before use.

F   Chloramine T solution, 1%
Dissolve 1 g of chloramine T in about 100 ml of H_2O. The solution is stable for at least one month.

G   Trichlorethylene, or CCl_4, or $CHCl_3$

H Na_2SO_4 anhydrous
All solutions including standards and blanks, should be made with glass distilled water which has subsequently passed through a Wofatit F cation exchange column in the H^+ form. (See however note on H_2O, p. 56).

Procedure
Add 5 ml of solution (C) to a 50 ml sample in a 100–200 ml separatory funnel, mix, and add 2 ml of solution (F). Mix thoroughly again and allow to stand for exactly 5 minutes at room temperature (18–20°C). Then add 6 ml of solution (D) quickly, by means of a fast-running pipette, to the stirred solution. After 5 minutes, add 10 ml of solution (E) and mix again. When the pyrazolone blue turbidity has disappeared, add 10 ml of the organic solvent (G), then acidify with 2 ml of solution (B), mix, and immediately shake the solution for 2 minutes. Separate the organic phase. If any turbidity occurs, add about 0·5 g of anhydrous Na_2SO_4 (H).

It is essential to make standards with each series of determinations, because colour development is sensitive to small changes of temperature and to other factors. The standards should cover the range 10–400 μg of NH_3–N.

Measure the extinction of the reagent blank, standards and samples in suitable cells at a wavelength as close as possible to 450 mμ.

The colour of the extract is stable for at least 14 days. Evaporation of the solvent may be avoided by the use of containers with ground glass stoppers.

Interferences
The relatively serious interference of the reducing substances Fe^{2+}, S^{2-} and $SO_3{}^{2-}$ can be readily removed by a prior oxidation with $KMnO_4$ (slight excess of 0·1 N $KMnO_4$ at pH 2). The sample must then be readjusted to pH 6–7 with 1 N NaOH before starting the normal procedure. Aminoacids, amines, CN^- and CNS^- diminish the absorbance if present at high molar ratio levels (more than 10 molar ratio excess), since they compete with NH_3 for chloramine T and bis-pyrazolone.

Interferences from these causes can be removed by increasing the quantity of reagents (D) and (F).

Precision, accuracy, and range of application
The standard deviation is 1%. The accuracy is 3%, if a standard is run in the same series.

The method is suitable for 1–400 μg of NH_3–N without dilution.

Notes
(1) Care should be taken that the temperature of blank, standards and all samples in the series is the same.
(2) If the alkalinity is greater than 3 meq/l, the sample should be neutralized with 0·5 N HCl (free of NH_3) before the normal procedure is started.

5.3 NITRATE

LEVEL II

5.3.1. Colorimetric (tentative)
(Suitable for samples with a relatively low ratio of NO_2–N to NO_3–N).

Principle

NO_3^- is reduced to NO_2^- in strongly alkaline medium (pH $= 12$) by means of hydrazine sulphate. The reaction is catalysed by Cu^{2+}.

Reagents

A_1 KNO_3 standard solution, 200 μg/ml of NO_3–N See § 5.1.1.

B HCl, 1 N
Dilute 4 N HCl (§ 1.4.1) (25 ml → 100 ml).

C NaOH, 1 N
Dilute 10 N NaOH (10 ml → 100 ml).

D Reduction Mixture

D_1 Catalyst solution
Dissolve 0·039 g of $CuSO_4 . 5H_2O$ in 100 ml of H_2O.

D_2 Hydrazine sulphate solution
Dissolve 1·2 g of $N_2H_4 . H_2SO_4$ in 250 ml of H_2O. Mix 5 ml of solution (D_1) and 25 ml of solution (D_2). Make up with twice distilled H_2O to 50 ml. (This solution is usable for 2 days).

E Acetone (A.R.)
For other reagents see the determination of nitrites.

Procedure

Pass the filtered sample through a Wofatit F or similar cation exchange column (Na^+ form, height 18 cm, diameter 2 cm). Discard the first 50 ml of the filtrate. Take the next 40 ml, add 1 ml of solution (C) and 1 ml of solution (D), mix well, and allow to stand for 30 minutes at 28–30°C. Then add 0·5 ml of (E). After 5 minutes add 1 ml of (B) and determine NO_2^- as described in § 5.4.

Prepare standards covering the range 10–400 μg/l of NO_3–N, and run at least one internal standard with each sample.

Interference

The reduction step is strongly affected by the presence of particles and even by some dissolved organic substances. Samples should therefore be filtered before analysis and care should be taken to keep the reagent free from any precipitate. If the NO_3^- concentration allows, dilute the sample before the determination. Interference due to humic substances can be avoided by boiling the sample for 5 minutes after the addition of solution (C). After cooling to room temperature, the determination continues as described above.

Precision, accuracy, and range of application

The standard deviation is about 2%.

The accuracy can not be specified, since it is dependent on the presence of interfering substances. The method is suitable for 1–400 $\mu g/l$ of NO_3–N without dilution.

Notes

(1) If the sample is of soft water (total ion concentration about 1–1·5 meq/l) and it contains a relatively high concentration of nitrate, so that samples can be diluted 10 times, it is not necessary to run the sample through the cation exchange column.

(2) The result of this analysis represents the sum of $NO_3{}^-$ and $NO_2{}^-$. The absorbance of $NO_2{}^-$ when determined by procedure § 5.4, but in the presence of reagents (C) to (E), is lowered by 13%. Chemical reduction of $NO_2{}^-$ to NH_3 must also be considered (about 5% after 30 minutes reduction in the conditions specified here for fresh water samples). It is therefore necessary to subtract only 82% of the $NO_2{}^-$ originally present.

It will be apparent that this method is not altogether reliable, but it does have the advantage that *only* $NO_3{}^-$ can be reduced to $NO_2{}^-$. This method can therefore be used to check that most of the NH_3 distilled off after reduction with Devarda's alloy does indeed come from $NO_3{}^-$ specifically.

Calculation

$$NO_3\text{–N mg} = \text{mg (NO}_2\text{–N)}_{\text{found}} - \frac{0{\cdot}82}{1{\cdot}00} \times \text{mg (NO}_2\text{–N)}_{\text{orig. present}}$$

5.4 NITRITE

LEVEL I AND II

5.4.1. Colorimetric

Principle

In strongly acid medium, HNO_2 reacts with sulphanilamide (I) to form a diazonium compound (II)

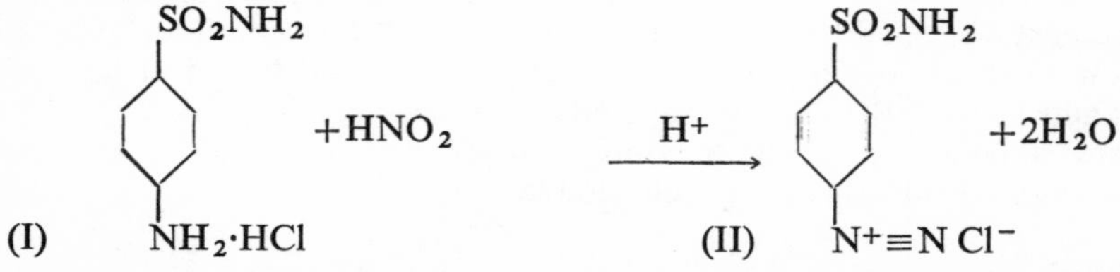

The diazonium compound (II) reacts with N-(1-naphthyl)ethylenediamine di-HCl (III) to form a strongly coloured azo-compound.

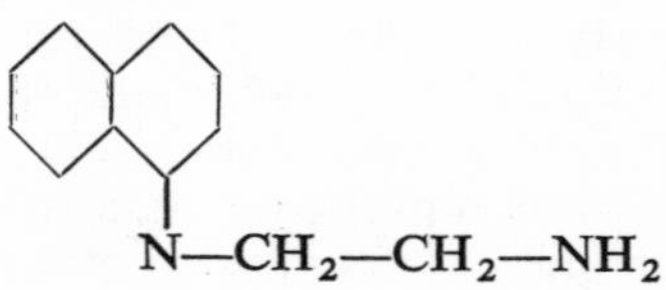

If any NO_2^- is left at this stage it will destroy the reagent (III), so that almost no colour will develop, and the sample will *appear* to contain almost no NO_2^-. Possible excess NO_2^- is therefore destroyed by adding ammonium sulphamate

$$O_2S\diagdown\diagup\begin{matrix}O\text{–}NH_4\\NH_2\end{matrix}$$

just before reagent (III). This situation also allows the use of as near perfect a reagent blank as may be obtained; ammonium sulphamate is added to the water sample as first (rather than third) reagent. All NO_2^- is thus destroyed before colour development.

(Note that the upper limit of the range of the method is much smaller than the amount of NO_2^- stoicheiometrically equivalent to the added sulphanilamide.)

Reagents

A_1 KNO$_2$ standard, 0·100 N (0·7 mg/ml NO$_2$–N)

Dissolve 1·064 g of KNO_2 (A.R., dried at 105°C for one hour) in H_2O. Add 1 ml of 5 N NaOH and dilute to 250 ml. The solution can be stored, but must be checked oxidimetrically.

To do this, mix 10·0 ml of A_1 with 25·0 ml 0·1 N KMnO$_4$ (standardized), acidify with 5 ml 4 N H_2SO_4. Wait 15 minutes and add a known excess of $(COOH)_2$. Then backtitrate with the KMnO$_4$ solution.

The KNO_2 solution (A_1) contains 700 mg/1 NO_2–N.

A_2 Diluted KNO$_2$ standard, 3·50 μg/ml NO$_2$–N

Dilute (A_1) 200 times (5 ml → 1000 ml). This solution contains 3·50 μg/ml NO_2–N.

B HCl, 6 N

Dilute 12 N HCl (see § 1.4.1).

C Sulphanilamide, 0·2%

Dissolve 2 g of sulphanilamide in 1 litre of H_2O.

D N-(1-naphthyl)ethylenediamine di-HCl, 0·1%

Dissolve 0·1 g of N-(1-naphthyl)ethylenediamine di-HCl in 100 ml of H_2O. The reagent can be kept for at least 2 months in a refrigerator and can be used even when it has become coloured.

E Ammonium sulphamate, 5%

Dissolve 5 g of $NH_4NH_2SO_3$ in 100 ml of H_2O. Store at room temperature.

Storage

The concentration of NO_2–N can change very rapidly due to bacterial conversions, either by oxidation of NH_3, or by reduction of NO_3^-. When prolonged storage is necessary the samples can be mixed with reagents (C) and (B) in the field. The samples can then be kept for at least 24 hours if put in a refrigerator. Filtration can be carried out after development of the colour.

Procedure

Mix 100 ml of sample containing not more than 35 μg of NO_2–N (or an aliquot diluted to 100 ml) in a 100/110 ml volumetric flask with 5 ml of suphanilamide solution (C), and 2 ml of HCl (B). After 3 minutes add 1 ml of ammonium sul-

F

phamate solution (E) followed after another 3 minutes by 1 ml of naphthylethylene-diamine solution (D). Dilute to 110 ml.

Prepare a blank by adding 1 ml of solution (E), and 2 ml HCl (B) before the sulphanilamide solution (C), is added. Measure the extinction of the reagent blank, standards and samples in suitable cells at a wavelength as close as possible to 530 mμ, after 15 minutes.

Prepare a calibration curve in the range of 1–35 μg of NO_2–N using the diluted standard (A_2). In this range the calibration curve is linear.

Precision and accuracy
Precision and accuracy are estimated at $1\frac{1}{2}\%$.

5.5 ORGANIC NITROGEN

LEVEL II

5.5.1. Colorimetric

A Dissolved organic nitrogen

Principle
Organic nitrogen (= org.–N) is determined by a wet digestion of filtered samples either after the removal of the inorganic nitrogen, or as the difference between the value obtained for total nitrogen and that for ammonia (§ 5.1.1). Thus org.–N = (org.-N)+(NH_3–N)−(NH_3–N).

Removal of NH_3 and NO_3^- (after reduction) by a previous distillation before the Kjeldahl destruction (see § 5.1.2) is suitable if the inorganic compounds are present in excess of the organic nitrogen compounds.

The less stable organic nitrogen compounds may hydrolyse to inorganic compounds (see p. 59), but the nitrogen in these organic compounds may be as easily available to algae as NH_3 and NO_3^- are. Biologically, therefore the distinction may be unimportant.

The Kjeldahl digest can also be used for Total Phosphate determination (§ 5.8). The digest must then be divided into two portions, one for the NH_3 determination and one for the Total-P determination.

Sampling and storage
Filter the samples immediately after collection. Millipore filters contain organic nitrogen, but they can be used if the filtrates only are analysed. Rinse the filters with distilled water before use. Blanks must also be filtered.

Because organic substances containing nitrogen may continuously be broken down to release NH_3, the only satisfactory methods of storage are to preserve with H_2SO_4, to deep-freeze to −20°C (after filtration), or to add $HgCl_2$. Direct investigation of fresh samples is, however, preferable.

Apparatus
The basic digestion vessel is the long-neck Kjeldahl flask (fig. 5.2). For macro determinations the volume may be as large as 800 ml, for micro determinations about 30 ml. Complete multiple units are available, with gas or electrical heaters, H_2SO_4 fume chimney and distillation equipment. For routine work these are very satisfactory.

Reagents

A H$_2$SO$_4$, (1+1) (See § 1.4.1)

Use the purest H$_2$SO$_4$, (A.R.) available. Some firms supply a "nitrogen free" grade. See note § 5.1.

B CuSO$_4$ solution, 10%

Dissolve 10 g of CuSO$_4$.5H$_2$O (A.R.) in 100 ml of H$_2$O.

C K$_2$SO$_4$(A.R.), solid (or Na$_2$SO$_4$(A.R.)).

D NaCl solution, 10%

Dissolve 10 g of NaCl (A.R.) in 100 ml of H$_2$O.

E NaOH, 10 N

(See § 1.4.1).

H$_2$O (see § 5.1.1)

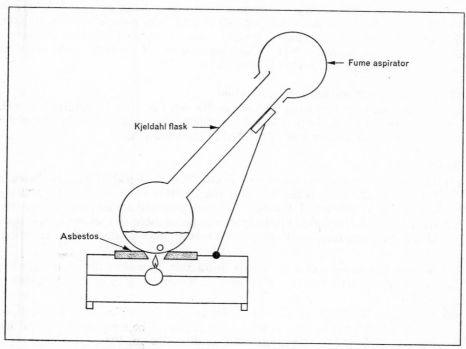

Figure 5.2. Kjeldahl digestion flask and simple digestion apparatus.

Procedure

Put not more than 40 ml of sample, preferably after procedure § 5.1.2, containing not more than 500 µg of nitrogen, in a 100 ml Kjeldahl flask (or smaller volume flask if only smaller samples are available) and mix with 4 ml H$_2$SO$_4$ (A), 10 drops (0·3 ml) of CuSO$_4$ solution (B),[1] 3·0 g of K$_2$SO$_4$ (C),[1] and 1 ml of NaCl (D)[1]. Add

[1] Not if after procedure § 5.1.2.

a quartz boiling chip or a glass bead. Heat the flask on a low flame for the first 10 to 30 minutes, until frothing stops. Then raise the temperature gradually until the sample is completely charred, and the acid boils and refluxes in one-third of the neck of the digestion flask. The flame should *not* be allowed to touch the flask above the part occupied by the liquid as this may lead to a loss of NH_3 because of the decomposition of $(NH_4)_2SO_4$.

Avoid heating at a temperature greater than about 380°C, because of undue volatilization of acid before all the organic matter is oxidized, and because some NH_3 may be lost. Rotate the flask at intervals and continue heating until the organic matter is destroyed. This should happen about one hour after the solution has cleared and has turned to a pale green colour. After digestion, allow the flask to cool. Dilute the contents with 10 ml of H_2O, and warm gently, if necessary, to dissolve the "cake" of $KHSO_4$. Transfer the digest quantitatively to the Parnas–Wagner (or other design) distillation apparatus (fig. 5.1) by rinsing three times with 5 ml of H_2O. Add 10 ml of 10 N NaOH (E) and close the tap A. Then follow procedure § 5.1.1.

For macro determination *either* collect the distillate in an excess of H_3BO_3 in an Erlenmeyer flask and then titrate with HCl (§ 5.2.2), *or* transfer an aliquot of the digest (containing not more than 500 μg of nitrogen) to the distillation apparatus. Distill off and determine the NH_3, after neutralization of the H_2SO_4 (A) by 10 ml of 10 N NaOH (E), as described in procedure § 5.1.1.

Precision, accuracy and range of application

Organic nitrogen content from 0·05 mg to 100 mg l/N, may be determined with an error of 0·05 mg l/N, the precision depending on the amount present, and on the accuracy of the apparatus and of the NH_3 determination.

Notes

(a) The distillation may be carried out directly from the Kjeldahl flask as shown in figure 5.3. The flask is heated (after the addition of excess NaOH) and the distillation is continued for two minutes after the steam has reached the receiving flask. The rate of heating should be adjusted so that the temperature in the receiving flask is 80–90°C after two minutes of distillation. (Jönsson, 1966.)

(b) Sudden temperature changes in the distillation apparatus (for instance when NaOH is added), or in the steam generator may result in liquid being sucked back.

(c) K_2SO_4 (or Na_2SO_4) are added in order to raise the boiling point of the digest to 345–370°C, without too much loss of H_2SO_4. The temperature should not exceed 380°C or loss of nitrogen will result. (Jackson, 1958.)

(d) The addition of NaCl is advisable for samples which have a low organic nitrogen and a relatively high nitrate content and which do not already contain Cl^-. The Cl^- will partly prevent the reduction of NO_3^- to NH_3, and will form products with NO_3^- (such as NOCl) which are to some extent volatile and do not interfere. The addition of NaCl is not necessary, if the NO_2^- and NO_3^- are removed after reduction as described in procedure § 5.1.

(e) All apparatus must be cleaned very thoroughly, and blanks should be run in advance and regularly in between series of determinations. Cleaning with a detergent (e.g. "OMO") followed by rinsing and steaming is sufficient. Not all

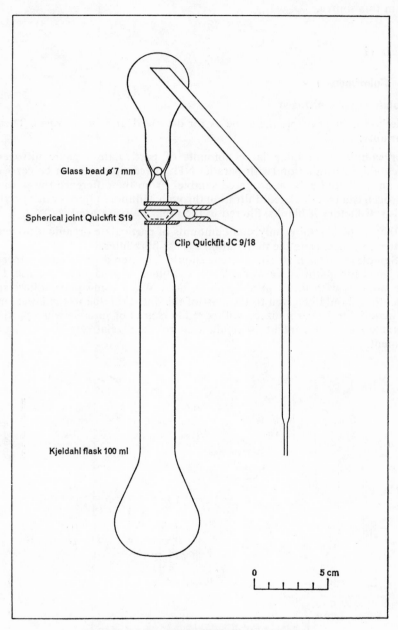

Glass bead ⌀ 7 mm

Spherical joint Quickfit S19

Clip Quickfit JC 9/18

Kjeldahl flask 100 ml

0   5 cm

Figure 5.3. Micro-Kjeldahl distillation apparatus.

detergents are satisfactory, and the composition of proprietary brands is altered from time to time. It is necessary therefore to beware of difficulties from this source.

LEVEL II

5.5.2. Colorimetric

Particulate organic nitrogen

The method is in principle the same as for dissolved organic nitrogen. There are two variants:

(1) For samples containing large amounts of particulate organic nitrogen the Kjeldahl determination (with parallel NH_3 determination) can be carried out on an unfiltered and on a filtered sample. From the difference the particulate nitrogen can be calculated. Filtration through Millipore filters—after prerinsing —is satisfactory if blanks, filtered in the same way, are used.

(2) If the sample contains only small amounts of particulate organic nitrogen, it is better to concentrate the material on a glass fibre filter.

Samples with a high silt content should be filtered on a hard paper filter designed for quantitative work. Wash the filters with H_2O before use. Digest the samples with filters in a Kjeldahl flask. When using paper filters special attention should be given to the start of the digestion due to the large amount of material to be carbonized. Millipore filters are not suitable when particulate organic nitrogen content is small, due to their relatively high organic N content.

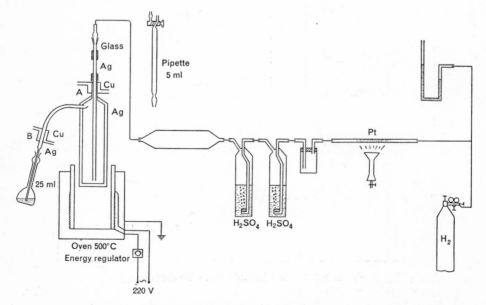

Figure 5.4. Scheme of micro organic N determination by digestion with NaOH and H_2.

LEVEL III

5.5.3. By digestion in a NaOH melt (Krogh and Keys, 1934; Duursma, 1961).

A micro method (fig. 5.4) for dissolved organic nitrogen or total organic nitrogen (dissolved plus particulate), is based on destruction of organic matter by H_2 at 500°C in a NaOH-melt in a silver tube. This method may be suitable for those circumstances where the Kjeldahl method is impracticable.

Small samples, e.g. volumes of 5 ml, are preferable to larger ones. The method is simple in principle, and requires for the digestion no reagents other than NaOH. The analyst must however have considerable experience of microchemical methods.

Satisfactory silver apparatus is not easy to obtain; lower quality silver is sometimes porous, causing some sweating of the alkali and therefore leakage. (Duursma, 1961).

ORTHO-PHOSPHATE AND TOTAL PHOSPHATE

5.6 ORTHO-PHOSPHATE

Principle

In strongly acid solutions ortho-phosphate ($= PO_4–P$) will form a yellow complex with molybdate ions, which can then be reduced to a highly coloured blue complex. If ascorbic acid is used as a reducing agent, the formation of the blue colour is stimulated by antimony. The method can be made more sensitive by extraction of the blue complex into an organic layer, or by extraction of the yellow complex before reduction. (See Olsen, 1967).

Storage

Filter the sample through a membrane filter, pore size about 0.5μ. Pre-rinse the filters with at least 250 ml H_2O. The determination must be carried out as soon as possible. If delay cannot be avoided the sample may be stored by deep-freezing, or by using polythene bottles treated for a week with a solution of 5% of I_2 in an 8% solution of KI, and washed with H_2O afterwards. This last method will not be suitable if more than a small amount of organic matter is present. If the extraction method § 5.6.3 for the yellow complex is used, the yellow organic solution may be kept for 24 hours.

LEVEL I

5.6.1. Colorimetric

Reagents

A **KH_2PO_4 standard, 40 µg/ml of $PO_4–P$** (See § 5.6.2).

B **H_2SO_4, 4 N** (See § 1.4.1).

C **Reagent mixture**

Mix the following dry reagents thoroughly: 48 g of $(NH_4)_6Mo_7O_{24}.4H_2O$, 1.0 g of sodium antimony tartrate and 40 g of ascorbic acid. This mixture is, if kept dry, stable for three months.

D   Mixed reagent solution

Dissolve 1 ± 0.2 g (a "constant spoonful") of the reagent mixture (C) in 100 ml of
$4 \text{ N H}_2\text{SO}_4$. Allow to stand for about 15 minutes before using. This reagent should
not be kept for more than one day. (Fishman and Skougstad, 1965).

Procedure

Mix 40·0 ml of sample and 10·0 ml of reagent (D) in an Erlenmeyer flask. Measure
the extinction of the reagent blank, standards and samples in suitable cells in a
simple colorimeter after at least 10 minutes. Alternatively match the colour against
a phosphate standard.

   If necessary the modifications (b) and (c) of method § 5.6.2 can be used to make
the determination more sensitive.

Precision and accuracy

The precision and accuracy are estimated at 5–10% depending on the colorimeter
available.

Interferences

See method at level II.

LEVEL II

5.6.2.   Colorimetric

Reagents

A KH_2PO_4 standard solution, 40 µg/ml of PO_4–P

Dissolve 0·1757 g of KH_2PO_4 (dry, A.R.) in H_2O and dilute to 1000 ml. This
solution contains 40 µg P per ml. Prepare a 40 fold dilution (25·0 ml → 1000 ml),
which contains 1 µg of P per ml. Add 2·5 ml of H_2SO_4 (1+1) and a few drops of
$CHCl_3$ as a preservative to both standard solutions before making up to volume.

B H_2SO_4, 4 N (See § 1.4.1).

C   Molybdate-antimony solution

Dissolve 4·8 g of $(NH_4)_6Mo_7O_{24}.4H_2O$ and 0·1 g of sodium antimony tartrate
$(NaSbOC_4H_4O_6)$ in 400 ml of $4 \text{ N H}_2\text{SO}_4$ (B) and make up to 500 ml with the same
acid. (Murphy and Riley, 1958 and 1962.)

D   Ascorbic acid (about 0·1 M)

Dissolve 2·0 g of ascorbic acid in 100 ml of H_2O. This solution is usable for one
week if kept in a refrigerator.

E   n-Hexanol, Reagent grade.

F   Isopropanol, Reagent grade.

Procedure

Modification a

Pipette 40·0 ml of the sample into a 50 ml volumetric flask. Add 5 ml of molybdate
(C) and 2 ml of ascorbic acid solution (D) and mix well. Dilute to 50 ml. Measure
the extinction of the reagent blank, standards and samples in suitable cells at a
wavelength as close as possible to 882 mµ, (or with a filter with maximum light
transmittance at 720–750 mµ) at least 10 minutes after mixing.

Modification b (Stephens, 1963)

If the extinction is below 0·100 but above 0·020 (using 5 cm cells) transfer the coloured sample quantitatively into a separatory funnel. Add 10 ml n-hexanol and shake vigorously for 1 minute. Discard the lower layer and transfer the hexanol to a 10 ml graduated cylinder. Adjust the volume to 10 ml with a few drops of isopropanol, which clears the solution. Transfer to cells which have at least as long a light path as those used in modification **a**, but which are nevertheless sufficiently filled by 10 ml. Measure the extinction of the reagent blank, standards and samples in suitable cells, at a wavelength as close as possible to 690 mμ (or with a filter with a maximum wavelength transmission at 720 mμ).

Modification c

If the extinction is still too low, larger volumes of the sample can be extracted, e.g. 100 ml or 200 ml. In these cases add 10 or 20 ml of solution (C) and 4 or 8 ml of solution (D). The extraction can still be carried out with only 10 ml n-hexanol. Make up to 10 ml with isopropanol. About 1 ml should be needed.

Prepare a calibration curve covering the range 50–500 μg/l of PO_4–P for modification **a**, 10–100 μg/l for modification **b**, and 2–20 μg/l for modification **c**.

Precision and accuracy

The precision for modification **a** is probably $1\frac{1}{2}\%$; for the others 2–5%, depending on the care with which the extraction is carried out. Extraction is 90–95% complete, the proportion extracted varying with temperature and solvent/solution ratio. The accuracy depends on the calibration curve for the extraction methods. The best results will be obtained with an internal standard. The minimal requirement is that standards be run with each series. The calibration curve for this method is linear up to about 0·5 mg/l of PO_4–P. If necessary, the linear range may be extended to about 3 mg/l (Harwood, van Steenderen and Kuhn, 1969).

Interferences

Cu^{2+}, Fe and silicate (up to 10 mg/l of Si) do not interfere. Arsenate produces a colour similar to that produced by phosphate. Humic acids and oxidizable organic material interfere and must be removed, using the method § 5.7.2.

LEVEL II

5.6.3. Colorimetric (tentative)

Principle

Extraction of the yellow phosphomolybdate in isobutanol and reduction with $SnCl_2$ to the blue compound. (Proctor and Hood, 1954, and Golterman and Würtz, 1961.)

Reagents

A **KH_2PO_4 standard** (See § 5.6.2).

B **H_2SO_4, 4 N** (See § 1.4.1).

C **Molybdate solution, 5%**
Dissolve 25 g of $(NH_4)_6Mo_7O_{24}.4H_2O$ in 500 ml of 4 N H_2SO_4.

D **$SnCl_2$ solution, 0·1%**
Dissolve 2 g of hydrazine sulphate (anti-oxidant) in 1 litre of 0·6 N H_2SO_4. Cool to about 10°C and add 1 g of $SnCl_2.2H_2O$. This solution becomes clear after about 12 hours in a refrigerator and can be kept at 4°C for 4–8 weeks at least.

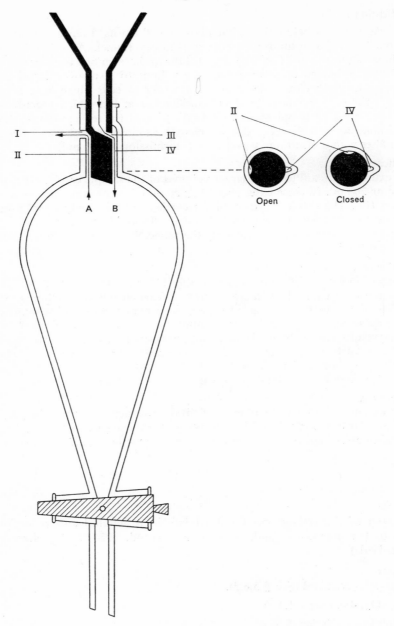

Figure 5.5. Phosphate extraction funnel.

In the neck of the separatory funnel a hole (I) is made; opposite this hole lies a small groove (IV), similar to those in dropping bottles. The small funnel has a similar groove (II) in its solid lower half, and a hole (III) leading to the interior of the separatory funnel. When the two holes are placed opposite the grooves, liquid can be poured into the separatory funnel (via arrow B), while the air can escape (via A). When the small funnel is turned 90° the separatory funnel is closed and can be shaken. The funnel is made water-repellent by treatment with Desicote.

E Isobutanol

Use A.R. grade or distill the laboratory reagent quality. Use the fraction 107–108·5°C.

F Ethanol 96% (Normal quality).

G KMnO$_4$, 0·1 N

Dissolve 3 g of KMnO$_4$ in 1 litre of H$_2$O.

Apparatus

The apparatus shown in fig. 5.5 is convenient for the extraction technique.

Procedure

Mix 50 ml of sample in a separatory funnel with 6·0 ml of 4 N H$_2$SO$_4$ and with 5 ml of molybdate reagent (C).

The yellow complex with phosphate is formed, though it may not be apparent if the phosphate concentration is low.

Add 15 ml of isobutanol (E) and shake for 15 sec. Discard the aqueous layer and wash (shake) with 5 ml of 4 N H$_2$SO$_4$ (B) plus 10–20 ml of H$_2$O. Remove the aqueous layer quantitatively. (Allow the organic layer to fill the bore of the stopcock of the funnel). Dry the funnel outlet. Rinse the organic layer with ethanol into a suitable volumetric flask (25 or 50 ml) and add 0·25 ml (for 25 ml flask) or 0·50 ml (for 50 ml flask) of SnCl$_2$ solution (D). Dilute to volume with ethanol. Measure the extinction against a reagent blank in suitable cells at about 720 mμ within 30 minutes. If the blue colour is too weak a larger sample can be used with proportionally increased quantities of H$_2$SO$_4$ and molybdate reagent. 15 ml more isobutanol (E) must be added than is necessary for saturation (about 10 ml per 100 ml sample).

If desired, 10–20 ml of n-hexanol may be substituted for n-butanol.

Precision and accuracy

A precision and accuracy of 1–2% may be obtained.

Interferences

When the water has a high C.O.D. difficulties arise. These can be avoided by adding to the sample—after 7 ml of 4 N H$_2$SO$_4$—sufficient 0·1 N KMnO$_4$ that the colour does not disappear in 15 minutes. (This can be done in the separatory funnel). Remove the excess of KMnO$_4$ by adding isobutanol and shaking. Then add the acid molybdate reagent. When large amounts of humic acids are present it may be possible to remove them by the procedure just described. They can alternatively be removed by extraction of the acidified sample with isobutanol, until the organic layer is no longer coloured. The organic layers can be collected and evaporated to dryness with 1 ml of 4 N H$_2$SO$_4$. The phosphates that were extracted with humic acids will dissolve in the H$_2$SO$_4$. (It is not known whether or no phosphates are partly split off from the humic acids during the extraction). The phosphates can be determined after destruction of these humic acids (see § 5.7).

When no silicates are present at concentrations greater than 0·05 mg/l the normality of the acid during the extraction may be changed to 0·4 N. Add no extra acid to the sample before the molybdate reagent.

5.7 TOTAL PHOSPHATE

LEVEL II

Principle (see Olsen, 1967)

Phosphate bound to organic substances ($=$ org$-$P) and polyphosphate do not react with the molybdate reagent. These compounds must therefore be hydrolysed in order to convert the phosphate to H_3PO_4. High temperature and a high acidity are essential for the digestion.

Analysis of the hydrolysate of filtered water gives the quantity Total Dissolved Phosphate ($=$ Tot$-P_{diss}$). Subtraction of the PO_4-P then gives the Hydrolysable Phosphate ($=$ Poly$-P+$Org$-P_{diss}$). In unpolluted waters this fraction is usually organic phosphate only. In polluted waters the polyphosphate concentration may be high.

Analysis of the hydrolysate of the unfiltered sample gives Total$-P$. Subtraction of the Tot$-P_{diss}$ then gives the Particulate Phosphate ($=$ Part$-P$). This last can also be determined by hydrolysis of the filter residue, if the filters are, or are washed, phosphate free.

Two methods are recommended for digestion:

A H_2SO_4, with or without H_2O_2

This allows determination of organic nitrogen as well. (See § 5.5.1; the $CuSO_4$ catalyst added for the Kjeldahl digestion does not interfere in the P-determination).

B $HClO_4$

Suitable for fresh and saline water. (Robinson, 1941).

If large numbers of samples are to be analysed a persulphate digestion may be convenient (Menzel and Corwin, 1965). The method is not given here in detail. Adjustment of the acidity of the digest from A or B with NaOH may be needed before the inorganic determination § 5.6.2 can be made.

Reagent blanks and standards should be run through the digestion stage together with the samples.

Sampling and storage

Any conventional sampler may be used, but the greatest care is needed to avoid contamination. It is best to measure and put unfiltered samples directly from the sampler into the reaction vessel. Filtration should be done immediately after collection, and the measured filtrate stored in the reaction vessel.

Two other satisfactory methods of storage can be recommended:

(1) Place 50 ml or other appropriate volume of sample in a boiling tube. Add 2 drops of 4 N H_2SO_4 and cover with a (phosphorus-free) plastic film such as "Parafilm". Store at room temperature.

(2) Place the sample in a polyethylene bottle with polyethylene stopper. Freeze the sample immediately and store at $-20°C$. Frozen samples should be thawed completely and mixed carefully before analysis.

Phosphorus may be released from living cells on freezing, or from dying cells. This can increase the proportion of dissolved phosphorus if unfiltered samples are frozen, melted, and later filtered. The total amount of phosphorus should not change.

If glass bottles must be used, Pyrex or Jenaglass (borosilicate) is usually satisfactory. Ordinary (lime-soda) glass must be avoided.

Reagents

A H$_2$SO$_4$ (1+1) (See § 1.4.1).

B HClO$_4$ solution

Dilute HClO$_4$ (A.R. s.g. = 1·69 = 70%) 10 times (0·1 litre → 1 litre).

C HCl solution, 1·3 N

Dilute 4 N HCl (see § 1.4.1) (0·25 litre → 0·75 litre).

D NH$_4$OH solution, 1·8 N

Dilute NH$_4$OH solution (A.R. s.g. = 0·91) (0·15 litre → 1 litre).

E KI solution, 5%

Dissolve 5 g of KI in 100 ml of H$_2$O.

F CuSO$_4$ solution, 10%

Dissolve 10 g of CuSO$_4$.5H$_2$O in 100 ml of H$_2$O.

G H$_2$O$_2$, 30% A.R.

Check that a PO$_4$-free grade is used.

Special apparatus

Use special Kjeldahl flasks (about 75 ml capacity) with a neck about 30 cm long. These prevent the loss of P$_2$O$_5$ by volatilization. All glassware must be cleaned with hot chromic sulphuric acid. New glassware should then be filled with slightly acidic H$_2$O and left to stand for some weeks. Note that most detergents and laboratory cleaning solutions contain phosphorus and must be avoided.

5.7.1. Hydrolysis with H$_2$SO$_4$ digestion

Procedure

Put 50 ml of sample (or, if desired, a smaller volume) in the long necked Kjeldahl flask. Add 4 ml H$_2$SO$_4$ (A) and 10 drops (0·5 ml) of the CuSO$_4$ solution (F). Evaporate—if necessary add more sample—and heat to fuming. If much organic matter is present and black charred material is produced, cool, and add 10 drops of H$_2$O$_2$ (G). Heat until a clear solution is obtained and continue heating for 15 minutes. It is necessary to remove all the H$_2$O$_2$ before adding molybdate. To do this, cool and add about 5 ml of H$_2$O. Then heat to fuming to remove the last traces of H$_2$O$_2$. Cool, add 20 ml of H$_2$O, and boil.

If phosphate is to be determined by procedure § 5.6.2 the digest must be nearly neutralized with NaOH and then diluted to 100 ml (or smaller volume if desired). Take 40 ml for the phosphate determination. A second aliquot may be used for the determination of organic nitrogen, § 5.5.1. If procedure § 5.6.3 is used the neutralization is not necessary.

5.7.2. Hydrolysis with HClO$_4$ digestion

Procedure

N.B. This procedure is potentially dangerous. Boiling HClO$_4$, especially in contact with organic matter, and HClO$_4$ fumes, are explosive. This method should only be used if 5.7.1. or 5.7.3 are unsatisfactory. If it *is* used, the precautions given on p. 164 must be followed.

Mix 50 ml of sample with 10 ml of $HClO_4$ (B) (or transfer quantitatively all 50 ml of a sample stored in a tube with two washings of 5 ml $HClO_4$ (B)) into a 100 ml Erlenmeyer flask (Pyrex or Jena glass). Cover with a watch glass if easily oxidizable compounds are present. If very low phosphate concentrations are present 200 ml of sample may be evaporated with $HClO_4$ in a 1 litre Erlenmeyer flask with reflux ("cold finger"). Reduce the volume of solution to about 10 ml by boiling. If interference from arsenic is expected add 2 drops of the KI solution (E). Continue the evaporation—gradually lowering the temperature when solid material begins to separate—until $HClO_4$ begins to reflux. Continue the refluxing for 10 minutes. If the digestion is not complete **COOL** and add more $HClO_4$ (B). Repeat the refluxing. Cool the flask and add 10 ml diluted NH_4OH solution (D) and evaporate again to dryness. Add about 25 ml of H_2O and 1 ml of 1·3 N HCl (C). Boil for 5 minutes, cool, and dilute to 50 ml in a volumetric flask. Use 40 ml for the phosphate determination of procedure § 5.6.2 or § 5.6.3. Run reagent blanks using 50 ml of H_2O, and at least one standard as losses of PO_4-P may occur.

Interferences

Arsenic forms the same complex with molybdate as phosphorus. It is removed by the addition of KI which reduces it to the volatile trivalent form.

During the $HClO_4$ digestion losses of up to 15% of the phosphate may occur; these may be avoided by using a special Kjeldahl flask with a neck about 30 cm long or by using a "cold finger".

5.7.3. Hydrolysis with H_2SO_4

Procedure

(Tentative—suggested if a large number of samples are to be analysed).

The samples may be hydrolysed by making them 0·3 N with respect to H_2SO_4 and heating in an autoclave at 135–140°C for 8 hours. If much organic material is present $(NH_4)_2S_2O_8$ may be added, up to a maximum of about 1 g, and the reaction time may be shortened to 2 hours.

Procedure § 5.6.3 (PO_4-P) can then be used directly omitting the 6 ml of 4 N H_2SO_4, shaking with isobutanol for at least 1 minute.

Procedure § 5.6.2 (PO_4-P) may be used, but with the molybdate-antimony solution made in 1·6 N H_2SO_4.

REACTIVE SILICATE AND TOTAL SILICA

The formulae of the compounds of silicon which are determined by these methods are not known. The terms "silica" and "silicate" are used here as a convenient description only. (See Golterman, 1967).

REACTIVE SILICATE

LEVEL II

5.8 Colorimetric

Principle

Between pH 3 and 4 silicate forms a yellow complex with molybdate ions which can then be reduced to a highly coloured blue complex.

Reagents

A Na$_2$SiF$_6$, standard solution* (100 µg/ml of SiO$_3$–Si)

Dissolve 671·4 mg of Na$_2$SiF$_6$ (A.R.) in 400 ml of H$_2$O, heating until solution is complete. Cool and dilute to 1000 ml. Store in a thick walled polythene bottle. This solution contains 100 µg/ml of Si.

A$_1$

Dilute solution (A) 10 times (10·0 ml → 100 ml). This solution contains 10 µg/ml of Si.

A$_2$

Dilute solution (A) 50 times (10·0 ml → 500 ml). This solution contains 2 µg/ml of Si.

B H$_2$SO$_4$, 1+1 (See § 1.4.1).

C Na$_2$MoO$_4$ solution, 5%

Dissolve 5 g of Na$_2$MoO$_4$ in 100 ml of 0·5 N H$_2$SO$_4$. Allow to stand for 48 hours before use.

D$_1$ SnCl$_2$, stock solution

Dissolve 40 g of SnCl$_2$ in 12 N HCl (s.g. 1·18) at room temperature and dilute to 100 ml with 12 N HCl. Allow to stand for 24 hours before use.

D$_2$ Diluted SnCl$_2$ solution

Dilute 1 ml of (D$_1$) with 100 ml of H$_2$O. Use immediately.

Procedure

Mix 20 ml of sample (pH 5–8) containing not more than 100 µg Si, (or an aliquot diluted to 20 ml) with 2 ml of solution (C). Allow to stand for 15 minutes, and add 5 ml of H$_2$SO$_4$ (B). Cool to room temperature and add 1 ml of the freshly prepared solution (D$_2$). Measure the extinction of the reagent blank, standards and samples in suitable cells at a wavelength as close as possible to 815 mµ, 10–15 minutes after mixing. A calibration curve—covering the range 5–100 µg of Si per sample—must be made. Run a blank using 20 ml of H$_2$O.

Tentative procedure

In waters with a very high silicate concentration it is possible that colloidal silicate dissolves after dilution (see Kobayashi, 1967). In this case dilution must be avoided and the yellow colour should be measured after the addition of the H$_2$SO$_4$. Measure the extinction at 365 mµ. As this is not the maximum of the absorption curve (see Golterman, 1967) the wavelength must be carefully checked, and the wavelength adjustment must be free from drift; a filter colorimeter is therefore actually preferable to most spectrophotometers.

Precision, accuracy and range of application

The precision is estimated at 1–2%. With a good calibration curve the precision and accuracy are equal.

The range of application is 0·1–5·0 mg/l SiO$_3$–Si for the blue method. The yellow method can be used in the range of 1·0–20·0 mg/l of Si.

---

* Na$_2$SiF$_6$ may be obtained from Riedel de Haën or Baker Co.

5.9 TOTAL SILICA

Principle

Silica may occur in the water in colloidal and in particulate form as well as in solution. That which passes through a 0·5 μ filter may be considered as soluble or colloidal. The particulate fraction is that retained by the filter. Particulate silica is made soluble by fusion with $NaKCO_3$ in a platinum crucible.

The silica is converted into sodium silicate and is then determined as described below. Particulate silica may be either determined directly, or obtained by difference between total and soluble plus colloidal silica.

Reagents

A H_2SO_4, 4 N (See § 1.4.1).

B $NaKCO_3$, 2%

Dissolve 20 g of $NaKCO_3$ (A.R.) in 1 litre of H_2O. Store in a polythene bottle.

Procedure

Evaporate a sample, containing not more than 100 μg of Si, to dryness together with 10·0 ml of $NaKCO_3$ (B) in a platinum crucible. Gently fuse the dry residue using a small flame at first and then a Meker burner for 5 minutes. An electric furnace at a temperature of 900°C is preferable. Cool. Dissolve the melt in 40 ml of H_2O, and transfer to a 100 ml polythene bottle. Rinse the crucible twice and add the rinsings. Add 1 ml of H_2SO_4 (A) slowly to the polythene bottle. After mixing, dilute the solution to volume in a 100 ml volumetric flask.

Avoid contamination from the outside of the crucible. (Platinum crucibles in an electric furnace are best placed on a platinum disc).

Then proceed as described for reactive silicate, § 5.8.

Interferences

(For reactive silicate and total silica procedures.)

The similar yellow and blue complexes with phosphate interfere, but are destroyed by the H_2SO_4 added. H_2SO_4 is more efficient than oxalic acid. When the phosphate concentrations are high a control is necessary. (Run a silicate blank, containing the same amount of phosphate as the sample, against a normal blank.)

In the yellow method self-colour and turbidity of the sample may interfere.

Keep reagents and samples in thick walled polythene flasks. Keep the samples in the dark. With some waters deep-freezing has led to errors due to precipitation of the silica (Kobayashi, 1967).

CHAPTER 6

DETERMINATION OF TRACE ELEMENTS

BORON, COBALT, COPPER, IRON, MANGANESE, MOLYBDENUM, VANADIUM, AND ZINC

6.0

LEVEL II AND III

General notes

Because of their low concentrations, the analysis of trace elements presents acute problems. In particular, contamination can very easily occur. For reliable results internal standards should be used, together with H_2O blanks (to check reagent blanks) as described in § 1.2.3.

The validity of each method for a particular situation should be checked.

It is suggested that analyses be made of samples which have been:

1. filtered
2. filtered and digested
3. not filtered
4. not filtered, but digested.

6.0.1. Sampling and storage

Samples, even those of surface waters, must be collected from below the surface film. Completely non-metallic samplers must be used and lowering cables or ropes should be of nylon or similar materials or coated with plastic. Even rubber should be avoided as it contains significant amounts of zinc. Samplers may be tested as sources of contamination by storing samples in them and removing aliquots for analysis at 15 minute intervals.

Containers used for field collection should be of polyethylene with stoppers of polyethylene or a similar acid resistant plastic. They must be washed before use with concentrated HCl or 50% HNO_3 and rinsed with H_2O. They may profitably be rinsed with sample just before filling. Analyses should be performed in borosilicate glass vessels which have been cleaned with strong acid. Running a blank of H_2O which has been stored in a representative manner is recommended. Long term storage is not recommended. If it is necessary to store samples for more than a few hours it should be done in the vessels in which final analysis will be done, i.e. samples for digestion should be stored in the digestion flasks, and the samples to be filtered should be filtered and stored in the flasks in which they will be analyzed. This will reduce problems caused by precipitation and adsorption. If gross storage for several days is unavoidable the samples should be filtered (if appropriate) and 10–25 ml of 4 N HCl should be added to each bottle. (This renders a later distinction between ferric and ferrous iron impossible).

81

6.0.2. Sample digestion

Several methods are available, including $HClO_4$ and $(NH_4)_2S_2O_8$ digestion. An ultraviolet photo-oxidation has been described by Armstrong *et al.* (1966), but is still in the experimental stage.

$HClO_4$ digestion

> **N.B. This procedure is potentially dangerous. Boiling $HClO_4$, especially in contact with organic matter, and $HClO_4$ fumes, are explosive. This method should only be used if the other methods are unsatisfactory. If it is used the precautions given on p. 164 must be followed.**

Boil the sample of 100–200 ml to near dryness in a long necked flask such as a modified Erlenmeyer flask or a volumetric flask. After cooling add 2 ml of 60–70% $HClO_4$ and heat the flask on a hot plate until the condensed $HClO_4$ vapours form a ring about half way up the neck of the flask. After one hour the contents should be clear and colourless. Cool the flask and add 50 ml water and one drop of phenolphthalein indicator. Neutralize the excess $HClO_4$ with 4 N NaOH. Then add 1 ml 12 N HCl. Dilute the sample to the appropriate volume for the analysis to be made. (See Robinson 1941, Smith 1953).

$(NH_4)_2S_2O_8$ digestion

Add a freshly prepared 5% solution of $(NH_4)_2S_2O_8$ to the sample in the ratio of 8 to 50 (V:V). Put the mixture in a water bath at 100°C for 60 minutes or autoclave at 120°C for 30 minutes (e.g. in pressure cooker). This method is convenient and rapid, but its utility for particulate matter is not yet proved. See Hansen and Robinson (1953) and Menzel and Corwin (1965).

6.1 BORON

Colorimetric

Principle

Boron forms a coloured complex with either carmine, resorcinol, or curcumin. The carmine complex method is that given here, and is taken from Standard Methods (1965). The resorcinol complex method (Glebovich, 1963) also seems suited to routine analysis. The curcumin method (Greenhalgh and Riley, 1962) is probably the most accurate and is suggested for critical work.

Reagents

A   Standard Boron solution, 100 µg/ml

Dissolve 0·5716 g of H_3BO_3 in H_2O and dilute to 1000 ml; 1·00 ml contains 100 µg B. (Since H_3BO_3 loses H_2O on drying at 105°C a pure reagent should be used and kept tightly stoppered to prevent absorption of moisture).

B H_2SO_4 (A.R., s.g. = 1·84) (See § 1.4.1).

C   HCl, 12 N (A.R.) (See § 1.4.1).

D   HCl, 1 N

Dilute 4 N HCl (see § 1.4.1) (0·25 litre → 1 litre).

E   NaOH, 1 N

Dilute 10 N NaOH (see § 1.4.1) (0·1 litre → 1 litre).

F   Carmine solution, 0·1 %

Dissolve 1 g of carmine (NF 40, or carminic acid, the main constituent of carmine) in 1 litre of H_2SO_4 (s.g. = 1·84). This may take up to 2 hours.

6.1.1.   Boric acid

Procedure

Put 2·00 ml sample into a small Erlenmeyer flask or 30 ml test tube, and add 2 drops (0·1 ml) of HCl (C) and, with great care, 10·0 ml of H_2SO_4 (B). Mix well and cool. Add 10·0 ml of carmine solution (F), mix well and allow to stand for at least 45 minutes. Measure the extinction of the reagent blank, standards and samples in suitable cells at a wavelength as close as possible to 585 mμ.

Prepare a calibration curve corresponding to 1–10·0 mg/l of Boron.

N.B. When the liquids are mixed, bubbles form. The mixing should therefore be efficient, and bubbles be allowed to dissipate before measuring the extinction.

6.1.2.   Total Boron

Procedure

Make a suitable aliquot just alkaline with 1 N NaOH (E), and then add a slight excess of NaOH. Prepare a blank containing the same amount of NaOH. Evaporate both sample and blank to dryness on a steam bath. Ignite at 500–550°C. Cool and add 2·5 ml of 1 N HCl (D). Make sure the solution is acid, and mix with a rubber tipped glass rod. Pour the solution into a conical centrifuge tube and centrifuge it until clear. Pipette 2·00 ml of the clear solution into an Erlenmeyer flask and proceed as above.

Precision, accuracy, and sensitivity

Results are estimated to be accurate and reproducible within ± 0·4 μg of B per sample. The sensitivity is 0·2 μg of B per sample. If higher sensitivity is required the curcumin method is recommended.

6.2   COBALT

Colorimetric

Principle

2 nitroso-l-naphthol yields a coloured complex with cobalt. The complex can be extracted into non-polar solvents. The excess reagent is removed from the organic phase with NaOH. The following procedure is modified from Sandell (1959).

Reagents

A   Standard Co solution, 100 µg/ml.

A₁

Dissolve 0·0404 g of $CoCl_2 . 6H_2O$ in water, add 3 ml of 4 N HCl, dilute to 100 ml. This solution contains 100 μg/ml of Co.

A$_2$

Dilute A$_1$ ten times with 0·1 N HCl (10 μg/ml of Co).

B   HCl, 2 N

Dilute 4 N HCl (see § 1.4.1); (50 ml → 100 ml).

C   NaOH, 2 N

Dilute 10 N NaOH (see § 1.4.1); (20 ml → 100 ml).

D   Sodium citrate, 40%

Dissolve 200 g of sodium citrate in H$_2$O and dilute to about 500 ml.

E   H$_2$O$_2$, 3%

Dilute H$_2$O$_2$ 30% (A.R.) (10 ml → 100 ml).

F   2 nitroso-l-naphthol solution, 1%

Dissolve 1·0 g of 2 nitroso-1-naphthol in 100 ml of glacial CH$_3$COOH. Add 1 g of activated carbon. Shake the solution before use and filter off the required amount. (This procedure keeps the reagent blank low).

G   CHCl$_3$

Procedure

Add 10 ml of sodium citrate solution (D) to 100–500 ml (exactly measured) of sample. Adjust the pH to 3–4 with 2 N HCl (B) or 2 N NaOH (C). Add 10 ml of 3% H$_2$O$_2$ (E), mix, and allow to stand for a short while. Then add 2 ml of reagent solution (F), mix, and allow to stand for at least 30 minutes at room temperature. Transfer to a separatory funnel and shake the funnel vigorously for 1 minute with 25 ml of CHCl$_3$ (G). Separate the solvent. Repeat the extraction twice with 10 ml portions of CHCl$_3$ (G). Dilute the combined extracts to 50 ml and transfer to a clean separatory funnel. Shake the funnel for 1 minute with 20 ml 2 N HCl (B), and then run the CHCl$_3$ layer into another funnel and shake it for 1 minute with 20 ml 2 N NaOH (C). Finally, separate the CHCl$_3$ layer for extinction measurement. Measure the extinction of the reagent blank, standards and samples in suitable cells at a wavelength as close as possible to 530 mμ. The colour is stable for at least 12 hours. Prepare a calibration curve in the range 5–200 μg of Co, dissolved in the same volume of H$_2$O as the samples.

Interferences

If the sample contains more than a few mg/l of Fe it should be pretreated with 2 N HCl sufficient to dissolve the Fe. Fe^{2+} interferes, but in this procedure it is oxidized by the H$_2$O$_2$ and kept from precipitation and extraction by the citrate. Ni^{2+} and Cu^{2+} could interfere but prevented from doing so by the HCl wash of the CHCl$_3$ extract. Unless the sample contains enough Ni^{2+} and Cu^{2+} to cause problems this step could be left out. The NaOH wash is still necessary.

Precision, accuracy, and sensitivity

Precision and accuracy are unknown. 200 μg of Co (in a final volume of 50 ml of CHCl$_3$) in a 1 cm cell have an extinction of about 1·0, Sandell (1959). Thus it is possible to determine as little as 1–2 μg.

6.3 COPPER

Colorimetric

Principle

Copper, reduced to its cuprous form, reacts with diquinolyl to form a coloured complex, which is extracted into an organic solvent for colorimetric estimation. (Riley and Sinhaseni, 1958).

Reagents

A Standard Cu solution, 1 mg/ml

Weigh accurately 100 mg of Cu (A.R. or electrolytic) in a quartz or Pyrex beaker. Dissolve it in 3 ml of HNO_3 (s.g. = 1·42), add 1 ml of H_2SO_4 (s.g. = 1·84) and evaporate under an infrared heater until dense white fumes are evolved. Allow to cool and then dissolve the residue in H_2O and dilute to 100 ml. This solution contains 1 mg of Cu per ml.

A_1 Standard Cu solution, 10 μg/ml

Dilute solution (A) 100 times (10·0 ml → 1000 ml). Solution (A_1) contains 10 μg/ml of Cu.

A_2 Standard Cu solution, 2 μg/ml

Dilute solution (A_1) 5 times (10·0 ml → 50·0 ml). Solution (A_2) contains 2 μg/ml of Cu. Prepare (A_1) and (A_2) freshly as required.

B $NH_2OH.HCl$ solution, 10%

Dissolve 10 g of $NH_2OH.HCl$ (A.R.) in about 80 ml of H_2O, filter, and dilute to 100 ml. If the reagent contains appreciable amounts of Cu^{2+}, extract it with 10 ml portions of a 0·01% solution of dithizone in CCl_4 (see § 6.8) until there is no change in the colour of the dithizone. Extract solution (B) with CCl_4 until all colour has been removed.

C Sodium acetate buffer solution, 1 N

Dissolve 136 g of $CH_3COONa.3H_2O$ in H_2O and dilute to 1 litre. If the reagent contains more than a trace of Cu, extract with dithizone as described above.

D Dinquinolyl reagent, 0·03%

Dissolve 0·03 g of 2:2′-diquinolyl in 100 ml of n-hexanol that has been redistilled over NaOH.

E Ethanolic hydroquinone solution, 1%

Dissolve 1 g of hydroquinone in 100 ml of redistilled ethanol.

Procedure

The analyses are made in 1 litre separatory funnels. Clean these by leaving them overnight filled with a (1+1) mixture of HNO_3 (s.g. = 1·42) and H_2SO_4 (s.g. = 1·84). Empty them, and rinse several times with H_2O.

Transfer 900 ml of sample to a 1 litre separatory funnel and add 10 ml of $NH_2OH.HCl$ solution (B) and 10 ml of buffer solution (C) (to adjust pH to 4·3–5·8). Add 8 ml of diquinolyl reagent (D) and shake the funnel for 5 minutes. Run the aqueous layer into another funnel, add to it 2 ml $NH_2OH.HCl$ solution (B) (to keep the Cu reduced), and 3 ml diquinolyl reagent (D). Extract again for 3 minutes. Repeat this extraction once more.

Combine the three hexanol extracts in a calibrated cylinder containing 0·5 ml hydroquinone solution (E). Dilute to 15 ml with hexanol. Measure the extinction of the reagent blank, standards and samples in suitable cells at a wavelength as close as possible to 540 mμ. The colour is stable.

N.B. Hexanol is recommended by Riley and Sinhaseni, but a 50/50 mixture of CCl_4 and isoamyl alcohol may be preferred as it is heavier than water. Reagent (D) may be made in this solvent mixture, and there is then no need to transfer the sample to another funnel for each extraction.

Interferences
None are likely in natural waters.

Precision, accuracy, and sensitivity
The method gave a dispersion of 2·5% with seawater containing 27·0 μg/l of Cu. Samples ranging from 2 to 100 μg/500 ml sample yielded a mean extinction of 0·0393 per μg of Cu^{2+}.

6.4 IRON

Colorimetric

Principle
Iron, after reduction to Fe^{2+}, reacts with bathophenanthroline to form a red compound which, if necessary, is extracted into hexanol and estimated colorimetrically (Lee and Stumm, 1960).

Iron can exist as Fe^{2+} or Fe^{3+}. The generally accepted approach is to determine total inorganic iron and Fe^{2+}, and to obtain Fe^{3+} by difference. Total iron, including organic Fe, may be estimated after a wet digestion.

For estimation of "available iron", see Shapiro (1967).

Reagents
A₁ Standard Fe^{2+} solution, 10 µg/ml
Dissolve 0·0702 g $(NH_4)_2SO_4.FeSO_4.6H_2O$ (Mohr's salt), in about 0·5 litre H_2O that contains 5 ml H_2SO_4 (1+1), and dilute to 1000 ml. This solution contains 10 μg/ml Fe^{2+}. Standardize the Mohr's salt with 0·100 N $KMnO_4$.

A₂ Standard Fe^{2+} solution, 1·0 µg/ml
Dilute 10 ml of this solution (A₁) to 100·0 ml with H_2O that contains 5 ml of H_2SO_4 (1+1) per litre. This solution contains 1·0 μg/ml of Fe^{2+}.

B Standard Fe^{3+} solution, 10 µg/ml
Add excess aqueous chlorine to an aliquot of 10 μg/ml standard Fe^{2+} solution. Boil to remove unreacted aqueous chlorine. Dilute the cool solution to the original aliquot volume.

C HCl, 4 N (See § 1.4.1).

D NH₄OH, 4 N

Dilute NH_4OH (s.g. $= 0.91$) (0.3 litre $\rightarrow 1.0$ litre).

E CH₃COONa, 10%

Dissolve 10 g of CH_3COONa (or 15 g of $CH_3COONa.3H_2O$) in 100 ml of H_2O contained in a 125 separatory funnel. Add 2 ml 0·001 M bathophenanthroline (G), and mix well. Add 10 ml n-hexanol, and extract. Repeat the extraction in a second separatory funnel to ensure complete removal of iron. Store the solution in a glass stoppered bottle.

F NH₂OH.HCl, 10%

Dissolve 10 g of $NH_2OH.HCl$ in 100 ml H_2O.

$NH_2OH.HCl$ often contains appreciable amounts of iron. If no sufficiently pure grade can be found, the iron must be removed. To do this dissolve 10 g of $NH_2OH.HCl$ in 100 ml of H_2O contained in a 125 ml separatory funnel. Add 2 ml 0·001 M bathophenanthroline (G)and 10 ml n hexanol, and extract. Repeat the extraction to ensure complete removal of iron. (The small amount of n-hexanol left in the solution is not detrimental.)

The solution has a pH of 1·5–1·75. Store in a glass stoppered bottle.

G Bathophenanthroline solution, 0·001 M

Dissolve 0·0332 g of 4 : 7-diphenyl-1,10-phenanthroline ($C_{24}H_{16}N_2$, mol wt 332) in 50 ml of ethanol, and dilute to 100 ml with iron-free water. Store the solution in a glass stoppered bottle.

H n-Hexanol

Reagent grade n-hexanol may be used without further purification. Technical grade material must be distilled before use.

J Ethanol, 95%

Re-distill commercial grade ethyl alcohol to remove iron.

Procedure

6.4.1. Total Iron (*inorganic or, if following digestion, inorganic plus organic*).

Add 5 ml of 4 N HCl (C) and 2 ml of 10% $NH_2OH.HCl$ (F) solution to a 50 ml sample, or to a neutral digested sample diluted to 50 ml. Add a glass bead, and boil for 15 minutes, cool, and make up to approximately the initial volume with H_2O. Add 5 ml of bathophenanthroline (G), mix, and add 4 ml 10% CH_3COONa solution (E). Adjust the pH to 4–5 with 4 N NH_4OH (D) added drop by drop. This point may be determined with a pH indicator paper (Congo red), or as the point where the solution becomes cloudy. Transfer the solution quantitatively to a 125 ml separatory funnel, add 10·0 ml n-hexanol (H), and shake the funnel for 3 minutes. Discard the aqueous layer. Run the hexanol solution into a 50 ml cylinder, rinse the funnel contents into this with 95% ethanol (J) from a squeeze bottle, and make up to 50 ml with the ethanol. Measure the extinction of the reagent blank, standards and samples in suitable cells at a wavelength as close as possible to 533 mμ within 10 minutes.

6.4.2. Fe²⁺

Proceed as for Total Iron (§ 6.4.1), but do *not* add $NH_2OH.HCl$ (F), and do *not* boil. Do not let the sample stand in the acidified condition but carry the procedure through immediately. If it is not possible to continue at once, the sample may be stored for several hours in a full, stoppered bottle but the acid should not be added until the procedure can be completed.

Interferences

Lee and Stumm (1960), from whose method this procedure has been modified, state that Co and Cu (both of which can form yellow complexes with batho-phenanthroline) do not interfere. $HClO_4$ in high concentrations causes precipitation of bathophenanthroline. If this is a problem in the particular circumstances then the persulphate digestion method should be used. Fe^{3+} interferes in the Fe^{2+} deter-mination, giving a small amount of colour with the reagents. Its contribution can be estimated from a curve prepared by making the Fe^{2+} analysis on a series of standards containing only Fe^{3+}. Lee and Stumm suggested in their original method that the sample be boiled with acid (p. 1572, § 3.3). If any organic matter is present however, Fe^{3+} will be converted to Fe^{2+} (Shapiro, 1965; O'Connor, Komolrit, and Engelbrecht, 1965), and this step is therefore best omitted for Fe^{2+} determinations.

Precision, accuracy and sensitivity

Using a 4 cm cell 1 μg of Fe^{2+} per litre of sample gives an extinction of 0·001. If desired, the hexanol may be diluted less for greater sensitivity.

6.5 MANGANESE

Colorimetric

Principle

Mn is oxidized to MnO_4^- which is then estimated colorimetrically. Either KIO_4 or $(NH_4)_2S_2O_8$ may be the oxidizing agent. The persulphate method, which is des-cribed here, is simpler, as the sample need not be evaporated to remove chloride. The procedure is from Sandell (1959) and Standard Methods (1965). See Morgan and Stumm (1965) for a discussion of methods.

Manganese can exist in natural waters as soluble Mn^{2+} which is oxidizable to MnO_4^- by $(NH_4)_2S_2O_8$, and also as insoluble higher valence forms such as MnO_2 which are not oxidizable to permanganate. Filtration does not necessarily separate these forms in natural waters, so determination of manganese may become rather complicated. Oxidation of organic matter by wet ashing will also leave the mangan-ese in its oxidized state. Separate procedures are therefore suggested; one for soluble manganous ion (§ 6.5.1), one for total inorganic manganese (§ 6.5.2), and one for total manganese (§ 6.5.3).

Reagents

A   Standard Mn solution, 50 µg/ml

Dissolve 3·2 g of $KMnO_4$ in H_2O and make up to 1 litre. Heat for several hours near the boiling point, then filter through a sintered glass filter and standardize against $(COOH)_2$ of accurately known concentration, approximately 0·1 N. From the $KMnO_4$ solution prepare a standard containing 50 mg/l of Mn. To 1 litre of this add 5 ml H_2SO_4 (1+1) and then 10% $NaHSO_3$ solution in single drops, with stirring, until the permanganate colour disappears. Boil to remove the excess SO_2, and cool. Dilute again to 1000 ml with H_2O.

B H_3PO_4 (s.g. = 1·69).

C NH_2OH.HCl solution, 10%
Dissolve 10 g of NH_2OH.HCl in 100 ml of H_2O.

D_1 Hydroquinone solution, 1%
Dissolve 1 g of hydroquinone in 100 ml of H_2O.
or

D_2 H_2O_2, 30%

E   Special Hg/Ag solution
Dissolve 75 g of $HgSO_4$ in 400 ml of HNO_3 (s.g. = 1·42) and 200 ml of H_2O. Add 200 ml of H_3PO_4 (s.g. = 1·69), and 35 mg of $AgNO_3$. Dilute the cooled solution to 1 litre.

F $(NH_4)_2S_2O_8$ (A.R.) Dry.

Procedure

6.5.1.   Soluble Mn^{2+} (the sample need not to be filtered).
Add 5 ml of solution (E) and 3 g of $(NH_4)_2S_2O_8$ (F) to 90 ml of the sample, or to an aliquot diluted to 90 ml. Bring to boiling in about 2 minutes over a flame (do not heat on a water bath). Remove the flask from the flame, allow to stand for one minute and then cool under the tap. Dilute to 100 ml with H_2O.
  Measure the extinction of the reagent blank, standards and samples in suitable cells at a wavelength near 525 or 545 mμ. The colour is stable if the persulphate is in excess. If the solution was cloudy, during measurement add 1 drop of 1% hydroquinone solution (D_1), or 1 drop of 30% H_2O_2 (D_2). Stir and measure the extinction again. The difference is the extinction due to permanganate.

6.5.2.   Total inorganic manganese
(Filtered or unfiltered samples may be used).
Acidify a 90 ml sample with 3 ml H_3PO_4 (B). Add 2 drops NH_2OH.HCl solution (C), and heat to boiling. Cool and proceed as in § 6.5.1.

6.5.3.   Total manganese
Following wet digestion, proceed as in § 6.5.1.

Interferences

Fe^{3+} could interfere but in this procedure it is kept from doing so by the H_3PO_4. Interference by Cl^- is prevented by the special solution (E) (up to 100 mg of NaCl per sample).

Precision, accuracy, and sensitivity

The error in the determination of 0·05–5 mg of manganese per sample in the absence of interfering substances is usually not more than 1%. Method § 6.5.1 probably measures some organic Mn^{2+} if it exists, due to oxidation of some of the organic matter by the persulphate. The chief problem with this method is its low sensitivity (1 mg/l). For this reason a more sensitive method (Strickland and Parsons, 1965) is also given here, which may be suitable. It may be used in place of the previous method for all Mn fractions.

6.5.4. Manganese (tentative).

Principle

Mn^{2+} ions are oxidized to MnO_4^- by KIO_4 in a sodium acetate buffer. The $KMnO_4$ is then used to oxidize leucomalachite green and the extinction measured at about 620 mμ. (Strickland and Parsons, 1965). This method may be used to determine other Mn fractions following the filtration or digestion described in § 6.5.1–6.5.3.

Reagents

A   Standard manganese solution, 0·5 µg/ml

See § 6.5.1, but dilute 100 fold just before use.

B   Acetate buffer, 0·5 M

Dilute 30 ml CH_3COOH, glacial (A.R.), to 1000 ml with H_2O. Add carefully to this 5 N NaOH solution (A.R.) until the pH of the buffer lies in the range of 4·1 to 4·2. Store the solution in a thick walled polyethylene bottle. The solution is stable for many months.

C   KIO₄ solution, 0·2%

Dissolve 1·0 g of KIO_4 (A.R.) in 500 ml of H_2O, and add one small pellet (about 0·2 g) of NaOH. Store the solution in a dark glass bottle out of direct sunlight. The solution is stable for several weeks if stored in the dark, but slowly decomposes when exposed to strong light. For accurate work the solution should be made up every few days.

D   Leucomalachite Green solution, 0·08%

Dissolve 0·20 g of leucomalachite green (= 4.4-Bisdimethylaminotriphenyl-methane) which has been recrystallized from alcohol in 250 ml of pure acetone. This solution is stable but should not be allowed to evaporate. The development of a slight green colour does no harm.

Procedure

Put 30 ml of sample into a 50 ml stoppered graduated measuring cylinder. Add acetate buffer (B) from a polyethylene wash bottle, to make the total volume in the cylinder 45 ml. Place the cylinder in a water bath at a temperature between 23 and 26°C, with a thermostat with accuracy of ± 1°C. After the solution has reached the bath temperature (15 to 30 minutes) add 5·0 ml of KIO_4 solution (C) from a pipette. Mix the solution thoroughly and leave in the bath for a further 10 to 15 minutes. Then add with rapid mixing, 1·0 ml of solution (D) from a pipette and return the cylinder to the thermostatically controlled bath.

Between 4 and 5 hours after adding the solution (D) measure the extinction of the reagent blank, standards, and samples, in suitable cells at a wavelength as close as possible to 615 mμ.

Interferences

Iron interferes, but its extinction is very low compared to that resulting from the same molar concentration of Mn. The extinction for a given Mn concentration increases as the concentration of salts decreases. Internal standards are therefore essential.

Precision, accuracy, and sensitivity

According to Strickland, as little as 0·1 μg/l can be detected. Precision and accuracy are unknown.

6.6 MOLYBDENUM

Principle

Molybdenum is co-precipitated with MnO, and determined colorimetrically with KCNS. The procedure of Bachman and Goldman (1964) has proved satisfactory. An alternative procedure by Chan and Riley (1967) may be more sensitive, but is more complicated.

Reagents

A$_1$ Standard Mo solution, 100 μg/ml

Dissolve 0·0750 g of MoO_3 (A.R.) in 10 ml of 0·1 N NaOH, dilute with H_2O to about 50 ml, make slightly acidic with HCl, and make up to 500 ml with H_2O. 1 ml contains 100 μg of Mo.

A$_2$ Standard Mo solution, 10 μg/ml

Dilute A$_1$ tenfold with 0·1 N HCl. Prepare fresh solution each week.

B Buffered MnSO$_4$ solution

Dissolve 1·0 g of $MnSO_4 . H_2O$ in 150 ml of H_2O. Mix 30 ml of this solution with 120 ml of glacial acetic acid and 50 ml of 4 M sodium acetate (544 g/litre of $CH_3COONa . 3H_2O$).

C KMnO$_4$ solution, 1%

Dissolve 1 g of $KMnO_4$ in 100 ml of H_2O.

D SnCl$_2$ solution, 10%

Dissolve 10 g of $SnCl_2 . 2H_2O$ in 100 ml of 1 N HCl. Filter if cloudy. Prepare fresh solution each week.

E KCNS reagent

E$_1$ HCl, 1·3 N

Dilute 4 N HCl three times (100 ml → 0·3 litre).

E$_2$ $(NH_4)_2SO_4 . FeSO_4$ solution, 1%.

Dissolve 1 g of $(NH_4)_2SO_4 . FeSO_4 . 6H_2O$ in 100 ml of 0·2 N H_2SO_4. Prepare fresh solution each day.

E$_3$ KCNS solution, 10%

Dissolve 10 g of KCNS in 100 ml of H$_2$O.

Mix 160 ml of 1·3 N HCl (E$_1$) with 10 ml of (NH$_4$)$_2$SO$_4$.FeSO$_4$ solution (E$_2$) and 30 ml of the KCNS solution (E$_3$). *Prepare fresh solution each day.*

F   Solvent mixture of isoamyl alcohol and CCl$_4$

Mix equal volumes of A.R. products.

G   CaCl$_2$ dry, (A.R.)

Procedure

Put 1 litre of sample in a 2 litre flask and heat to boiling. Remove source of heat, and add with vigorous stirring, 10 g of CaCl$_2$ (G), 20 ml of the buffered MnSO$_4$ solution (B), then 2 ml of the KMnO$_4$ solution (C). Stir occasionally until the hydrated Mn(OH)$_2$ forms and coagulates. Allow to cool to room temperature, collect the precipitate on a filter such as a Whatman GF/B, or a 47 mm membrane filter (ca. 1·2 μ pore size). At this point the precipitate may be stored for later analysis. Place the filter flat on the bottom of a 150 ml beaker or roll it and place it in a test tube. Add 5 ml of the KCNS reagent (E). Mix, by swirling, until the precipitate dissolves and transfer the solution to a 60 ml separatory funnel. Wash the filter with three additional 5 ml portions of the KCNS reagent (E), adding each to the separatory funnel. To the funnel add 3·0 ml of the SnCl$_2$ (D) and mix. Add exactly 5·0 ml of the solvent mixture (F) and shake the funnel vigorously for 1$\frac{1}{2}$ minutes. Allow the aqueous and organic phases to separate. Separate the organic phase by filtering the bottom layer through a hard filter paper (e.g. Whatman no. 541) directly into the spectrophotometer cells. The filter paper removes water droplets and any insoluble matter which may be present. Wait about 10 minutes for any trace of pink, due to Fe(CNS)$_3$, to disappear.

Measure the extinction of the reagent blank, standards and samples in suitable cells at a wavelength as close as possible to 465 mμ. The colour is stable.

Interferences

The only interference likely to be present in natural waters is caused by iron, which produces a pink colour due to Fe(CNS)$_3$. After 10 minutes the iron reduces, and the interference disappears. In cases where much iron is present, wash the organic layer with SnCl$_2$ solution (D).

Precision, accuracy, and sensitivity

Recovery of added molybdenum averaged 99% for concentrations of 2·0–10·0 μg/l. Standard deviation was 2%.

6.7   VANADIUM

There is insufficient interest, at present, in the occurrence of V in fresh waters to justify the inclusion of a detailed method in this Manual. Such methods may be found in Chan and Riley, (1966) and in Fishman and Skougstad (1964).

6.8 ZINC

Principle

Zinc reacts with dithizone in weakly acidic medium to form a red compound, which is extracted with CCl_4 and estimated colorimetrically. See O'Connor (1963).

Reagents

A   Standard Zn solution, 1 mg/ml

Dissolve 1·00 g of granulated Zn (A.R.) in a slight excess of 4 N HCl (about 10 ml). Make up to 1 litre with H_2O. 1 ml contains 1 mg of Zn. Dilute standards should be freshly prepared.

B   HCl, 4 N

Dilute 12 N HCl three times (1 + 2). Select a supply with a low blank, or redistill a 50% solution.

C   Acetate buffer, 4 N

Mix equal volumes of 4 N CH_3COONa (544 g of $CH_3COONa.3H_2O$ in H_2O, dilute to 1 litre) and 4 N acetic acid (240 ml of $CH_3COOH \rightarrow$ 1 litre). Extract with dithizone solution (E) and subsequently with CCl_4 to remove zinc and colour. Store in dithizone-cleaned polyethylene bottles.

D $Na_2S_2O_3$ solution, 50%

Dissolve 500 g of $Na_2S_2O_3.5H_2O$ in H_2O and dilute to 1 litre. Remove zinc as described for reagent (C).

E   Dithizone solution, 0·01%

Dissolve 10 mg of dithizone in 100 ml of CCl_4. ($CHCl_3$ may be used instead). Keep in refrigerator.

E_1 Dithizone solution, 0·001%

Dilute solution (E) 10 times (10 ml $\rightarrow$ 100 ml). Solution E_1 is usable for a few days only.

Procedure

Put 100 ml of the sample into a 125 ml separatory funnel and add HCl (B) to about 0·05 N (0·5–1·0 ml of 4 N HCl). Add 4 ml of buffer solution (C), 4 ml of $Na_2S_2O_3$ solution (D) and 10 ml of dithizone solution (E_1). Shake the funnel vigorously for 2 minutes. Separate the solvent and repeat the extraction with fresh dithizone. Combine the extracts and make up to a known volume with CCl_4. Measure the extinction of the reagent blank, standards and samples in suitable cells at a wavelength between 520–540 mμ (this measures the red zinc dithizonate) or at 620 mμ (this measures the unreacted dithizone). Protect the solution from strong light.

Interferences

The most likely interferences in fresh water are due to Pb and Cu. Their reaction with dithizone is prevented by the $Na_2S_2O_3$ solution. If much Co or Ni is present it may be necessary to use KCN as a complexing agent. This is not usually necessary.

Precision, accuracy, and sensitivity

No figures available, but sensitivity is high. 1–2 μg of Zn per 100 ml of sample can easily be detected.

LEVEL III

There are many techniques, besides colorimetry, for determining the concentration of trace elements. None of these are ever likely to be field procedures.

In approximate order of equipment expense they include:

	Literature	*Notes*
Bioassay	Rodhe (1948); Shapiro (1967), (Fe); Harvey (1957) N; Goldman (1965); Hutner, Provasoli and Baker (1961).	
Chromatography		Widely used for organic substances, but little for trace elements.
(*a*) Polarography		Sensitivity rather low.
(*b*) Cathode ray polarography		Sensitivity about 100 times better.
Amperometric titration		Excellent for Mn (0·0003 mg/l sensitivity), but sensitivity for other trace elements too low.
Flame emission photometry		Sensitivity too low for trace elements.
Atomic absorption flame photometry	Fishman and Downs (1966) (Cu, Mn, Zn); Willis, (1962) (Pb); Fabricand, Sawyer, Ungar and Adler (1962); Malissa and Schöffman (1955), and references in 4.3.4. The method seems promising for Cu, Fe, Mn and Zn.	Sensitivity rather low for trace elements; concentration is usually necessary.
Emission spectroscopy	Haffty (1960); Silvey and Brennan (1962); Kopp and Kroner (1965).	Less sensitive than colorimetric methods, but estimates many elements at the same time.
Neutron activation	Meinke (1955).	Most sensitive technique known for most trace elements except Fe and, perhaps, Mo.

With the exception of bioassay all of these methods are capable of yielding results on several trace elements in a single small sample. Bioassay is however of outstanding interest, since it gives an estimate of how much of a substance is actually available to at least one organism.

CHAPTER 7

DETERMINATION OF ORGANIC SUBSTANCES

7.1 ORGANIC CARBON

LEVEL III

Principle

The first stage in the analysis of organic carbon in fresh water is to oxidize the carbon quantitatively to CO_2. This may be done by one of three methods. The next stage is to transfer the CO_2 produced, quantitatively, to an apparatus for CO_2 determination. The last stage is the measurement of CO_2.

The oxidation may be made by chromic acid in H_2SO_4 (§ 7.1.1) or, by persulphate (§ 7.1.2), or by combustion in O_2 (§ 7.1.7, particulate carbon only).

Oxidation of organic compounds in water samples is generally complete, but for some artificial organic compounds the recovery by wet combustion methods may be incomplete. These compounds are, however, unlikely to occur in natural water samples. It is essential to check the technique by using a standard of oxalic acid, $(COOH)_2$. (See 7.3.1).

Interferences

Impurities in the apparatus may easily give extra CO_2; adsorption of CO_2 on the walls and by cleaning solutions may lead to results which are numerically too small. Chlorine, and acid oxides produced during the oxidation will interfere with CO_2 measurement and must therefore be removed. The dimensions of the equipment depend on the concentrations involved. If the dimensions are small CO_2 is removed more quickly than it would be from a larger apparatus.

The following descriptions of the techniques of organic carbon determination are given in outline, and more details will be found in the appropriate references.

Sampling and storage

Only specially cleaned glass-fibre or silver filters are permissible for filtration If glass fibre filters are to be used later for the determination of particulate carbon, they should be preheated for 10 hours at 550°C. They should be stored in a dust free place. The sample should be filtered as soon as possible after sampling, to avoid decomposition of organic compounds.

There is no ideal method of storage. The addition of 2 ml H_2SO_4 (1 + 1) per 0·5 litre is the usual method and is effective for at least some weeks. Hydrolysis may occur, but at 5°C this process is slow. Deep-freezing is, in principle, the best method, but plastic containers may give off organic matter, and glass containers will sometimes break, so this method cannot be relied on.

If no living plankton cells are present another method may be used to separate dissolved from particulate fractions. Transfer the sample from the sampling bottle to a glass-stoppered 500 ml bottle, which already contains 2 ml H_2SO_4 $(1+1)$. Place this bottle for 24 hours in a completely undisturbed place. The particulate matter will settle to the bottom of the bottle. An aliquot of the supernatant liquid can then be withdrawn. Great care should be taken not to disturb the sediment.

Dissolved organic carbon

7.1.1.   Oxidation with chromic acid

Apparatus

The apparatus used by Effenberger (1962), which is especially suitable for polluted water, is shown in fig. 7.1. Organic carbon can be estimated even when in combination with inorganic carbon. The CO_2 is determined conductometrically (§ 7.1.5).

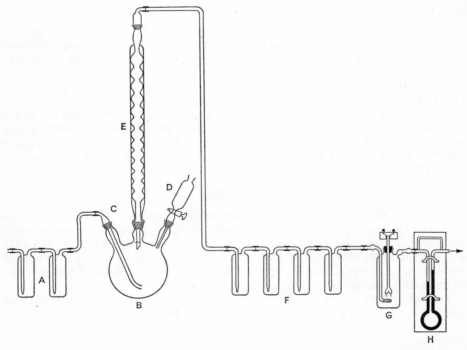

Figure 7.1. Apparatus for dissolved organic carbon determination according to Effenberger (1962).

A   Wash-bottles for CO_2 absorption from the carrier gas (air). Contents: 50% KOH solution.
B   Reaction vessel.
C   Air-inlet.
D   Oxidation mixture.
E   Reflux-condenser.
F   Wash-bottles, containing successively $K_2Cr_2O_7 + H_2SO_4$, $KI + H_2SO_4$, $Na_2S_2O_3$, and concentrated H_2SO_4.
G   Conductivity absorption cell.
H   Manometer.

The apparatus used by Krey and Szekielda (1965), which is particularly suitable for rapid analysis of small quantities of water, is shown in fig. 7.2.

The apparatus used by Duursma (1961) is shown in fig. 7.3. The principle on which this works is the same as that used by Krey and Szekielda.

Reagents

A   H₂SO₄ (1+1) (See § 1.4.1).

B   Oxidation mixture

Dissolve 10 g of $Ag_2Cr_2O_7$ and 42 g of $K_2Cr_2O_7$ in 400 ml of H_2SO_4 (A.R. s.g. = 1·84) at about 90°C. Free the mixture of carbon by heating at 125°C for 8 hours while passing a stream of CO_2 free and H_2O free O_2 through it at a constant rate. Avoid a higher temperature as auto-oxidation causes a precipitate in the mixture.

Fine crystals of $Ag_2Cr_2O_7$ can be obtained by adding slowly 50 g of $K_2Cr_2O_7$ in 800 ml of H_2O to a boiling solution of 50 g of $AgNO_3$ in 500 ml of H_2O (to which 4 ml conc. HNO_3 have been added). Collect the precipitate on a sintered glass filter and dry the precipitate at 100°C. (Commercial products must sometimes be purified by heating in H_2SO_4 at 125°C for 8 hours).

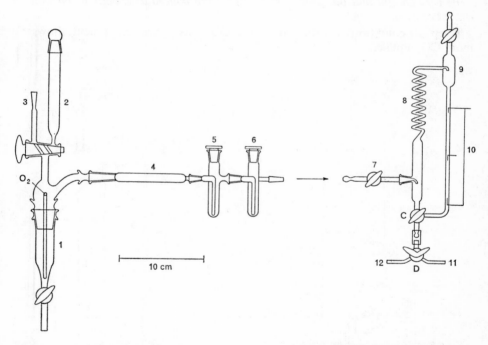

Figure 7.2. Apparatus for dissolved organic carbon determination according to Krey and Szekielda (1965).

   1. Reaction vessel.
   2. Oxidation-mixture.
   3. Entrance for the sample.
   4. Catalyser and absorption tube (550°C).
   5. Absorption vessel with Mg(ClO₄)₂.
   6. Absorption vessel with concentrated H₂SO₄.
   7. Inlet with tap for CO₂.
   8. Absorption space of CO₂.
   9. Separation chamber for O₂ and NaOH.
   10. Tube with electrodes for conductivity measurement.
   11. Tube connected with stock solution of NaOH.
   12. Outlet.
   C and D are taps.

H

Procedure

Place the sample in the reaction vessel (see fig. 7.1, 7.2 or 7.3) with 0·04 ml H_2SO_4 (A) per ml of sample. Drive off the inorganic CO_2 by heating for $1\frac{1}{2}$ minutes just below boiling temperature. This CO_2, plus the O_2 introduced at a constant rate, should be allowed to escape at once from the reaction vessel. The O_2 is purified from CO_2 by sodium asbestos or sodium hydroxide, and from H_2O by passage over $CaCl_2$, and is passed into the apparatus at a constant speed. The best rate must be determined. Close the reaction vessel again immediately, so that no CO_2 can enter. No oxidation mixture should be introduced until the CO_2 absorption equipment shows that the apparatus is in equilibrium.

Now add to the sample an equal volume of the oxidation mixture. The temperature will rise to about 100°C. Then heat further to 130°C.

Be very careful that this procedure is always reproduced as exactly as possible on every occasion.

Keep all conditions constant until the CO_2 absorption equipment shows no more CO_2 uptake.

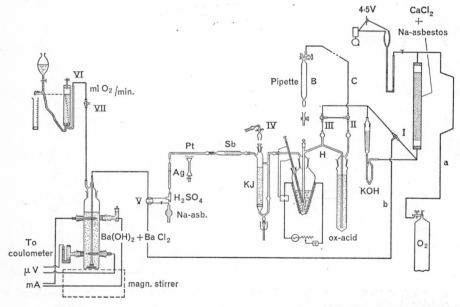

Figure 7.3. Apparatus for dissolved organic carbon determination according to Duursma. For a detailed description of the apparatus see the original paper, Duursma (1961).

Range of application and accuracy

Dissolved organic carbon at concentrations from 0·2 to 20 mg/l of C can be determined with an accuracy of ± 0·03 mg/l of C, if complicated apparatus and techniques are used.

Note

Each series of determinations must start with blanks and standards to check that the apparatus is working correctly. A repeatable blank can be obtained only if details of operation are carefully standardized. For this reason, continuous working is preferable.

Liquids suck back easily if either the O_2 supply or the heating of the reaction vessel is irregular.

7.1.2. Oxidation with persulphate

Apparatus

The apparatus used by Menzel and Vaccaro (1964) is shown in fig 7.4.

The 10 ml pyrex ampoules are heated in a muffle furnace at 700°C for one hour to remove any traces of organic carbon. At this temperature the ampoules are soft, and may fuse together. Care should therefore be taken to keep them apart. Heating with a solution of 40 ml of 3% H_3PO_4 and 20 g of $K_2S_2O_8$ at 130°C in an autoclave for two hours is equally satisfactory.

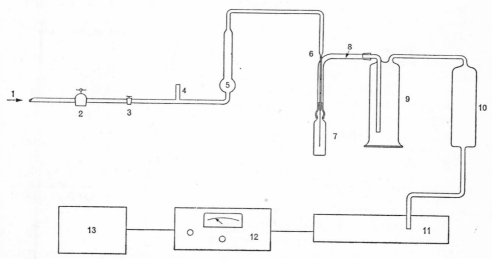

Figure 7.4. Schematic diagram of equipment used in the detection of CO_2, resulting from the oxidation of dissolved organic carbon, Menzel and Vaccaro (1964).

1. Nitrogen supply.
2. Regulator.
3. Needle valve.
4. Flow meter.
5. Ascarite tube.
6. Hypodermic needle.
7. Ampoule.
8. Rubber tubing.
9. Gas washing bottle.
10. Mg(ClO₄)₂ drying tube.
11. Infra red CO_2 analyzer.
12. Amplifier.
13. Recorder.

Reagents

A H_3PO_4, 3%

Dissolve 3 ml H_3PO_4 (A.R.) in 100 ml double distilled H_2O.

B $K_2S_2O_8$, dry.

Procedure

Inject 5 ml filtered sample into the 10 ml ampoule. Then add successively 0·1 g $K_2S_2O_8$ and 0·2 ml 3% H_3PO_4. Bubble N_2 gas, free of CO_2, through a 10 cm cannula into the ampoule at a rate of 200 ml/min for 3 minutes to remove all inorganic carbon. Place a vaccine stopper with a cut off fine hypodermic needle, inserted through it on top of the ampoule to restrict gas movement. Seal the ampoule in an oxygen-gas flame immediately. This operation is critical, as products of combustion from the flame may enter the ampoule. Details are given by Menzel and Vaccaro (1964).

Heat a batch of these samples at 130°C in an autoclave. Normally one-half an hour is sufficient, but for polluted waters, containing unusually stable compounds, a longer time may be necessary. The ampoules may at this stage be transported, and the CO_2 subsequently transferred (§ 7.1.3) and estimated with a sensitive CO_2 detector e.g. the infrared CO_2 analyser (§ 7.1.7). Storage of the samples is no problem.

7.1.3.   Transfer and purification of CO_2

The CO_2 formed during the oxidation must be transferred to the detector by flushing with O_2 or N_2.

During this transfer Cl_2, oxides of nitrogen and sulphur (formed during the oxidation) and water-vapour must be removed. CO must be oxidised to CO_2.

Passage through a KI solution (40 g in 50 ml 4 N H_2SO_4), followed by metallic antimony and then a silver-manganese catalyst is a suitable combination for this purpose. H_2SO_4 and $Mg(ClO_4)_2$ absorb H_2O; H_2SO_4 also absorbs the nitrogen- and sulphur-oxides. Antimony and silver (a 5 cm long tuft of very fine silver wool) can be used to retain halogens. Platinum (a 10×4 cm roll of fine meshed platinum-gauze in a quartz tube) or more effectively the silver-manganese catalyst convert CO to CO_2. This latter catalyst also combines with halogens and sulphur-oxides.

The silver-manganese catalyst is prepared as follows:

Dissolve 40 g $MnSO_4.4H_2O$ in 200 ml double-distilled H_2O. Add a solution of 20 g $AgNO_3$ in 50 ml H_2O to which has been added 20 ml concentrated NH_4OH. Filter through a sintered glass filter, wash the precipitate free of $SO_4{}^{2-}$ and dry at 120°C. Decompose at 400–500°C (avoid heating at greater than 550°C) for 2 hours.

All reagents should be of high purity. Regular replacement is necessary. Solutions must be made with double or triple distilled H_2O (distillation from $H_3PO_4 +$ $KMnO_4$ solution). Those ground glass joint surfaces which are in contact with the oxidation mixture or H_2SO_4 should be sealed with H_2SO_4 (s.g. = 1·84).

Special procedure for CO_2 transfer following persulphate combustion

The neck of the sealed ampoule is inserted into the rubber tubing (fig. 7.4), and N_2 is flushed through the system until the IR analyser indicates the complete removal of extraneous CO_2. The gas flow is then shut off, the tip of the ampoule is crushed, and the cannula is inserted into the solution. The gas flow is started again and kept constant. The gas is washed by the acid KI solution and dried by $Mg(ClO_4)_2$.

7.1.4.   Determination of CO_2 by absorption in excess $(Ba(OH)_2$; back-titration with HCl. (Kay, 1954)

Reagents

A $Ba(OH)_2$, 0·05 N

Dissolve 16 g of $Ba(OH)_2.8H_2O$ and 20 g of $BaCl_2$ in 2 litres of boiled H_2O. Store the solution in a container which is connected directly to a burette. Exclude CO_2 from both. Allow any $BaCO_3$ precipitate to settle before transferring the solution to the burette.

B HCl, 0·025 N

Dilute 0·100 N HCl (250 ml → 1000 ml).

C Mixed indicator

Mix 10 ml of 0·1% Thymol Blue (in 50% alcohol) with 30 ml of 0·1% phenol-phthalein in 50% alcohol. At pH = 9 the colour changes from red-violet (alkaline) to clear yellow (acid).

Procedure

Backtitrate the excess of $Ba(OH)_2$ with HCl using the mixed indicator to locate the end point.

Note

The $Ba(OH)_2$–HCl titration method can only be used for waters which have a relatively high concentration of organic carbon. 1 ml of HCl is equal to 0·15 mg of C per sample. No direct check for completion of the reaction is possible.

7.1.5. Determination of CO_2 by absorption in excess NaOH; change in conductivity. (Effenberger (1962); Szekielda and Krey (1965))

The CO_2 is absorbed in a solution of NaOH or $Ba(OH)_2$, which results in a decrease of the conductivity of the solution. NaOH is preferable because there is then no precipitate on the electrodes, or on the container surfaces, although the change in conductivity is smaller than with $Ba(OH)_2$. The concentration of NaOH or $Ba(OH)_2$ should be between 0·01 N and 0·02 N.

The two fixed platinum electrodes in the absorption vessel (see figures 7.1 and 7.2) form one arm of a Wheatstone bridge. To measure the conductivity an A.C. voltage of approximately 10 Volts can be used. The frequency should be not less than 1000 cycles per second. The temperature must be kept constant.

The apparatus must be standardized empirically at the same temperature. A standard of $(COOH)_2$, see § 7.3.1 (made with boiled H_2O) can be used. There should be a linear relationship between CO_2 and conductivity.

7.1.6. Determination of CO_2 by coulometric titration (Duursma, 1961)

Just as with the conductometric determination, this method makes it possible to follow the arrival of CO_2 from the combustion chamber continuously. The advantage of the coulometric method is that conditions in the apparatus are always constant, and the apparatus is immediately ready for the next analysis.

The CO_2 is absorbed (fig. 7.3) in a $BaCl_2$ solution which is maintained at a fixed pH of 9·6 by electrolysis. The anode is separated from the absorption solution by an agar salt bridge.

By measuring the amount of electricity (current multiplied by time), the amount of absorbed CO_2 can be calculated. Absorption of 1 mg carbon as CO_2 requires 16·084 Coulombs (i.e. 804·2 seconds of electrolysis with a constant current of 20 mA), to maintain the pH constant.

By plotting coulombs against time the course of CO_2 absorption can be followed.

7.1.7. Determination of CO_2 by infrared gas analysis (Montgomery and Thom, 1962; Menzel and Vaccaro, 1964)

If small amounts only of CO_2 are available for determination, a particularly sensitive technique is necessary. Measurement of absorption of infra-red radiation

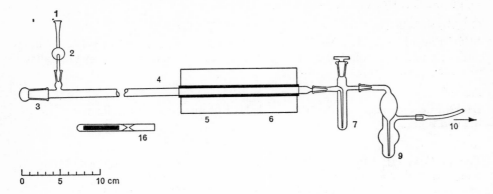

Figure 7.5. Apparatus for particulate organic carbon determination, Szekielda and Krey (1965).
1. Inlet for O_2.
2. Bubble counter.
3. Stopper.
4. Quartz-combustion tube.
5. Combustion zone.
6. Catalyser-zone.
7. Absorption vessel for H_2O by $Mg(ClO_4)_2$.
9. Absorption vessel for nitrogenoxides by concentrated H_2SO_4.
10. Towards CO_2 inlet (7) in fig. 7.2.
16. Quartz tube with iron for transporting the filter in the combustion tube magnetically.

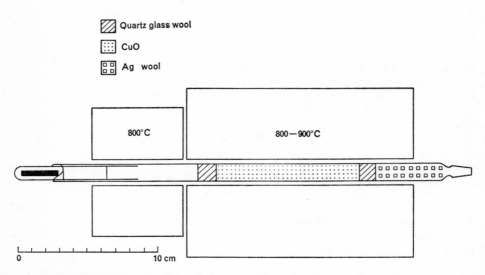

Figure 7.6. Details of combustion tube of apparatus fig. 7.5.

due to CO_2 in the gas mixture is a suitable technique. Following the persulphate oxidation (§ 7.1.2 and fig. 7.4) no other method of CO_2 estimation is sufficiently sensitive, but it can of course also be used following chromic acid oxidation (§ 7.1.1).

The measurement can be made either directly in the purified gas stream or after collecting the CO_2 in an evacuated container. The IR analyser must be calibrated empirically (Montgomery and Thom, 1962).

The use of a commercially available apparatus is described by Busch (1967).

7.1.8. The determination of particulate carbon (See Szekielda and Krey, 1965)

Principle

The particulate material is collected on a glass fibre or silver filter. After drying, the filter is heated at a high temperature in a stream of O_2, and the liberated CO_2 is determined conductometrically. A simplified diagram of the apparatus is given in figure 7.5. The method can also be used in combination with an infrared gas analyser. The CO_2 should then be absorbed as in the dissolved organic carbon method. Oxygen instead of nitrogen is used as the carrier gas (Menzel and Vaccaro, 1964).

Accuracy, sensitivity and range of application

The range of application is 50–1000 $\mu g/l$ C; The standard deviation of 10 samples containing 0·34 mg/l C was 15 $\mu g/l$ C. Accuracy is about 4%.

7.2 BIOCHEMICAL OXYGEN DEMAND (B.O.D.)

ALL LEVELS

Principle

The rate of removal of O_2 by organisms using the organic matter in water may be measured.

This test, called *biochemical oxygen demand* is especially useful as an easy, though only approximate, index of organic pollution (or of sewage treatment plant efficiency). The B.O.D. test is commonly made by measuring O_2 concentration in samples before and after incubation in the dark at 20°C for 5 days. Preliminary dilution and aeration of the sample are usually necessary to ensure that not all the O_2 is used during the incubation. Sometimes a culture of bacteria is added so that more of the organic matter will be used up during the incubation.

(For detailed instructions see Standard Methods (1965).)

The importance of short experimental times and the stoicheiometry of the reactions involved is stressed by Busch (1966).

In waters that are not heavily polluted, the bacterial degradation of the organic matter is slow and often continues for 10, 20, or more days (Straškrabová-Prokešová, 1966). The standard B.O.D. method is not usable under these conditions, but a simplified method can give some information about differences between lakes or rivers or about seasonal changes in the dissolved organic matter in one water body (Stangenberg, 1959).

Procedure

If the O_2 content of the original sample is very low, the sample should be aerated for 5 or 10 minutes. Place portions of the sample into 3 glass stoppered bottles

(125, 250, or 300 ml) and immediately determine the O_2 concentration in one bottle. (See § 8.1.1 or § 8.1.2). Incubate the remaining 2 bottles in the dark at a standard temperature (e.g. 20°C) or at the temperature of the original sample for 1 to 5 days. Then determine the remaining O_2. Subtract this value from the original value of O_2 to give B.O.D.

CHEMICAL OXYGEN DEMAND (C.O.D.)

LEVEL II

7.3 C.O.D. DUE TO DISSOLVED ORGANIC COMPOUNDS

Principle

The concentration of organic compounds in lake water can be estimated by their oxidability by oxidizing substances such as $K_2Cr_2O_7$ and $KMnO_4$.

Organic carbon and O_2 are indirectly related because the reaction is:

$$C_xH_{2y}O_z + \left[x + \frac{(y-z)}{2}\right] O_2 \rightarrow x\, CO_2 + y\, H_2O$$

The amount of carbon oxidized can therefore be calculated from the amount of O_2 taken up only if the ratio of $(y-z)$ to x is known. This ratio is, however, in most cases unknown. The C.O.D. method is, however, simpler than a carbon determination, and is directly comparable to the biochemical oxygen demand (B.O.D.), which estimates the organic compounds available for bacterial activities.

C.O.D. also has particular significance when photosynthesis is expressed in the same units; as mg/l O_2. (See opening address, Golterman, 1967).

$K_2Cr_2O_7$ is the most suitable oxidizing agent. The reaction is:

$$Cr_2O_7{}^{2-} + 14H^+ + 6e^- \rightarrow 2Cr^{3+} + 7H_2O$$

so that

$$1.0 \text{ M/l } Cr_2O_7{}^{2-} \text{ is } 6.0 \text{ N}$$

It cannot, however, be used for samples containing more than 2 g/l Cl^- because of the oxidation of Cl^- to Cl_2. In these cases $KMnO_4$ must be used, though the results are more variable because $KMnO_4$ is self oxidizing. When $K_2Cr_2O_7$ is used $HgSO_4$ must be added to mask the chloride in the range 0.2 to 2 g/l of Cl^-.

Ag_2SO_4 is used as a catalyst for the oxidation. It is particularly effective for short straight-chain alcohols and acids.

The oxidation is carried out with an excess of $K_2Cr_2O_7$. The C.O.D. is estimated either by the determination of unused $Cr_2O_7{}^{2-}$ (§ 7.3.1) or by the spectrophotometric determination of the Cr^{3+} formed (§ 7.3.2).

(See Burns and Marshall, 1965, Maciolek, 1962).

Sampling and storage

The water samples should be taken with water-sampling bottles, which do not release organic substances into the water. Filtration through glass-fibre filters is recommended, but hard paper filters may be used if the sample has a high C.O.D. The filters should be prerinsed with water.

The analysis should be made as soon as possible and the samples kept cold (4–8°C) beforehand. For long storage deep-freezing is recommended.

Apparatus

Autoclave and 250 ml flat bottom boiling flasks with covers, or 250 ml flat bottom boiling flasks with ground-glass connections to 30 cm Liebig (straight tube single surface) condensers.

For method 1a: Dead stop titrator (see § 9.13) or pH meter.

For method 2: Spectrophotometer or colorimeter with filters with maximum transmittance close to 500 mμ and 585 mμ, and with narrow band with a sharp cut off.

7.3.1. Oxidability by $K_2Cr_2O_7$ (with back-titration)

Reagents

A Standard oxalic acid, 0·0125 N (10 ml = 1 mg C.O.D.)

Dilute 0·100 N $(COOH)_2$ (See § 1.4.1) (25 ml → 200 ml).

B $K_2Cr_2O_7$, 1·000 N

Dissolve 49·035 g of $K_2Cr_2O_7$ (A.R., dried for 2 hours at 105°C) in H_2O (double distilled) and dilute to 1000 ml.

C_1 H_2SO_4 (s.g. = 1·84, A.R.)

C_2 H_2SO_4 (1+1) A.R. (See § 1.4.1).

D Ferrous solution, 0·25 N. *Either D_1 or D_2 may be used.*

D_1 Fe–ES solution, 0·25 N

Dissolve 95·5 g of Fe-ethylenediamine sulphate.$4H_2O$ (available from Merck or Baker) in H_2O, add 1 ml of H_2SO_4 (1+1) and dilute with H_2O to 1000 ml.

D_2 $Fe(NH_4)_2(SO_4)_2$, 0·25N

Dissolve 98 g of $Fe(NH_4)_2(SO_4)_2 . 6H_2O$ in H_2O. Add 40 ml of H_2SO_4 (1+1) and dilute to 1000 ml.

Standardize the Fe solution (D_1 or D_2) against a $K_2Cr_2O_7$ solution (B).

E NH_2SO_3H (Sulphamic acid), (dry, A.R.)

F Diphenylamine indicator, 0·5%

Dissolve 0·50 g of diphenylamine in 20 ml of H_2O and add, with caution, 100 ml of H_2SO_4 (s.g. 1·84).

G Ag_2SO_4 (dry, A.R.)

H $HgSO_4$ (dry, A.R.)

Procedure

Mix 70 ml of sample containing not more than 16 mg C.O.D. (as O_2) or an aliquot diluted to 70 ml, in a 250 ml flask with powdered $HgSO_4$ (H) in the ratio $HgSO_4$: $Cl^- = 10 : 1$ (Cl^- less than 2 g/l). Add, with caution, 20 ml of H_2SO_4 (C_1). Then add successively 100 mg of Ag_2SO_4 (G) and 10·00 ml of $K_2Cr_2O_7$ (B). Attach the condenser to the Erlenmeyer flask, and put the flask in a water bath. Either boil for 3–6 hours or autoclave the covered flasks at about 135°C (3 atmospheres pressure) for 3–6 hours. Cool the flask, and then:

EITHER

Titrate the excess of $K_2Cr_2O_7$ with reagent (D_1) using a dead stop end point titrimeter or a potentiometric titrimeter. (See § 9.12 and § 9.13). Graph the meter readings against ml of reagent.

OR

Add 1 ml of indicator (F) and titrate the excess of $K_2Cr_2O_7$ with reagent (D_2). At the end point the colour changes sharply from turbid blue to brilliant green.

Run a blank using 70 ml of double-distilled H_2O, and all reagents.

Calculation

$$\text{C.O.D. mg/l} = \frac{(\alpha - \beta) \times \text{N} \times 8 \times 1000}{\text{ml sample}}$$

where

C.O.D. = chemical oxygen demand in mg/l O_2

α = ml titrant used for blank (about 40 ml)

β = ml titrant used for sample (about 39 ml, for waters with a C.O.D. = $\sim$ 30 mg/l O_2)

N = normality of the titrant.

Precision and accuracy

It will be apparent that extreme care in the titration is necessary. The titration error is about $\frac{1}{4}$ mg C.O.D. per sample or 4 mg/l C.O.D. The precision depends therefore on the amount of carbon present (= the relative amounts of α and β). The precision is low for waters containing a low C.O.D. The use of a piston microburette renders the titration more precise. Since the capacity of a piston microburette is usually not more than 5 ml, the solution must in this case be made up to volume after the oxidation, and an aliquot taken for titration.

7.3.2. Oxidability by $K_2Cr_2O_7$ (measurement of Cr^{3+} produced, see de Graaf and Golterman, 1967).

Reagents

See § 7.3.1, but without (D), (F) and (H).

Procedure

Mix sample and reagents in a 100 ml volumetric flask as in procedure § 7.3.1, but omit the Ag_2SO_4 (G). After cooling, make up to 100 ml with H_2SO_4 (C) (about 2 ml). Mix again and transfer the solution to the 250 ml flask. Heat for 3–6 hours in a water bath at 100°C. Run a blank as in procedure § 7.3.1.

Within 3 hours, but after cooling, measure the extinctions of reagent blanks, standards and samples against H_2O blank in suitable cells at a wavelength as close as possible to both 500 mμ and 585 mμ.

Calibration curve

Prepare a calibration curve covering the range 1 up to 16 mg C.O.D. by using known amounts of $(COOH)_2$ (A) and using exactly the same method as described above. The calibration curve should be identical with a calibration curve using $K_2SO_4 \cdot Cr_2(SO_4)_3$ boiled for the same time in H_2SO_4 under the same conditions.

Calculation

The extinction of the sample at 585 mμ has two components. The major one is due to the Cr^{3+} produced in the reaction. The minor one is due to the unused $K_2Cr_2O_7$, the concentration of which is lower in the sample than in the blank. The decrease in extinction due to this cause is determined at 500 mμ because Cr^{3+} shows no extinction at this wavelength. If a colorimeter is used a check should be made to ensure that the extinction of Cr^{3+} at 500 mμ is 0. (If not try filter with maximum at 490 mμ.)

The extinction of the Cr^{3+} produced is

$$E_{Cr^{3+}}^{585} = E_{sample}^{585} - \frac{E_{sample}^{500}}{E_{blank}^{500}} \times E_{blank}^{585}$$

Precision

The extinction produced by a sample containing 1 meq/l C.O.D. in a 5 cm cell is about 0·030. The precision is about 1 mg/l of O_2 (corresponding to $E = 0·005$) which can be improved, when using a 20 cm cell by a factor of 4.

Notes

(1) The colour of the Cr^{3+} ion is stable for 3 hours; afterwards the violet hydrate may be formed in significant amounts.

(2) Ag_2SO_4 cannot be used as it causes turbidity.

Interferences: (method § 7.3.1 and § 7.3.2).

Fe^{2+} and H_2S interfere and must be removed by bubbling air through the sample.

NO_2^- interferes, but can be removed by adding 10 mg of sulfamic acid per mg of NO_2–N to the dichromate solution.

7.3.3. Oxidability by KMnO$_4$

For brackish waters the alkaline oxidation method is often applied, in spite of difficulties with incomplete oxidation and reproducibility. Cl^- interferes less than in the acid-dichromate method.

The method should always be used by analyzing batches of a number of samples together with blanks and standards.

Apparatus

(The following apparatus has proved convenient. It is not, of course, essential to the method.)

An ordinary domestic enamelled pan with lid is used as a water bath (fig. 7.7). A frame is put inside about 10 cm above the bottom. On this frame up to 20 Erlenmeyer flasks can be placed together for heating and afterwards for cooling (fig. 7.8).

Reagents

A Standard (COOH)$_2$, 0·100 N (See § 1.4.1).

B KMnO$_4$, 0·1 N

Dissolve 3·16 g of $KMnO_4$ + 16 g of NaOH in double or triple distilled H_2O. Dilute to 1 litre. Allow to stand in the dark for several days. Filter through a glass filter and standardize against (COOH)$_2$. Store in a refrigerator.

C Na$_2$S$_2$O$_3$, 0·1 N

Dissolve 15·81 g of $Na_2S_2O_3$ in 1 litre of H_2O. Add 1 g of Na_2CO_3 as preservative. Allow the solution to stand for a day before standardizing.

D H$_2$SO$_4$, 4 N (See §1.4.1).

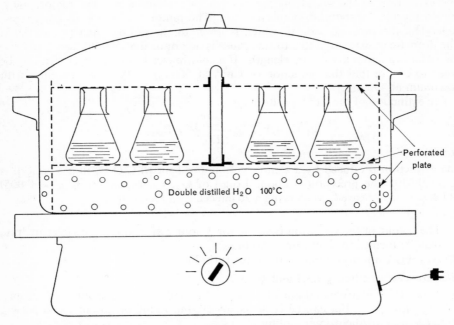

Figure 7.7. Batch of 100 ml Erlenmeyer flasks, covered with beakers in an ordinary enamelled pan. The flasks can be handled all together in the frame.

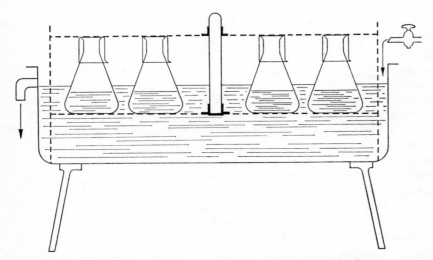

Figure 7.8. Cooling of the batch of Erlenmeyer flasks for C.O.D. determination.

E   KI solution, 10%
Dissolve 10 g of KI in 90 ml of H_2O.

F   Starch solution, 1%
Heat 1 g of soluble starch in 100 ml H_2O until it dissolves.

Procedure
Add 50 ml of sample or an aliquot containing not more than 0·8 mg C.O.D. (16 mg per litre), to a 100 ml Erlenmeyer flask. With each series run two or three blanks (double distilled H_2O) and at least two standards. Heat the water bath to boiling point. Add 5·0 ml of $KMnO_4$ (B) to each flask and place the batch in the water bath for exactly one hour. Cool for 10 minutes (fig. 7.8). Add 5 ml of KI (E) and directly afterwards 10 ml of 4 N H_2SO_4 (D). Titrate with thiosulphate (C), and when the solution has become pale yellow add 1 ml of the starch solution. Continue the titration until the blue colour disappears.

Calculation
$$\text{C.O.D. mg/l} = \frac{(\alpha - \beta) \times \text{N} \times 8 \times 1000}{\text{ml sample}}$$

where: α = ml thiosulphate for the blank

β = ml thiosulphate for the sample

N = normality of the thiosulphate

when $\beta > 0·9 \times \alpha$ the solutions of $KMnO_4$ and $Na_2S_2O_3$ must be diluted (0·05 or 0·01 N).

CHEMICAL OXYGEN DEMAND DUE TO PARTICULATE ORGANIC COMPOUNDS

7.3.4.   Oxidability
If more than about 25–50% of the total organic matter is present in particulate form it is possible to determine the C.O.D. in the total sample and in the filtrate (see § 7.3.1 or § 7.3.2). The difference gives the C.O.D. of the particulate matter. If the particulate matter is present in smaller proportion, or if the highest accuracy must be obtained, the particulate matter should be accumulated on a glass-fibre filter, and the filter can then be introduced in a quantity of double distilled water for analysis by method § 7.3.1 or § 7.3.2. The filter should be prewashed with dilute H_2SO_4, and rinsed with H_2O.

7.3.5.   Loss on ignition
This method is practicable for waters with a high concentration of particulate organic matter. The results are given as the loss in weight of oxidizable material per litre of water.

Reagents

A   HCl, 2 N
Dilute 4 N HCl (see § 1.4.1).

B H_2O_2, 30%.

Procedure

Dry some glass fibre or ash free paper filters (5 cm diameter is suitable) at 100°C for one hour. Place them in a desiccator, and determine the weight of each to at least the nearest mg. Store them in a clean place. Heat the crucibles for one hour at 800–900°C in an electric furnace. Let them cool to about 200°C, and then place them in a desiccator. After cooling to room temperature determine their weight. Filter the sample. One litre is often a suitable volume to use. Release the vacuum and put 5 ml of 2 N HCl (A) on the filter. The carbonates present will dissolve in a few (about 5) minutes. Then suck the acid through and wash twice with 5 ml H_2O.

Dry the filters in an oven at 100°C for one hour and determine the weight in the same way as before. The difference from the original weight of the filter is the total amount of particulate matter less that of carbonate (P mg). Place the dry filter in a crucible of known weight. Ash the filter (if paper) over a flame, but take care not to ignite the paper. The crucible should be held in a slightly oblique position. Cool and add 1 ml of 30% H_2O_2 (B) to the ash and allow to dry in an oven at 100°C or carefully over a flame.

Heat the crucible at 800–900°C for one hour and determine the weight as before. This weight minus that of the empty crucible (+glass fibre filter if appropriate) is that of the residue (Q mg).

Calculation

$$P - Q = \text{mg ignition loss per sample}$$

$$\frac{P - Q}{P} \times 100 = \text{percentage organic matter in the particulate matter.}$$

Note

When clay minerals are a component of the particulate matter, a small part of the loss of weight on ignition is due to the loss of water which is strongly bound to the clay minerals.

7.3.6.

LEVEL III

The method § 7.3.1 or § 7.3.2 can also be used at level III, using a recording potentiometric device, and it can easily be completely automated.

7.4 DISSOLVED ORGANIC COMPOUNDS

LEVEL III

By fluorescence in ultraviolet light

Principle

The method for determination of dissolved organic matter by fluorescence in ultraviolet light is based on the presence of six membered ring structures of melanoidine groups. Many of these groups are fluorescent. The proportion of fluorescent groups in dissolved organic matter is not constant. Since fluorescent substances are relatively resistant to decomposition these products may however characterize water bodies in mixing processes.

The filtered water sample is irradiated with U.V. light in a quartz cell. The fluorescent light, emitted perpendicular to the U.V. beam, is measured by a photo cell or photo multiplier. The instrument made by Karl Zeiss, Oberkochen, Germany is satisfactory. That made by many firms is not sufficiently sensitive to measure the very low levels of fluorescence in natural waters.

A calibration curve, which is not linear, can be made with quininebisulphate in $0.01 \, \mathrm{N} \, H_2SO_4$.

For further information see Kalle (1955/56), Duursma (1961), Duursma and Rommets (1961).

7.5 CARBOHYDRATES

LEVEL II

7.5.1. Colorimetric

Principle

Carbohydrates are estimated using the colour produced in the reaction of the furan derivatives of the sugars—formed by dehydration with strong H_2SO_4 at 100°C—with the anthrone reagent in strong H_2SO_4. Prior hydrolysis is not necessary as this takes place during the development of the colour.

Different carbohydrates react at different rates with the reagent (Yemm and Willis, 1954). After 5 minutes pentoses for example yield an extinction coefficient of about 50%, and fructose 200%, of the value of glucose, the substance that is usually used for calibration.

Although glucose reaches a maximum extinction after 5 minutes heating, 15 minutes is chosen as the recommended heating time because the extinction coefficients of the different sugars differ less after this period.

Reagents

A   Glucose standard solution, 100 µg/ml

Dissolve 100·0 mg of glucose in 1000 ml of H_2O. This solution will keep for short periods, but only if stored at 0°C. Just before use prepare dilutions containing 10, 25, 50 and 100 µg/ml of glucose.

B   Anthrone solution, 0·1 %

Dissolve 0·1 g of anthrone in 500 ml of H_2SO_4 (s.g. 1·84). Add this solution carefully to 200 ml H_2O.

Add 1 g of thiourea as antioxidant. The solution can then be kept for up to 2 weeks in a refrigerator. Otherwise a fresh solution must be prepared each day.

Procedure (total sugar)

Layer 5 ml of a sugar solution, or of a suspension or extract of organisms, containing not more than 100 µg of glucose equivalent per ml, on 25 ml of anthrone reagent (B) in a tall reagent tube (18 × 180 mm). Stopper loosely with corks. Mix and place all the tubes together in a boiling water bath for exactly 15 minutes. Cool the tubes together in a beaker with running tap water as quickly as possible. Measure the extinction of the reagent blank, standards, and samples against H_2O, in suitable cells within 3 hours using a wavelength between 620 and 630 mµ.

Note

The use of an ethanol containing anthrone solution has been described by Fales (1951) and Hewitt (1958). The ethanol is incorporated to stabilize the coloured products, but less is known about the reaction rates of the different sugars. The reagent is prepared as follows:

Dissolve 0·4 g of anthrone in 200 ml of H_2SO_4 (s.g. = 1·84). Add this solution to a flask containing 60 ml of H_2O and 15 ml of 95% ethanol. Measure the extinction of the coloured product at 620 mμ.

Acid soluble carbohydrates

Hydrolyse the dry cells, or a cell suspension, with a final H_2SO_4 concentration of 0·5 N in a boiling water bath for 30 minutes. Centrifuge (3000 rpm) and use 5 ml as described for the procedure above.

LEVEL II/III

7.5.2. Volumetric

Principle

Sugars and polysaccharides are hydrolysed to monosaccharides in HCl (Blažka, 1966b). The reducing capacity of the sugars is then determined by a micro ferricyanide back-titration (Hanes, 1929, Hulme and Narain, 1931). The ferrocyanide which is formed is precipitated with Zn^{2+}. The method estimates total reducing capacity and is not specific for carbohydrates.

The advantage of the ferricyanide method over the anthrone method is that the total reducing value of a mixture of sugars is the sum of the different components. The reactions involved with the ferricyanide titration are nearly stoicheiometric. Comparison with procedure § 7.5.1 is useful.

Reagents

A   Glucose standard solution, 100 μg/ml
See § 7.5.1, reagent (A).

B   HCl, 1 N
Dilute 4 N HCl (See § 1.4.1.)

C   Glacial CH$_3$COOH
Use a grade which is free of reducing substances.

D   NaOH, 2 N
Dilute 4 N NaOH (See § 1.4.1.)

E   Thiosulphate solution, 0·01 N (See § 8.1.2.)

F   Alkaline K$_3$Fe(CN)$_6$ solution, about 0·025 N
Dissolve 8·25 g of $K_3Fe(CN)_6$ and 10·6 g of Na_2CO_3 in 1 litre of H_2O.

G   KI solution, 2·5%
Dissolve 12·5 g of KI, 25·0 g of $ZnSO_4$, and 125 g of NaCl in H_2O and dilute to 500 ml.

H   Soluble starch (See § 8.1.2)

Procedure

Heat the dry residue of a water sample with 10·0 ml of 1 N HCl (B) at 100°C for 30 minutes. The acid soluble carbohydrates are thus extracted, and sucrose is converted to glucose plus fructose. Add 50 ml of 2 N NaOH, centrifuge or filter, and mix 10·0 ml of extract with 10·0 ml of ferricyanide solution (F) in test tubes. Place the test tubes in a boiling water bath for 15 minutes. Cool in running cold tap water for 3 minutes and add 5 ml KI solution (G). I_2 is liberated and insoluble Zn ferrocyanide is formed. Titrate the I_2 with $S_2O_3^{2-}$ (E), as described in § 8.1.2. Run blanks through the whole procedure.

Calibration and calculation

Calculate (ml $S_2O_3^{2-}$)$_{eq}$
  [i.e. ml $S_2O_3^{2-}$ equivalent to the amount of ferricyanide reduced by the sugar in the sample, thus:

$$(ml\ S_2O_3^{2-})_{blank} - (ml\ S_2O_3^{2-})_{sample}]$$

Make a calibration curve, plotting (ml $S_2O_3^{2-}$)$_{eq}$ against mg of glucose in the range of 0·1 − 3·0 mg of glucose. The relation between amounts of sugar and of ml of 0·01 N ferrocyanide reduced is:

$$sugar = b[(ml\ S_2O_3^{2-})_{eq} + a]$$

a having the value of 0·05 ml of 0·01 N $S_2O_3^{2-}$

and b = 0·340 (glucose)

  = 0·341 (fructose)

  = 0·338 (invert sugar)

  = 0·455 (maltose)

If other sugars are present in substantial amounts the values for these sugars must be determined.

Precision and accuracy

The method is accurate to 0·0067 mg of sugar (mean value for 4 sugars).

7.6 LIPIDS OR FATS

LEVEL II

Principle

The lipids are extracted from the organisms by a nonpolar solvent. Lipids often contain compounds with double bonds which are easily oxidized, especially during drying. It is therefore better to use fresh material—which must be kept for short periods only—and to evaporate solutions containing lipids under vacuum or under N_2.

The extracts are washed with water and the lipids are transferred to dry ether. After evaporation of the ether the lipids are determined gravimetrically or by a carbon determination (see § 7.1 or § 7.3). Methanol and ethanol-ether are recommended, although other solvents give the same results (Blažka, 1966b).

The method is not specific, although few biochemicals other than lipids dissolve in dry ether. A specific determination would involve hydrolysis with KOH, methylation of the fatty acids produced followed by a gas chromatographic determination (see e.g. Farkas and Herodek, 1964, and Otsuka and Morimura, 1966).

Note

The method described here uses ether. The vapour of ether is heavier than air and dangerously inflammable. Naked flames and electrical sparks must not be allowed in the laboratory.

Reagents

A   Methanol

Use a normal laboratory grade.

B   Ether, normal grade

Use the normal laboratory grade, free from peroxides.

Check for peroxides by shaking the ether with an equal volume of 10% KI solution. Leave to stand overnight. A yellow colour indicates the presence of peroxides. They can be removed by shaking the ether with an acid solution of $FeSO_4$. After discarding the water layer the ether is dried over Na_2SO_4 and then redistilled (but NOT OVER A NAKED FLAME).

C   Ethanol-ether, $1+1$

Mix equal volumes ethanol (96%) and ether, both normal grades, but free from peroxides.

D Na_2SO_4, anhydrous.

Procedure

Obtain the fresh particulate material by centrifuging. Homogenise larger animals in methanol. Add 5 ml methanol (A) and leave to stand for 20 minutes. Decant the methanol into a crystallising or evaporating basin and wash the particulate material successively with 5 ml of methanol (A) and twice with 5 ml of ethanol-ether (C). Combine and evaporate the extracts. Carefully extract the dry residue thus obtained with dry ether (B). Shake the ether with H_2O in a separatory funnel. Discard the water layer and dry the ether with Na_2SO_4. Filter the ether through a G3 sintered glass filter (15–40 μ pore size) into a crystallising dish, and evaporate.

If sufficient lipids are present (about 5 mg) the final determination may be made gravimetrically.

More sensitive is an oxidation with dichromate, preferably procedure § 7.1.1 + § 7.1.4, or § 7.3.2.

Note

All evaporations must be made in a vacuum desiccator or under N_2 in order to avoid oxidation of unsaturated fatty acids. If the *ether* extracts are being evaporated the vacuum must be applied slowly.

7.7   PROTEINS

LEVEL   II

Colorimetric

Introductory

Proteins may be estimated approximately by multiplying the N-content (see § 5.5) by the factor 6.25. They may be estimated more accurately by the biuret reaction

(Krey, 1951) or with an acetonyl-acetone reagent (Keeler, 1959). The last is 10 times as sensitive as the biuret reaction.

In the biuret method albumin is used as a standard; casein is used in the acetonyl-acetone method.

Agreement between the three methods is poor. Unfortunately attempts do not appear to have been made to correlate the different methods using the same standard substances.

More specific is the determination of α-amino-N (van Slyke, Dillon, MacFadgen and Hamilton, 1941). Amino acids may be separated quantitatively by ion exchange chromatography. They may be separated and qualitatively determined by paper chromatography (Lederer and Lederer, 1957).

The two colorimetric methods are described here in detail.

7.7.1. Biuret method

Principle

Biuret, $H_2NCONHCONH_2$, and all compounds containing two —$CONH_2$ or —$CNHNH_2$ groups at two adjacent C-atoms (or at two C-atoms bound together either by a N or by a third C-atom) form a violet coloured complex with Cu^{2+} in strongly alkaline conditions.

A correction must be made for the self colour of the reagent and for turbidity.

Proteins are hydrolysed and released from planktonic organisms (both animal and plant) by alkaline hydrolysis.

Reagents

A Albumin standard solution, 1 mg/ml of albumin

Dissolve 100 mg of albumin in 100 ml of 0·2 N NaOH.

B NaOH, 2 N

Dilute 10 N NaOH, see § 1.4.1.

C CuSO₄ solution

Dissolve 1·2 g of $CuSO_4.5H_2O$ in 60 ml of H_2O. Add 50 ml of (ethylene) glycol, to keep the Cu^{2+} in solution in the alkaline conditions of this procedure.

Procedure

Collect the plankton organisms on a filter (for phytoplankton a membrane filter may be used). Suspend the material for 12–24 hours in 10 ml of 2 N NaOH (B). (For animal material a homogenate in 0·2 N NaOH may be used. This is quicker than the extraction with NaOH). Dilute with H_2O to 0·2 N NaOH (10 ml to 100 ml with H_2O) and filter through a hard paper filter or membrane filter. Measure the extinction at 530 mμ and at 750 mμ (self colour). Add 0·5 ml of CuSO₄ solution (C) and measure the extinction of the reagent blank, standards and samples against H_2O, in suitable cells at 530 mμ and 750 mμ after 30 minutes.

Prepare a calibration curve in the range 0·1–0·6 mg of albumin in 10 ml.

Calculation

Subtract the extinction of the blank at 530 mμ and 750 mμ from that of the samples. Find the "true biuret colour" by subtracting the extinction at 750 mμ from that at 530 mμ

Sensitivity

The lowest quantity of protein that can be estimated is about 30 μg per sample. Krey (1951) reports a precision of 5–10%. The accuracy depends on the type of protein used for standardization and on the type of protein in the sample, and cannot therefore be specified.

Interferences

Humic acids interfere in the case of nanoseston (Blažka 1966a).

7.7.2. Acetonylacetone reaction method

Principle

Proteins, certain amino acids and amines form pyrroles with acetonylacetone. The pyrroles form coloured complexes with p-dimethylaminobenzaldehyde (Keeler, 1959).

Reagents

A   Standard protein solution, 1 mg/ml

Dissolve 100 mg of egg albumin or casein in 100 ml of 0·2 N NaOH.

B   Acetonylacetone reagent

Add 1 ml of acetonylacetone to 50 ml of 1 N Na_2CO_3. (5 g of Na_2CO_3, or 14 g of $Na_2CO_3.10H_2O$, per 100 ml of H_2O).

C   Dimethylaminobenzaldehyde solution. (Ehrlich reagent)

Dissolve 0·8 g of p-dimethylaminobenzaldehyde.HCl in a mixture of 30 ml of methanol plus 30 ml of 12 N HCl.

D   Ethanol, normal laboratory grade

Procedure

Mix 5 ml of the sample or extract (obtained as in procedure § 7.7.1) with 5 ml acetonylacetone reagent (B) in a test tube. Cover the tubes, mix, and place the tubes in a boiling water bath for 15 minutes. Cool and add 35 ml of ethanol (D) and 5 ml of Ehrlich reagent (C).

Measure the extinction of the reagent blanks, standards and samples against H_2O in suitable cells at 530 mμ after 30 minutes. Prepare a calibration curve in the range of 0·05–5·0 mg of protein per sample.

All volumes may be reduced by a factor of 5, which may be useful if a 5 cm cell holding 10 ml is available. The range of application is then 0·01–1·0 mg of protein.

7.8. DETERMINATION OF CHLOROPHYLL AND PHAEOPHYTIN

Several types of chlorophyll occur in plants; the most important quantitatively is usually chl–a. Chlorophylls are easily altered (for example in even mildly acid conditions or strong light at room temperature). The products are phaeophytins. The absorption spectra of chlorophyll and phaeophytin are all slightly different, and may be used for quantitative estimations. Quantitive extraction is difficult, especially with green algae. Different solvents and temperatures should be compared.

LEVEL I

7.8.1. Colorimetric

Principle

In cases where there is little phaeophytin present, and most of the chlorophyll is chl–a, an approximate estimate of chl–a may be got from the extinction at 665 mμ of a methanol or acetone extract. The results are expressed, as if all the chlorophyll were chl–a, as chl–a equivalent.

Apparatus

Colorimeter and filter (see § 7.8.2).

Reagents

Acetone, ethanol or methanol (reagent grade) with 0·1% MgCO$_3$ (solid) added.
Filters retain some water. The organic solvent concentration should be such that, after adding it to the filter, the final concentration of organic solvent is 90%.

Procedure

Filter off the particulate matter from a known volume of water sample. Either glass fibre or membrane filters may be used. Roll the filter, put it in a centrifuge tube, and add a sufficient (measured) volume of ice cold solvent to cover the filter. Cover the tubes, and put them in a refrigerator for 24 hours or, if the solvent is methanol, heat to near boiling in a very dim light. Decant the solvent, and if turbid, centrifuge. Measure the extinction in a suitable cell.

Calculation

If $E^{1\,cm}$ is the extinction of the extract in a 1 cm cuvette;

μg chl–a equivalent/ml of solvent = $11·9 \times E^{1\,cm}$ (acetone); $13·9 \times E^{1\,cm}$ (ethanol and methanol). See Talling and Driver, 1963.

LEVEL II

7.8.2. Colorimetric or spectrophotometric

Principle

The absorption spectrum of chlorophyll has a maximum in acetone at 663 mμ. Chlorophyll can be converted to phaeophytin by the addition of an acid, which removes Mg from the chlorophyll molecule. Both molecules occur in natural conditions. Phaeophytin also absorbs light at 663 mμ, but less strongly than the same concentration of chlorophyll. From the decrease in extinction, when the sample is acidified the amount of chlorophyll can be calculated.

An approximate correction for other coloured compounds, and for turbidity, can be made by subtracting the extinction at 750 mμ (where chlorophyll and phaeophytin absorb an insignificant amount of light).

Accurate measurement of the concentration of chlorophylls is extremely difficult. The method described here is easy and rapid in use but the results should be interpreted with great care. For example the two most common chlorophylls, *a* and *b*, both absorb light at 663 mμ and the extinction coefficients are not accurately known (see table 7.1). [For further information see Report of SCOR (1966)].

Apparatus

(1) Filter assembly for 47 mm diameter filters including filtering flask and device for producing a vacuum.

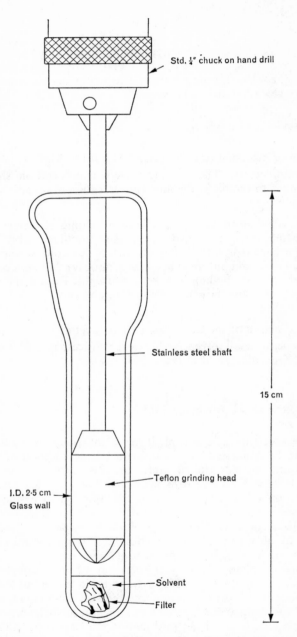

Std. ¼″ chuck on hand drill

Stainless steel shaft

15 cm

Teflon grinding head

I.D. 2·5 cm
Glass wall

Solvent

Filter

Figure 7.9. Grinding apparatus for chlorophyll extraction. Conventional tissue grinder (Arthur Thomas, U.S.A.).

(2) Whatman GF/C or Gelman A filters.

(3) Grinding apparatus (see fig. 7.9). It is convenient to have this driven electrically at about 1000 rpm, but a hand drill may also be used. Samples may even be ground by hand.

(4) 15–20 ml screwcap test tubes.

If no spectrophotometer is available a colorimeter and suitable optical filter may be employed. If possible the device should be standardized by comparing a range of extinction readings on a spectrophotometer with the colorimetric readings. The optical filter should have suitable cutoff properties so that it transmits only light within the principal chlorophyll absorption region centred about 663 mμ. Suitable filters are Corning 2–58, Wratten no. 26 and Schott RG/2. The correction at 750 mμ (described in the Procedure), cannot be made with this apparatus.

Reagents

A MgCO$_3$ (reagent grade, powdered)

Make a suspension in H$_2$O in a plastic bottle.

B Acetone (90%, reagent grade).

C HCl, 4 N (See § 1.4.1).

Procedure

Place a filter (2) on the tower and apply vacuum. Deposit a film of MgCO$_3$ on the filter by filtering a suspension of it in H$_2$O. (The MgCO$_3$ increases retention of particles on the filter). Pour a suitable measured volume of the fresh water sample through the filter and suck dry. Remove the filter, fold in half so that the side having precipitate is not exposed and drop it into the grinding tube. Add 2 ml of 90% acetone, insert the pestle and grind for 30 seconds at about 1000 rpm to release pigments from the cells. Remove the pestle and wash with 2 ml of 90% acetone, catching the washings in the grinding tube. Wash the contents of the grinding tube into the screwcap test tube and make up to a known volume, generally 10 ml. Centrifuge for 30 seconds. Measure the extinction of the supernatant in a suitable cell, with a ground stopper or lid (see fig. 7.10), at 663 mμ and at 750 mμ:

$$^UE_{663} \quad \text{and} \quad ^UE_{750}$$

Pour the contents of the cuvette back into the screwcap test tube, add 0·1 ml of 4 N HCl (C), and recentrifuge. Measure the extinction again at 663 mμ and 750 mμ:

$$^AE_{663} \quad \text{and} \quad ^AE_{750}.$$

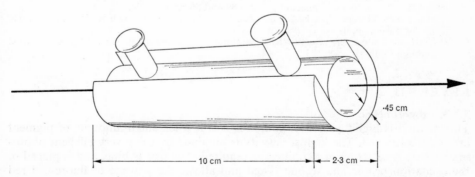

Figure 7.10. Brass cuvette holder for small volume, long light path cuvettes. Fits Beckman D.U. type spectrophotometer. Arrow indicates light path.

Calculations

Compute the unacidified corrected extinction ($^U E^{1\ cm}_{663}$) and the acidified corrected extinction ($^A E^{1\ cm}_{663}$) by

$$^U E^{1\ cm}_{663} = \frac{^U E_{663} - {}^U E_{750}}{\text{lightpath (cm)}} \qquad {}^A E^{1\ cm}_{663} = \frac{^A E_{663} - {}^A E_{750}}{\text{lightpath (cm)}}$$

Calculate the total pigment ($P_t = Chl + Php$)

$$P_t = {}^U E^{1\ cm}_{663} \times \frac{1000}{K} \times \frac{\text{vol. extract (ml)}}{\text{vol. filtrate (1)}} = \mu g/l$$

where K is the extinction coefficient (see note E).
Calculate the extinction due to chlorophyll

$$E^{1\ cm}_{chl} = 2 \cdot 43 \, (^U E^{1\ cm}_{663} - {}^A E^{1\ cm}_{663})$$

Compute the extinction due to phaeophytin

$$E^{1\ cm}_{phae} = {}^U E^{1\ cm}_{663} - E^{1cm}_{chl}$$

Calculate the quantities of either chlorophyll or phaeophytin

$$P_{chl\ or\ phae} = E^{1\ cm}_{chl\ or\ phae} \times \frac{1000}{K_{chl\ or\ phae}} \times \frac{\text{vol. extract (ml)}}{\text{vol. filtrate (1)}} = \mu g/l$$

where K is the extinction coefficient (respectively 89 and 56, see note E).

Notes
A. If samples are to be stored for some reason, they should be stored in a darkened desiccator at around 0°C. It is, however, emphasized that best results are obtained when samples are analysed immediately. In no circumstances should extracts be stored for longer than 12 hours.
B. On the whole, methanol extracts better than 90% acetone. The specific absorption values are, however, not well known and changes in the pigment structure occur rapidly in methanol.
C. In the acidification step, 100% chlorophyll solution will yield a ratio $^U E / ^A E$ of 1·7 or slightly higher. If the extract contains nothing but phaeophytin, the ratio will be 1·0 (see fig. 7.11).
D. From fig. 7.11 $^U E / ^A E$ can be converted directly to percentage as chlorophyll or phaeophytin.
E. There is about 25% difference in the extinction coefficients, given by different workers (table 7.1). Because of the nature of the methods used for obtaining these values, one might recommend using the highest extinction coefficient for chlorophyll *a*. The recommended values for chlorophyll and phaeophytin are 89 and 56 respectively.
   Much data however has been published using the value 65 which is close to the value given for phaeophytin.
F. If very small algae are absent, then membrane filters and method § 7.8.1 may be used (avoiding grinding).

LEVEL III

7.8.3. Fluorimetric

This method is highly sensitive, and so is useful when small amounts of pigment are to be estimated. The high sensitivity is obtained by using very efficient photomultipliers. A selection of two filters is required. The first is blue, and is placed in the excitation beam. The second is red and allows the passage of fluoresced red light to the photomultiplier tube.

For details see Yentsch and Menzel (1963), Holm-Hansen *et al.* (1966).

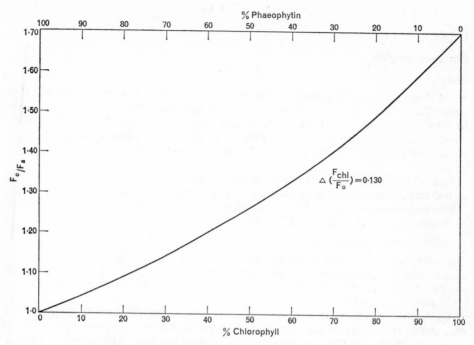

Figure 7.11. Relationship between percentages of chlorophyll and phaeophytin and the acid ratio.

Table 7.1. Extinction coefficient (K) for chlorophyll *a* in aqueous acetone.

Reference		Extinction coefficient (K)[1] for wavelength		Acetone concentration
		665 mμ	664–663 mμ	
Zscheile	1934	65·0	68·5	90%
MacKinney	1940	84·0	—	100%
MacKinney	1941	76·0	82·0	80%
Zscheile, *et al.*	1942	—	82·0	80%
Richards	1952	66·7	71·0	90%
Vernon	1960	90·8	92·6	100%
			91·1	90%
Parsons and Strickland	1963	89·0	90·0	90%

[1] The extinction coefficient $K = \dfrac{\log_{10} I/I_0}{C.l}$

where *l* is the light path in centimeters and C is the concentration in g/l.

7.9 SEPARATION OF CHLOROPLASTIC PIGMENTS BY THIN-LAYER CHROMATOGRAPHY

LEVEL III

Chromatographic

Principle

The substances to be separated are placed in a spot or streak near the edge of a thin layer of adsorbent on a glass plate. As in paper chromatography, a solvent is made to pass across the adsorbent layer. If the solvent and adsorbent are correctly chosen, the substances to be separated move across the plate at different rates, because of differences in their chemical structure, and come to form discrete spots or streaks.

The method is rapid—a complete run may take only 30 minutes. It is also possible to use larger amounts of material than in paper chromatography.

For application of the technique to pigment separations see Madgwick (1966), Bollinger *et al.* (1965) and Stahl (1965).

Procedure: Plate preparation

The adsorbent is very finely ground sugar (icing or confectionary sugar) plus 3% starch. Stir the sugar/starch slowly into isopropanol (4+3) until the mixture is smooth. Even mixtures are easily obtained using a domestic blender, or by stirring vigorously in a beaker.

Apply the adsorbent in a layer approximately 3 mm thick to a 20 by 20 cm glass plate. There are commercially available spreaders that will apply the adsorbent at an even thickness. One can however use a glass rod for this purpose, as shown in fig. 7.14.

Dry the coated plates under an infrared lamp for one hour. They then have stable sugar coatings; but as they are highly susceptible to damage from water and moisture in the air, they must be stored in a desiccator.

Extraction of pigment and streaking of plates

Filter the water sample on a glass fiber filter which has been previously coated with $MgCO_3$ (see § 7.8.1 for details). Air dry the filter and algae for 30 minutes. If the air is moist, dry the filters in a desiccator. Extract the filter and algae in 2 or 3 ml of 100% acetone, and centrifuge and prepare for streaking. Apply the extract with a 100 μl pipette in a long narrow band approximately 2 centimeters from the bottom of the plate. Nitrogen blown across the plate causes almost immediate evaporation of the solvent. In this manner as much as 2 ml of solvent, rich in pigment, can be applied in a short time. If the extract is made in more than 2 ml of solvent, concentrate the pigment by evaporation before streaking on the plate.

Development of the plate

Place the plate vertically in a small rectangular tank (approximately $10 \times 20 \times 20$ cm) with 100 ml of a mixture of petroleum ether and n-propanol, 100: 0·5 in the bottom. Variation of the n-propanol content influences the separation of the various pigments and their respective RF values. RF values for various pigments are not always constant, but the pigment bands always remain in the sequence shown in figs. 7.12 and 7.13. Development usually takes from 20 to 30 minutes, and this, of course, depends upon the degree of separation desired.

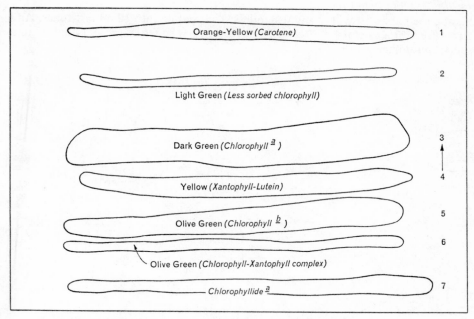

Figure 7.12. Thin-layer chromatogram, extract from green algae.

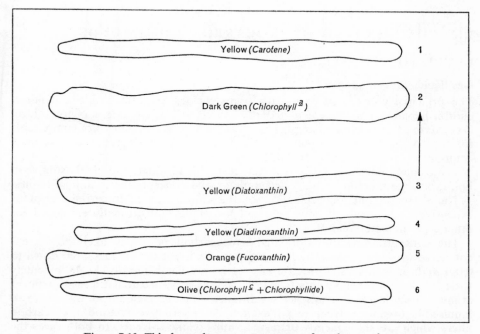

Figure 7.13. Thin-layer chromatogram, extract from brown algae.

Identification of pigments

Scrape the bands off with a small stainless steel spatula into 10 ml test-tubes. Add 2 ml of 85–90% acetone and centrifuge. Decant the supernatant and analyze in a spectrophotometer.

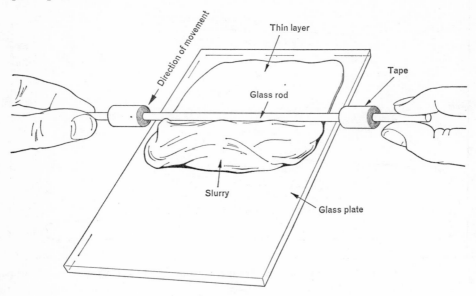

Figure 7.14. Glass rod for applying adsorbent.

7.10   CHLORINATED HYDROCARBON COMPOUNDS

LEVEL III

Gas liquid chromatography

The principal chlorinated hydrocarbon insecticides are DDT, aldrin, dieldrin, endrin, heptachlor toxaphene and BHC. Under normal conditions of use, aldrin is converted to dieldrin and heptachlor to heptachlor epoxide, both of comparable toxicity to the parent substances, while DDT is slowly degraded to less toxic compounds, mainly TDE and DDE.

These compounds are stable, relatively insoluble in water, and highly soluble in lipids, and are therefore rapidly accumulated and concentrated in animal tissues.

The detection and determination of the chlorinated hydrocarbons requires expensive and specialised apparatus and techniques not normally employed for other types of water analysis.

The concentrations of chlorinated hydrocarbon pesticides likely to be encountered in water are usually less than 0·01 mg/l, but can be measured down to 0·001 μg/l, or with special procedures even lower. The higher level can be acutely toxic to fish and other aquatic fauna, while long-term accumulation is significant at much lower levels. In analysis the substance is first extracted from water into an immiscible organic solvent (e.g. hexane). An alternative method uses carbon filters which are subsequently extracted with organic solvents. In both cases the organic solvent is evaporated to a small volume to concentrate the residues, Breidenbach, *et al.* (1964), Holden and Marsden (1966).

Extracts from seriously polluted waters, from mud, or from organisms usually require more treatment before analysis.

The solvent extract, which may contain residue concentrations in the range 0·001–1·0 mg/l is analysed by gas-liquid chromatography, during which the components are separated and quantitatively determined. An electron-capture detector is used, as it is particularly sensitive to chlorinated organic molecules. Less sensitive is a microcoulometric detector, which is however specific for halogens; Teasley and Cox (1963).

Where sufficient residue is available (usually several μg) separation by paper or thin-layer chromatography, and detection either in situ or after re-extraction of the separated constituents and injection into the gas chromatograph, can be performed; Goodenkauf and Erdei (1964), Kovacs (1963).

7.11 DETERMINATION OF DISSOLVED VITAMIN B_{12}, THIAMINE AND BIOTIN

LEVEL III

Bioassay

Principle

As the concentrations of vitamins in fresh water are generally very low, they can only be estimated by bioassay. In bioassay the growth, in the water sample, of an organism that needs the compound in question for its growth, is compared with the growth of the same organism in solutions of known concentrations of the vitamin.

Detailed procedures for the bioassay of dissolved vitamin B_{12}, thiamine, and biotin in fresh water systems are available in Kavanagh (1963). More recently, rapid and sensitive algal bioassay methods for these vitamins in sea water have been developed [Carlucci and Silbernagel (1966a), (1966b), (1967a), (1967b)] and it is recommended that these be adapted for fresh water assays. *Cyclotella nana* (13–1), *Monochrysis lutheri*, and *Amphidinium carteri* are used to assay vitamin B_{12}, thiamine, and biotin, respectively.

Outline of procedure for seawater

Samples are collected as aseptically as possible, sterilized by passage through a membrane filter, and frozen at $-20°C$ until assayed. Prior to assay the samples are thawed, refiltered if any question exists as to sterility, supplemented with sterile nutrients, dispensed into appropriate vessels, inoculated with the test alga, and incubated in the light. After 46 hours (96 hours in the biotin assay) $Na^{14}CO_3$ is added and then the cultures are incubated for two more hours. The algal cells are collected on a filter and ^{14}C uptake measured. The ^{14}C uptakes are proportional to vitamin concentrations in ecologically significant ranges. A standard curve is prepared using known additions to a vitamin-free (charcoal-treated) seawater. A known amount of the vitamin is also added to a portion of each sample to serve as an internal standard. From the amount of vitamin recovered in the internal standard the inhibitory properties of the samples can be calculated and these factors accounted for when reporting the actual vitamin concentrations. If facilities for using ^{14}C are not available, the assay cultures are incubated for two or three more days and cell numbers determined. After a sufficient incubation period, cell numbers are proportional to vitamin concentrations.

Range of application

The range of vitamin concentrations in seawater which can be assayed are: vitamin B_{12}, 0·05–3·0 ng/l; thiamine, 2–35 ng/l; and biotin, 0·2–6 ng/l (1 ng $= 10^{-9}$g).

Notes

The analyst should refer to the original papers for the detailed procedures for these assays. The modification necessary for fresh water analysis is to dilute the sample with a NaCl supplemented, charcoal-treated seawater (artificial or natural seawater may be used) so that the final concentration of salts in the diluted sample is 28–35 $^o/_{oo}$. The analyst may find it more useful and practical to modify these assays so that fresh water algae can be used as the test organisms. A list of algae requiring vitamins has been compiled by Lewin (1961).

7.12 OTHER SPECIFIC ORGANIC COMPOUNDS

LEVEL III

Some specific organic compounds may be estimated by bioassay involving bacterial uptake systems. These systems are stereospecific transport systems, whose kinetics may be described by the equations of the enzyme-substrate relationship (Michaelis–Menten equation). As uptake of ^{14}C labelled compounds is used, rather than growth, concentrations as low as 5 μg/l can be measured. Natural bacterial populations may be used, to obtain an indication of which compounds are present, and also to estimate their maximum concentration, and their rate of use, Wright and Hobbie (1966), Hobbie (1967). Quantitative analysis may be made adding bacterial cultures to filtered lake or river water, Hobbie and Wright (1965).

CHAPTER 8

DETERMINATION OF DISSOLVED GASES

8.1 OXYGEN

General principles

The determination of O_2 may be carried out with an O_2-detecting electrode or by a titrimetric method. The electrode methods are most useful when a large number of measurements are required in the field, and possess the special advantage that the collection of separate samples in bottles is not necessary, because an electrode may be lowered over the side of a boat to give direct measurements.

The titrimetric methods are mainly based on the technique described by Winkler. (See § 8.1.2.)

If the content of organic matter in the water is high (as in eutrophic lakes), or the concentration of O_2 is in excess of 20 mg/l, or if the titration must be delayed, the Bruhns modification of the Winkler method is most useful. This modification is described here in detail. Many other variants have been devised for particular situations.

It is possible to buy field kits for estimating the I_2 colour produced in the Winkler method. The manufacturer's instructions must be followed carefully. Apparatus of this type is supplied by British Drug Houses and by Hach Chemical Company.

Additional methods have been described by Roskam and Langen (1963), Montgomery and Cockburn (1964) and Montgomery *et al.* (1964), Knowles and Lowden (1953), Hart (1967), and Rebsdorf (1966).

LEVEL I

8.1.1. Titrimetric

Principle

Hydroxides of manganese are formed as in the Winkler method (see § 8.1.2).

The excess of $Mn(OH)_2$ is then converted to $MnCO_3$, which is not affected by O_2. The determination is completed as in the Winkler method.

Reagents

A H_3PO_4, (s.g. = 1·75).

B NaOH, 10 N (See § 1.4.1).

C $(NH_4)_2CO_3$, 50%

Dissolve 500 g of $(NH_4)_2CO_3$ in 900 ml of H_2O on a water bath at 60°C, cool, and dilute to 1 litre. After 1 week some crystals should be present. If not, add a further 100 g of $(NH_4)_2CO_3$ at 60°C and cool rapidly.

D $MnSO_4 . 5H_2O$, 50%

Dissolve 500 g of $MnSO_4 . 5H_2O$ in H_2O and dilute to 1 litre.

E   KI (or NaI), dry

Store in a brown bottle.

F   NaHCO$_3$ (or KHCO$_3$), dry

In addition, reagents (A), (B) and (F) of § 8.1.2 are necessary.

Procedure

Determine the volume of a glass stoppered bottle of approximately 100 ml capacity, by subtracting the weight of the bottle and stopper from the weight of the bottle when filled with water with the stopper in place. Use this bottle for taking the sample. Add 1 ml each of reagents (D) and (B), replace the stopper, and shake the bottle by inverting and rotating the bottle several times for about 10 sec. When the precipitate has settled to the lower third of the bottle repeat the mixing. When the precipitate has settled completely add 4 ml of reagent (C), replace the stopper, and shake well. After settling, decant about 50 ml of the supernatant to allow sufficient air to enter the bottle to oxidise Fe^{2+} salts to Fe^{3+}. If the acidification must be postponed for more than 1 hour, add about 1 g of reagent (F) and shake. The precipitate is stable for several days. If the sample was believed to contain interfering amounts of organic matter or NO_2^-, however, as much of the supernatant as possible must be siphoned off instead of decanting 50 ml; it is then necessary to add 50 ml of H_2O.

Add 1 g of reagent (E) and 5–6 ml of reagent (A). Titrate the liberated I_2 with $S_2O_3^{2-}$ as described under level II (§ 8.1.2).

Note

For approximate work reagent (C) may be omitted and 1 g of reagent (F) added directly to the bottle before some of the water is decanted.

Calculation

As for level II (§ 8.1.2).

LEVEL II

8.1.2.   Titrimetric

Principle

O_2 combines with $Mn(OH)_2$ forming higher hydroxides which, on subsequent acidification in the presence of I^-, liberate I_2 in an amount equivalent to the original dissolved O_2 content of the sample. The I_2 is then determined by titration with $Na_2S_2O_3$. NO_2^- interference (up to 5 mg N/l) is eliminated by the use of NaN_3 (sodium azide).

The recommended procedure employs a reagent devised by Pomeroy and Kirschman (1945), which contains a much higher concentration of KI than the reagent used formerly. The advantages are that errors due to the volatilization of I_2 and to interference by organic matter are reduced, that the hydroxides dissolve more readily, and that the starch end point is sharper.

Apparatus

The bottles should be of good quality, with narrow necks and well fitting ground glass stoppers. In normal use bottles are kept clean by the acidic iodine solution of the Winkler procedure and require no treatment apart from rinsing with H_2O. Contaminated bottles must be discarded.

Sampling

Special care is needed in sampling for dissolved O_2. For accurate work a displacement sampler, in which the contents of the sample bottle are automatically changed at least three times, is necessary.

For very shallow water the sample may be taken in a syringe and analysed by a small-scale technique such as that of Fox and Wingfield (1938).

The bottle or sample container must always be completely filled and reagents or preservatives must be added immediately after sampling.

Reagents

A KIO_3, 0·100 N

Dissolve 3·567 g of KIO_3 (A.R., dried 105°C) in H_2O and dilute to 1000 ml. Dilute further as required.

B_1 $Na_2S_2O_3$, approximately 0·025 N

Dissolve 6·2 g of $Na_2S_2O_3 . 5H_2O$, in H_2O. Add a pellet of NaOH or 1 g of Na_2CO_3 and dilute to 1 litre. Store in a brown bottle.

B_2 $Na_2S_2O_3$, 0·0125 N or 0·0025 N

Dilute the 0·025 N $Na_2S_2O_3$ solution to the required strength and store in a brown bottle. The strength required will depend on the size of the sample: for 250 ml bottles (and for the B.O.D. test) 0·0125 N $Na_2S_2O_3$ is normally used. For smaller samples, 0·0025 N may be used without loss of accuracy.

For standardization, which should be repeated frequently (at least each week), pipette 10·00 ml of 0·025 N KIO_3 solution into a conical flask containing 100 ml of H_2O and add 1 ml of alkaline iodide-azide solution (D), followed by 2 ml of H_3PO_4 (C). Mix *thoroughly* then titrate with the 0·0125 N $Na_2S_2O_3$, adding 2 ml of starch solution (F) or about 0·5 g of starch-urea just before the end point. If the strength of $Na_2S_2O_3$ is other than 0·0125 N, adjust the concentration of standard KIO_3 and alter the volumes of H_2O and reagents in proportion, so that an actual dissolved O_2 titration is simulated as closely as possible in the standardization.

C H_3PO_4, (s.g. = 1·75).

D   Alkaline iodide-azide solution

Dissolve 400 g of NaOH in 560 ml of H_2O, add 900 g of NaI (A.R.) and keep the solution hot until the NaI has dissolved. Cool the solution and dilute to 1 litre. Decant or filter, if necessary, after standing overnight. No I_2 should be liberated when 1 ml is diluted to 50 ml and acidified. For work in which the highest accuracy is not required, a reagent containing 500 g of NaOH and 150 g of KI (or 140 g of NaI) per litre may be used.

If only impure NaI (I_2 containing) is available, dissolve 900 g in 560 ml of H_2O, add a few drops of CH_3COOH and stir with 1 g of Zn dust until the solution is colourless. Filter and add 400 g of NaOH without delay, then cool and dilute to 1 litre.

Mix 1 litre of alkaline KI reagent with 300 ml of a 2·5% NaN_3 solution.

E $MnSO_4 . 5H_2O$, 50%

Dissolve 500 g of $MnSO_4 . 5H_2O$ in H_2O, filter if necessary, and make up to 1 litre. No iodine should be liberated when 1 ml of reagent is added to 50 ml of acidified KI iodide solution.

F   Starch indicator, 1%

Disperse 1 g of starch in 100 ml of water and warm to 80°–90°C. Stir well, allow to cool, and add 0·1 g salicylic acid. Alternatively use powdered starch-urea complex ("cold water soluble starch"), which can be purchased ready for use ("Thiodene").

G   Polyviol MO5/140 (Wacker–Chemie GmbH or Bush Beach; alternative to starch as end point indicator)

This is a polyvinyl alcohol. The colour change is from orange to colourless.

Procedure

The whole procedure must be carried out away from direct sunlight.

To the sample add 1 ml of $MnSO_4$ solution (E) just below the neck of the bottle and 1 ml of alkaline iodide-azide solution (D) at the surface (the fine points of pipettes may be cut off so that they empty quicker, or hypodermic syringes may be used). Incline the bottle, replace the stopper carefully so as to avoid inclusion of air bubbles and thoroughly mix the contents by inverting and rotating the bottle several times during about ten seconds. When the precipitate has settled to the lower third of the bottle, repeat the mixing and then allow the precipitate to settle completely leaving a clear supernatant.

In the absence of organic matter the estimation of the dissolved O_2 by acidification and titration may be postponed at this stage, provided that the bottles are kept in the dark. It is of course, vital that air be excluded from the bottle during the period between precipitation and acidification; this should be assured if bottles with well-fitting stoppers are used, but even then the period should not exceed a few hours. Bottles may be stored by immersion in a vessel containing cold water.

Add 2 ml of H_3PO_4 (C). Replace the stopper and mix the contents thoroughly by rotation (a bubble of CO_2 may form at this stage, but this is not important). Normally the precipitate will dissolve almost instantaneously; if it does not, allow to stand for a few minutes and repeat the mixing. In any case mix the contents of the bottle again immediately before measurement.

Measure into a conical flask the whole sample or a suitable volume (say 50 ml) of the solution and immediately titrate the I_2 with $Na_2S_2O_3$ (B_1 or B_2) solution, using as indicator 2 ml of starch solution (F) or about 0·5 g of starch-urea, added only towards the end of the titration. For very precise work an amperometric or dead stop method may be used to detect the end point.

Notes

A.   The procedure applies to sample bottles of nominal capacity 125 ml. If bottles of very different size are used (e.g. 250 ml) the amounts of reagents must be adjusted in proportion.

B. I_2 is volatile and therefore the titration must be carried out as quickly as possible and with the minimum of exposure to the air. For very low concentrations of dissolved O_2, polyviol MO5/140 (G) may be used instead of starch.

Interferences

A modification of the "iodine-difference" method, suitable for the determination of dissolved O_2 in swamp water, has been described by Beadle (1958). Another modification of the Winkler method which has been used for waters with a high organic content is the bromination procedure of Alsterberg (1926). Success with Alsterberg's procedure requires the use of an alkaline KI reagent with a high concentration of KI (as described under level II). The sodium salicylate reagent, which destroys the excess of Br_2, must be freshly prepared and colourless; it is best prepared from crystalline sodium salicylate. Br_2 destroys $NO_2{}^-$, hence NaN_3 is not required.

Calculation

LEVELS I AND II

Allowance is made in the formula given below for the slight displacement of sample by the $MnSO_4$ and alkaline KI reagents, which contain very little dissolved O_2. Where N is the normality of $S_2O_3{}^{2-}$ (B),

$$O_2 \text{ mg/l} = \frac{\text{ml of titrant B} \times N \times 8 \times 1000}{\text{ml of sample titrated} \times \left(\dfrac{\text{ml of flask–2}}{\text{ml of flask}}\right)}$$

If the contents of the whole flask are titrated

$$O_2 \text{ mg/l} = \frac{\text{ml of titrant B} \times N \times 8 \times 1000}{\text{ml of flask–2}}$$

If the percentage saturation of dissolved O_2 is required, it may be calculated from the formula

$$\text{Percentage saturation} = \frac{O_2 \text{ concentration} \times 100}{\text{solubility}}$$

The solubility of O_2 in fresh water in equilibrium with air at 760 mm Hg is given in table 8.1.

For the solubility of oxygen in saline water see Carpenter (1966).

The percentage saturation of O_2 in *fresh* water may be calculated approximately from fig. 8.1., which is from Hart, 1967. A further nomogram, for converting mg/l of O_2 to percent saturation depending on temperature and atmospheric pressure is also given by Hart (1967).

LEVEL II AND III

8.1.3. Electrode methods

Principle

O_2 passes by diffusion to a reducing electrode, either uncovered as with the dropping Hg-electrode of the polarographic method, or through a membrane in the galvanic cell method. The combination of a polarographic cell covered with a membrane has also been used but proved unsuccessful, due to the great electronic amplification necessary. The quantity of O_2 reduced in unit time is proportional to the concentration of O_2 in the water, and the resulting current is measured on a meter. In detail the chemical principles of the two methods are entirely different. For further information see Mackereth (1964), Kolthoff and Sandell (1952) and Kolthoff and Lingane (1952).

H_2O containing a known concentration of O_2 is required for calibration of the electrode. Either the O_2 content of the calibration water may be found by the method § 8.1.2, or H_2O at a known temperature may be bubbled or stirred with air at a known barometric pressure until there is no further change. The percentage saturation is then 100 and the concentration of O_2 may be found from table 8.1.

Apparatus

The construction of a membrane covered cell has been described by Mackereth (1964), and a temperature-compensation circuit has been published by Briggs and Viney (1964). Temperature compensated cells may be obtained commercially. A dropping mercury device for field use has been described by Føyn (1955, 1967).

Table 8.1. Solubility of O_2 in water in equilibrium with air at 760 mm Hg pressure and 100% relative humidity [from Montgomery, Thom and Cockburn (1964)].

Temperature of sample °C	Solubility mg/l	Temperature of sample °C	Solubility mg/l
0	14·63	18	9·64
1	14·23	19	9·27
2	13·84	20	9·08
3	13·46	21	8·91
4	13·11	22	8·74
5	12·77	23	8·57
6	12·45	24	8·42
7	12·13	25	8·26
8	11·84	26	8·12
9	11·55	27	7·97
10	11·28	28	7·84
11	11·02	29	7·70
12	10·77	30	7·57
13	10·53	31	7·45
14	10·29	32	7·33
15	10·07	33	7·21
16	9·86	34	7·09
17	9·65	35	6·98

If the barometric pressure at the time of sampling is not 760 mm Hg then the saturation values at the actual pressure will differ from those given in the table according to the formula

$$S_x = \frac{SP_x}{760}$$

where S_x = solubility at pressure P_x.
  S = solubility at 760 mm Hg.
  P_x = observed pressure in mm Hg.
It is therefore necessary in accurate work, to note the barometer reading at the time of sampling. For less accurate work the average barometric pressure may be estimated from the altitude (table 8.2).

Table 8.2. Variation of mean atmospheric pressure with altitude [Dussart and Francis-Boeuf (1949)].

Altitude (m)	Average atmospheric pressure (mm Hg)	Factor	Altitude (m)	Average atmospheric pressure (mm Hg)	Factor
0	760	1·00	1300	647	1·17
100	750	1·01	1400	639	1·19
200	741	1·03	1500	631	1·20
300	732	1·04	1600	623	1·22
400	723	1·05	1700	615	1·24
500	714	1·06	1800	608	1·25
600	705	1·08	1900	601	1·26
700	696	1·09	2000	594	1·28
800	687	1·11	2100	587	1·30
900	679	1·12	2200	580	1·31
1000	671	1·13	2300	573	1·33
1100	663	1·15	2400	566	1·34
1200	655	1·16	2500	560	1·36

Membrane-covered cell instruments may be bought from

> The Lakeland Instruments Co.
>
> Electronic Instruments Ltd.
>
> Honeywell, Inc.
>
> Yellow Springs Instrument Co., Inc.   (see § 10.3).

Some of these instruments require daily calibration. Where automatic temperature compensation is not provided in the instrument, the temperature of the water must be noted and a correction applied according to the manufacturer's instructions.

Procedure

Use the apparatus according to the author's or manufacturer's instructions, calibrating and cleaning the electrode as often as experience shows to be necessary. The instructions regarding response time and turbulence should be noted carefully.

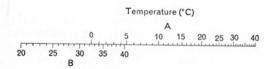

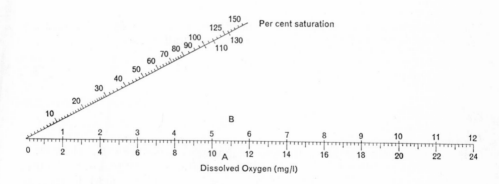

Figure 8.1. Draw a line connecting the temperature with the oxygen content, using the A scales for temperature and dissolved O_2. The percentage saturation is then read from the point at which the line crosses the central scale. For temperature above 20°C improved accuracy may be obtained by the use of the B scales, but these scales may only be used when the percentage saturation does not exceed 100. Finally, correct the percentage saturation to standard pressure, if this differs markedly from 760 mm, using the formula:

$$\text{True percentage saturation} = \text{percentage saturation from nomogram} \times \frac{760}{P_x}$$

A further nomogram, for converting mg/l of O_2 to per cent saturation depending on temperature and atmospheric pressure is also given by Hart (1967).

LEVEL III

8.1.4.

The "dead stop" technique (see § 9.13) is recommended for this level. This method can easily be automated.

No further level III techniques are recommended but attention is drawn to the highly precise modification of the Winkler method described by Carpenter (1965).

Both the membrane and the dropping mercury electrode techniques may be used with continuous recording.

8.2 DETERMINATION OF METHANE

LEVEL II

8.2.1.   Combustible-gas Indicator Method

Principle

The partial pressure of CH_4 in the gas phase (which is in equilibrium with the solution) may be determined with a combustible gas indicator. The combustible gas is oxidised catalytically on a heated Pt filament, which is part of a Wheatstone bridge network. The electrical resistance of the filament depends on the heat of oxidation of the gas. Frequent calibration is necessary (Rossum, Villarruz and Wade, 1950). The method is relatively simple and quick.

Precision, accuracy and sensitivity

The sensitivity is about 0.2 mg/l CH_4. The precision may be 2%. The accuracy varies between 2% and 10% depending on the calibration curve.

LEVEL III

8.2.2.   Combustion-Absorption Method

Principle

CH_4 is transferred to the gas phase and catalytically oxidised to CO_2. The CO_2 is estimated by the volume change on absorption in KOH. The methods of procedures § 7.1.4–7 may also be used. For further details see Larson (1938) and Mullen (1955).

Precision, accuracy and sensitivity

The sensitivity is 2 mg/l of CH_4. The precision and accuracy depend on the gasometric operations and may be less than 5%.

LEVEL III

8.2.3.   Gas chromatographic method

The determination of CH_4 in the gas chromatograph is relatively simple. The gas must be transferred from the dissolved phase to the gas phase with an inert gas, which serves as a carrier gas as well. The apparatus must be calibrated frequently

8.3 DETERMINATION OF OXYGEN, NITROGEN AND TOTAL CARBON DIOXIDE

LEVEL III:

Gas chromatographic.

The use of a gas chromatographic method for O_2, N_2 and total CO_2 has been described. The method is relatively simple and rapid. It has the advantage that the three gases are determined in one sample. For further details see Jeffery and Kipping (1964), Park (1965), Park and Catalfomo (1964), Swinnerton, Linnenbom and Cheek (1962 a and b, 1964).

8.4 DETERMINATION OF HYDROGEN, CARBON DIOXIDE AND METHANE

LEVEL III

Gas chromatographic (tentative).

Ray (1954) has separated the components of a mixture of H_2, CH_4, CO_2, ethylene and ethane by gas-solid chromatography. Although the method has not yet been applied in limnochemistry, the application of the method for gases dissolved in fresh water seems not to involve serious problems.

CHAPTER 9

ELECTROCHEMICAL PROPERTIES OF WATER

THEORETICAL ADDENDUM TO CHAPTER 3

9.1 SPECIFIC CONDUCTANCE

The specific conductance (conductivity) of a solution is a measure of its capacity to convey an electric current. Conductivity is related to the concentration of ionized substances present in the solution and to the temperature of the solution. Even pure H_2O has a measurable conductivity. After absorbing CO_2 from the air, and other substances from the glass in which H_2O is kept, the conductivity of distilled water is normally about 10^{-6} Ohm^{-1}cm^{-1} or 1 μmho/cm.

It is quite frequently reported as micromho, rather than as micromho/cm. This is strictly speaking incorrect, but widely accepted.

Kohlrausch has measured a value as low as 0.05 μmho. This indicates that water acts as a very weak binary electrolyte according to the following equation:

$$H_2O \rightleftharpoons H^+ + OH^- \tag{9.1}$$

From this conductivity it can be calculated that the concentration of H^+ and OH^- is about 10^{-7} Mol/l.

By more accurate measurements—using electrode potentials—a value of exactly 10^{-7} has been found at 24°C (0.83×10^{-7} at 20°C).

According to the law of homogenous equilibrium

$$[H^+][OH^-] = K[H_2O] = K_w \tag{9.2}$$

where K_w is known as the ionization constant of water. This "constant" depends upon temperature.

Substituting the value 0.83×10^{-7} for $[H^+]$ and $[OH^-]$ in equation (9.2), the value of K_w becomes 0.68×10^{-14} at 20°C. K_w increases with the temperature because the degree of ionization is greater at higher temperatures. The conductivity depends therefore on the temperature. It is inconvenient to write the concentration of H^+ as 0.93×10^{-7} (or $0.000,000,093$) Mol/l. The terms pH and pK are therefore used. They are defined as:

$$pH \equiv -\log_{10}[H^+] \qquad pK \equiv -\log_{10}K$$

where K is the ionization constant.

The variation of pK_w and pH with temperature is shown in table 9.1.
It should be noted that the concentrations of *both* H^+ and OH^- increase with temperature, in contrast to what happens after the addition of an acid to water as is described in § 9.2.

The conductivity of solutions is the sum of the conductances of the individual species of positive and negative ions. The conductance of an ion is determined partly by its mobility in the electric field. (The mobility is expressed in cm/sec per V/cm, thus in $cm^2/(V sec)$, in which V is the potential difference.)

The mobility of the ions depends on the temperature, so the conductance of a solution depends on the temperature. The conductance also depends on the concentration and the degree of ionization of the salts involved. This causes a non-linear relationship between conductivity and concentration (See table 3.2).

The conductance gives no indication of the nature of the substances in solution but any increase or decrease in their concentration will be reflected in a corresponding increase or decrease in conductance.

The amount of dissolved ionic matter in mg/l in a fresh water sample may be estimated by multiplying the specific conductance by an empirical factor, varying from 0·55 to 0·9 depending on the soluble compounds in the particular water (for KCl, 0·51; for NaCl, 0·48; for $Ca(HCO_3)_2$, 1·6). A rough approximation to the concentration in meq/l of either cations or anions may be obtained by multiplying the conductance in μmho by 0·01.

Table 9.1. Variation of pK_w and pH of pure H_2O with temperature. (From Handbook of Chemistry and Physics.)
Note that some authorities report $pK_w = 14 \cdot 000$ at 22°C.

Temperature (°C)	pK_w	pH
0°	14·943	7·47
15°	14·346	7·17
20°	14·167	7·08
24°	14·000	7·00
25°	13·997	7·00
30°	13·833	6·92

Conductivity can be used for conductometric titrations of, for instance, alkalinity and chloride. In soft water the conductometric method has advantages over the alkalinity titration method using a pH meter. In all cases, but especially at low Cl^- concentrations, the conductometric method has advantages over the potentiometric method, as in the conductometric method use is made of all the readings, except those close to the end points, to construct the straight lines used in estimating the end point. This makes use of most of the measurements, in contrast to the electrometric end point determination, in which it is mainly those points close to the end point which are used. The conductometric method is therefore especially useful for waters with a low HCO_3^- or Cl^- concentration. For a typical titration curve, see fig. 9.2.

9.2 pH.

In a neutral solution the concentration of H^+ is equal to that of OH^-. If an acid is added, the $[H^+]$ is increased and consequently the $[OH^-]$ is decreased according to equation 9.2.

The pH of neutral water at 24°C is 7·0 since the $[H^+]$ is 10^{-7}. The addition for instance of 1 meq/l of a strong acid makes the $[H^+]$ in the water 10^{-3} eq/l: the pH becomes 3.

Weak acids are not completely ionized in water: an equilibrium is established between dissociated and undissociated molecules, the degree of ionization depending on the dilution.

Acetic acid for instance is dissociated according to:

$$CH_3COOH \rightleftharpoons CH_3COO^- + H^+ \tag{9.3}$$

Applying the law of homogeneous equilibrium

$$K = \frac{[CH_3COO^-][H^+]}{[CH_3COOH]} \tag{9.4}$$

If the degree of ionization in reaction (9.3) is called α

$$\alpha \equiv \frac{[CH_3COO^-]}{[CH_3COO^-] + [CH_3COOH]}$$

and V is the volume in which 1 Mol of the acid is dissolved then

$$[CH_3COO^-] = [H^+] = \frac{\alpha}{V}$$

and

$$K = \frac{\alpha^2}{(1-\alpha)V} \tag{9.5}$$

(This equation summarizes Ostwald's dilution law).

If $V = 1000$ litre (i.e. 0·001 N), $\alpha = 0·127$, as $K = 18·4 \times 10^{-6}$ for acetic acid; the H^+ concentration is then $0·127 \times 10^{-3}$: the pH $= 3·9$.

For very weak acids (p$K > 5$) the dissociation is often so small that $(1 - \alpha) \simeq 1$. Equation (9.5) then becomes:

$$K = \frac{\alpha^2}{V} \quad \text{thus} \quad \alpha = \sqrt{(KV)} \tag{9.6}$$

Equation (9.5) does not hold for acids with a $K > 0·5 \times 10^{-2}$ i.e. p$K < 2·3$. HCl for instance has, for practical purposes, no ionization constant, because it dissociates almost completely.

9.3 BUFFER SOLUTIONS

When a salt of a weak acid (for instance CH_3COONa) is added to a solution of the acid itself the following equilibria exist:

$$HAc \rightleftharpoons H^+ + Ac^-$$

$$NaAc \rightleftharpoons Na^+ + Ac^-$$

Since HAc is a weak acid, only a small proportion ionizes. On the other hand, nearly all the NaAc exists in the ionic form. Substituting in equation (9.4)

$$K = \frac{[NaAc]_{added} \cdot [H^+]}{[HAc]_{added}}$$

and thus

$$pH = pK + \log \frac{[NaAc]}{[HAc]} \tag{9.7}$$

If a small quantity of an acid is added to this solution the H^+ of the acid immediately combine with the acetate-ions and form undissociated acetic acid molecules leaving the $[H^+]$ practically unaltered. More exactly, or when a large quantity of acid is added (for instance x mol/l) the pH becomes

$$\text{pH} = pK + \log \frac{[\text{NaAc}]_{\text{added}} - [x]}{[\text{HAc}]_{\text{added}} + [x]} \qquad (9.8)$$

From this formula it can be seen that to cause a decrease of 1 unit in pH

$$\frac{[\text{NaAc}] - [x]}{[\text{HAc}] + [x]} \quad \text{must be} \quad \frac{1}{10} \cdot \frac{[\text{NaAc}]}{[\text{HAc}]}$$

Assuming a concentration of NaAc and HAc of 0·1 M (pH = 4·75), x must be about 0·08 eq/l H^+ to decrease the pH by 1 unit to pH = 3·75. Without buffer the pH would have dropped to 1·1. If a base is added the OH^- of the base combine with the H^+ from the acetic acid. More acetic acid then ionizes to replace the H^+ until equilibrium is established again at not much below the original H^+ concentration. By varying the relative proportions of sodium acetate and acetic acid, solutions of any desired initial pH (within certain limits), may be prepared. Standard buffer solutions of a definite pH are therefore prepared from mixtures of NaAc and HAc or from other weak acids and their salts, for instance H_3PO_4, or H_2CO_3 and Na_2CO_3. The last of these is the buffer system of most alkaline lakes. A particularly useful series of buffer solutions, with pH in the biologically important range, can be made from mixtures of Na_2HPO_4 and NaH_2PO_4.

Buffer solutions of high concentration are more stable over long periods of time than those containing small amounts of acid or bases which may very easily be affected by absorption of CO_2 from the air or by solution of alkali from the glass container, or even by H^+ or OH^- from the ionization of any indicator which is added. Useful buffer mixtures are described in § 3.2.1.

9.4 INDICATORS

One of the most common methods of determining pH is to add an appropriate indicator to the unknown solution and to compare the resulting colour with that of buffer solutions of known pH value containing the same indicator. The indicators selected for this purpose are for the most part weak organic acids or bases which are able to exist in two forms possessing different colours. Being weak acids or bases, the law of homogeneous equilibrium applies to them just as it does to any other weak acid or base. The equilibrium may be indicated by the following equations:

$$\text{HIn}' \rightleftharpoons \text{HIn} \rightleftharpoons H^+ + \text{In}^-$$

$$\frac{[H^+][\text{In}^-]}{[\text{HIn}']} = K$$

HIn has the same colour as In^-, its anion. HIn' is the tautomeric form of the undissociated molecule (HIn), and has a different colour from HIn and In^-. Very little HIn is present. The colour of the indicator is determined by the ratio $[\text{In}^-]/[\text{HIn}']$. Since this ratio multiplied by the $[H^+]$ is equal to a constant, the ratio and, therefore, the colour of the indicator itself is directly related to the $[H^+]$.

It has been found that the human eye can detect no further visible colour change when the ratio of $[\text{In}^-]/[\text{HIn}']$ becomes greater than approximately 91/9 or less than 9/91. That is, the visible colour change occurs within a hundred-fold change in the concentration of either In^- or HIn'. There is a corresponding hundred-fold change in $[H^+]$. The usable colour range, then, of indicators in general corresponds to a range of 2 pH units.

Although the range of any one indicator is thus limited, there is fortunately considerable variation in the ranges of the numerous indicators available, so that almost any $[H^+]$ may be determined by the proper selection of indicator. A list of some indicators is given in § 3.2.1.

9.5 INFLUENCE OF TEMPERATURE ON THE pH OF WATER SAMPLES

The most important buffer system in natural waters with a pH > 6·5 is the bicarbonate–carbonate system. The pH of this system can be calculated from

$$pH = pK + \log \frac{[HCO_3^-]}{[CO_2]}, \text{ see equation (9.7)}$$

Temperature has an influence on the pH because it affects the dissociation coefficients of acids, and the solubility of CO_2. When the pH of a water sample is measured at a different temperature from that at which it was collected, care must therefore be taken that the samples are stored in closed bottles without air bubbles. The pH can also be measured at the "in situ" temperature and corrected by calculation to a standard temperature for all samples. As a rule the pH decreases by about 0·1 pH unit with a temperature increase of 20°C.

When using colour indicators the temperature of the colour indicator itself must also be taken into account, as the dissociation coefficients of the indicators change as well. A particular colour shade does therefore not indicate the same pH at all temperatures. Most pH meters have a temperature compensating mechanism, (either a potentiometer, or a thermistor placed in the solution). It is important to realise that this corrects only for the temperature sensitivity of the electrodes and that the "true" pH of the solutions at the prevailing temperature is measured.

Additional complications are met if different parts of the electrode system are at different temperatures, and this situation is best avoided if possible.

It will be clear that no general advice can be given about temperature correction. The analyst must decide whether he requires the pH at the in situ temperature or at laboratory temperature, or at some other temperature. He must also decide how accurately he needs to know the pH, and then decide the appropriate procedure for himself.

9.6 THE CARBONATE, BICARBONATE, CARBONIC ACID SYSTEM

Many natural waters contain CO_3^{2-}, HCO_3^-, and free CO_2, all in equilibrium with each other. As an example consider a solution of $NaHCO_3$ in H_2O. (In most natural waters the dominant cation is Ca^{2+}, but the theory is more complicated than for Na^+). For a complete treatment see Stumm and Morgan (1970).

This salt, when added to the water dissociates into Na^+ and HCO_3^-. The latter react with the H^+, which originates from the dissociation of H_2O, to form H_2CO_3. In turn, H_2CO_3 dissociates into CO_2 (in solution) and H_2O, the CO_2 being in equilibrium with the CO_2 from the air.

The reactions are the following:

$$NaHCO_3 \rightarrow Na^+ + HCO_3^- \tag{9.9}$$

$$H_2O \rightleftharpoons H^+ + OH^- \tag{9.10}$$

$$HCO_3^- + H^+ \rightleftharpoons H_2CO_3 \tag{9.11$_1$}$$

$$H_2CO_3 \rightleftharpoons H_2O + CO_2 \tag{9.11$_2$}$$

$$HCO_3^- \rightleftharpoons H^+ + CO_3^{2-} \tag{9.12}$$

The equilibrium constant for reaction (9.11$_1$) and (9.11$_2$) together is called K_1, the apparent dissociation constant for the first ionization step of carbonic acid. The dissociation constant of (9.12) is K_2. At 25°C $K_1 = 4\cdot30 \times 10^{-7}$ and $K_2 = 5\cdot61 = 5\cdot61 \times 10^{-11}$. Both are temperature dependent; (see table 9.2).

Table 9.2. Temperature dependance of the first (K_1) and second (K_2) ionization constant of carbonic acid and of the ionization product K_w of water.

$$pK = -\log K$$

Temp. (°C)	0	5	10	15	20	25	ref.
pK_1	6·58	6·52	6·46	6·42	6·38	6·35	(1)
pK_2	10·63	10·56	10·49	10·43	10·38	10·33	(1)
pK_w	14·94	14·73	14·54	14·35	14·17	14·00	(2)

(1) Harned, H. S. and B. B. Owen. The Physical Chemistry of Electrolytic Solutions; 3rd ed. 1958.

(2) Bates, R. G. Determination of pH, Theory and Practice, 1964.

Due to the fact that $K_1 > K_2$, more of the HCO_3^- will follow equation 9.11$_1$ than will follow 9.12. As reaction 9.12 is therefore of little quantitative importance in most lake waters it is useful to sum reactions 9.9, 9.10 and 9.11:

$$NaHCO_3 \rightleftharpoons Na^+ + OH^- + CO_2 \tag{9.13}$$

It can be seen from (9.13) that when $NaHCO_3$ is dissolved in H_2O the solutions have a slight alkaline pH (pH = 8·3 for 10^{-3} M $NaHCO_3$).

The amount of CO_2 formed according to (9.11$_2$) is more than can dissolve in H_2O in equilibrium with the CO_2 in the air, which is 0·5 mg/l of CO_2 at 20°C under atmospheric CO_2 partial pressure.

The solubility of gases follows Henry's law and depends therefore on the partial pressure in the gas phase (0·03% for CO_2 = 0·23 mm Hg); and on the temperature.

The excess of CO_2 formed will—until the system is in equilibrium with the air— escape. The disappearance of the CO_2 and thus the decrease in $[H^+]$ due to this process allows the $[OH^-]$ to increase. Accordingly to reaction (9.12) CO_3^{2-} then increases.

As K_2 is much smaller than K_1 the solution becomes more strongly alkaline. The overall reaction, the summation of reactions (9.9, 9.10, 9.11 and 9.12) is:

$$2NaHCO_3 \rightleftharpoons 2Na^+ + CO_3^{2-} + H_2O + CO_2 \tag{9.14}$$

Reaction (9.14) will take place until the equilibrium between HCO_3^-, CO_3^{2-} and "equilibrium" CO_2 has established itself. ["Equilibrium" CO_2 refers to CO_2 in

equilibrium with HCO_3^- and CO_3^{2-}; it is not, in general, in equilibrium with air]·
The equilibrium position depends on K_1 and K_2 and on the pH of the solution·
Figure 9.1 gives the percentage of HCO_3^-, CO_3^{2-} and CO_2 present in a solution
in relation to the pH.

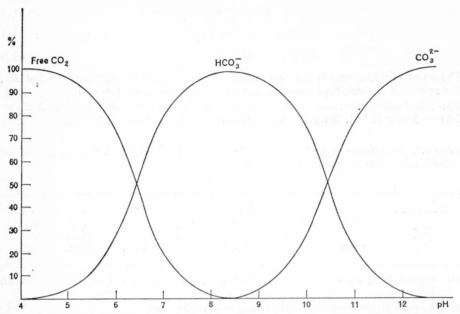

Figure 9.1. Relation between pH and % of total "CO_2" as free CO_2, HCO_3^- and CO_3^{2-}. From
Schmitt.

During photosynthesis the water becomes more alkaline in accordance with
reaction (9.14) owing to CO_2 uptake by algae.

In table 9.3 are shown the amounts of *free CO_2* (calculated from the equation

$$pH = pK + \log \frac{[HCO_3^-]}{[CO_2]}, \text{ see (9.7))},$$

the pH values, and the *changes of the pH with time*, of some $NaHCO_3$ solutions.
The pH of a fresh solution depends partly on the CO_2 already present. This effect
is more marked in very dilute solutions of $NaHCO_3$.

In most natural waters, where Ca^{2+} is the most common cation, the solubility

Table 9.3. pH values measured and concentration of CO_2 calculated in
$NaHCO_3$ solutions.

	0 hours		after 24 hours	
$NaHCO_3$	pH	CO_2 mg/l	pH	CO_2 mg/l
0·001 M in unboiled H_2O	7·2	6	7·94	1·1
in boiled H_2O	8·1	0·8	8·1	0·8
0·003 M in boiled H_2O	8·35	1·1	8·60	0·8
0·010 M in boiled H_2O	8·44	3·7	8·95	1·1

product of $CaCO_3$ determines the amount of Ca^{2+} and CO_3^{2-} (and thus the HCO_3^- concentration) that can be in solution together. (Solubility product, which is a constant at a given temperature, is obtained as $[Ca^{2+}] \times [CO_3^{2-}]$ in a saturated solution). Theoretically, in water in equilibrium with the air, the maximum concentration of $CaCO_3$ that can dissolve is 12·7 mg/l. For further discussion see Schmitt (1955) and Weber and Stumm (1963).

In many cases, however, metastable conditions persist for a long time with much higher Ca^{2+} concentrations (Hutchinson, 1957, page 670).

The solubility of $CaCO_3$ can also be increased by an extra amount of free CO_2.

Tillmans (1912) has given an approximative relation between $Ca(HCO_3)_2$ dissolved and the amount of free CO_2 necessary to keep the $Ca(HCO_3)_2$ in solution (table 9.4). This applies only to waters with a pH lower than 8·3 because the concentration of free CO_2 is negligible at greater pH values. These solutions are, however, not in equilibrium with the air.

Table 9.4. Relation between $CaCO_3$ concentration and free CO_2.

$CaCO_3$ in H_2O	equilibrium CO_2
1 meq/l	0·6 mg/l
2 meq/l	2·5 mg/l
3 meq/l	6·5 mg/l
4 meq/l	15·9 mg/l

The amount of free CO_2 present in excess of the equilibrium CO_2 is sometimes called "aggressive" CO_2 as it is able to react with alkaline carbonates or metals. It can be present only in waters not in equilibrium with the air, which renders its determination extremely difficult. Some indication can be found by comparing the existing pH with the equilibrium pH of the same solution. Titration with Na_2CO_3 or NaOH to an end point of pH 8·4 gives the quantity of "free CO_2" (= "aggressive" + "equilibrium"). In practice this is a difficult titration since air must be excluded, but at the same time CO_2 must not be removed.

9.7 TITRATION OF THE CARBONATE–BICARBONATE SYSTEM; ALKALINITY

A solution of $NaHCO_3$ has a pH > 7 and can be neutralized with HCl.

$$Na^+ + HCO_3^- + H^+ + Cl^- \rightarrow Na^+ + Cl^- + CO_2 + H_2O$$

The change of pH as HCl is added can be seen in fig. 9.2A_1. A measure of the "alkalinity" is given by the amount of HCl used to neutralize the alkaline reaction of the water. It is usually expressed in meq/l. At the end point the pH is not 7, but is, due to the H_2CO_3 still present, slightly lower. The titration can be carried out by detecting the end point with the colour change of an indicator with an indicator range below 6, for instance with methyl red (pH range 4·4–6·0). The titration can also be performed under N_2. The liberated CO_2 is partly removed and the titration curve follows more closely the pattern of a NaOH titration. This sharpens the end point, but does not alter its position. See fig. 9.2A_2.

As the mobility of HCO_3^- is less than that of Cl^- the conductivity of the water increases linearly up to the end point. Past the end point the increase of conductivity per unit of titrant added will be greater (but again constant) per quantity of HCl added. The titration can therefore be carried out with a conductometric end point determination (see fig. 9.2B).

The alkalinity of a water is determined by titration with strong acid. Bicarbonate ions are not the only ones which cause the alkalinity. The other main contributors are CO_3^{2-} and OH^-, and in exceptional cases even $H_3SiO_4^-$, $H_2BO_3^-$, NH_4^+, HS^-, organic anions, and colloidal or suspended $CaCO_3$. It is possible to calculate the concentration of total CO_2 (= free $CO_2 + HCO_3^- + CO_3^{2-}$) from the pH and the alkalinity of the water in question, if the alkalinity is caused only by HCO_3^-, CO_3^{2-} and OH^-.

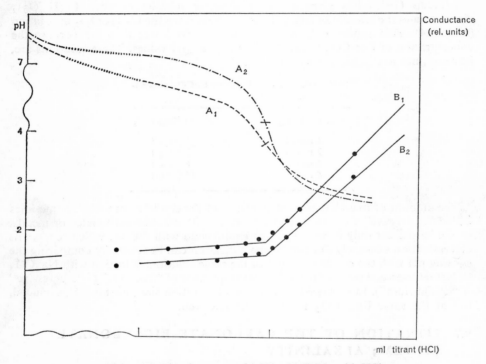

Figure 9.2. Titration curve of $0 \cdot 001$ N NaHCO$_3$ with HCl.
(Quéré automatic titrator).

A_1. Potentiometric titration.
A_2. Potentiometric titration under N_2 stream.
B_1. Conductometric titration.
B_2. Conductometric titration under N_2 stream.

Two types of alkalinity can be determined, which correspond to the two inflexion points of a titration curve (see fig. 9.3); Phenolphthalein Alkalinity (PA) and Total Alkalinity (TA).

The equivalence pH in a PA determination is equal to the pH of a NaHCO$_3$ solution of identical total ionic strength, temperature and concentration of total CO_2. For concentrations greater than about 0.2 mM/l of bicarbonate this pH is very near to $8 \cdot 3$, corresponding to the lower end of the range of phenolphthalein indicator.

The equivalence pH in a TA determination is equal to the pH of a CO_2 solution of identical ionic strength, temperature and concentration of total CO_2. This equivalence pH varies with the concentration of CO_2 present at the equivalence point, but it is usually within the pH values 4·2–5·4 (see table 3.5). At the equivalence point the situation is described by the following equations.

$$[CO_2]_{total} = [free\ CO_2 + H_2CO_3] + [HCO_3^-] + [CO_3^{2-}] \qquad (9.15)$$

$$[H^+] = [HCO_3^-] + [OH^-] + 2\ [CO_3^{2-}]$$

and

$$K_1 = \frac{[H^+]\ [HCO_3^-]}{[CO_2 + H_2CO_3]}$$

For alkalinities > 0·05 meq/l and conductivities < 400 μmho/cm the simplified equation (9.16) may be used for calculation of the equivalence pH with a calculated error of 0·01 pH unit:

$$pH = -\tfrac{1}{2}\log([CO_2]_T K_1) = \tfrac{1}{2}(pK_1 - \log[CO_2]_T) \qquad (9.16)$$

and for alkalinities > 0·2 meq/l equation (9.17) is sufficiently accurate:

$$pH = -\tfrac{1}{2}\log(K_1[CO_2]_T) \qquad (9.17)$$

Equivalence pH calculated by A. Rebsdorf according to equation (9.16) are given in table 3.5 for different values of $[CO_2]_T$ at 20°C, where $K_1 = 10^{-6.38}$. (The values are 0·3–0·4 units lower than those given in Standard Methods (1965), but agree with those of Weber and Stumm (1963), page 1569).

A loss of less than 10% of the total CO_2 will only make the end point 0·02 pH units higher than that given in table 3.5. It is fairly easy to keep losses to less than 10% in a routine titration if magnetic stirring is used.

9.8 DETERMINATION OF TOTAL CO_2

(a) By titration

For the determination of total CO_2 (used for primary productivity measurements by the ^{14}C method) a titration method and a calculation method may be used in waters where there is sufficient evidence that the alkalinity is caused mainly by CO_3^{2-}, HCO_3^- and OH^-.

The titration method is based on the principle that the difference in volume of titrant between the PA end point and the TA end point is equivalent to the total CO_2. The pH of the sample is first brought to 8·3 by careful addition of CO_2-free strong acid or base. Then the solution is titrated with strong acid to the TA end point as in a normal TA determination (fig. 9.3).

(b) By calculation

From a knowledge of the initial pH and the total alkalinity it is possible to calculate the concentration of total CO_2:

L

$$[CO_2]_T = (C.A.)_{eq} \frac{1 + \dfrac{[H^+]}{K_1} + \dfrac{K_2}{[H^+]}}{1 + \dfrac{2K_2}{[H^+]}} \qquad (9.18)$$

or, representing the last part of this expression by F_{20}, the value at 20°C,

$$[CO_2]_T = (C.A.)_{eq} F_{20} = [(T.A.)_{eq} - [OH^-]] F_{20}$$

where $(C.A.)_{eq}$ is carbonate alkalinity in eq/l and $[CO_2]_T$ is total CO_2 in mol/l.

In Chapter III, where the alkalinities (C.A. and T.A.) are expressed in meq/l the formula $(C.A.)_{eq} = (T.A.)_{eq} - [OH^-]$ is converted to $CA = TA - 10^3[OH^-]$. To avoid too many zeros it is convenient to introduce $\beta = 10^5[OH^-]$, so that $CA = TA - 0.01\beta$.
The value of β, depending on pH and conductivity can be found in Table 3.3.

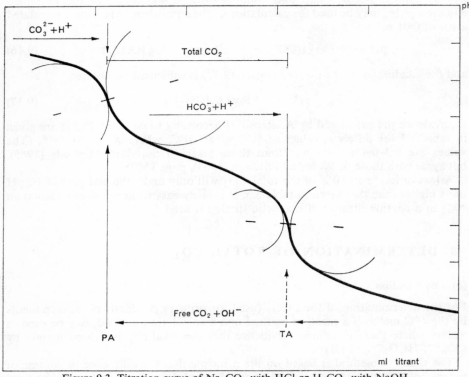

Figure 9.3. Titration curve of Na_2CO_3 with HCl or H_2CO_3 with NaOH.
(Quéré automatic titrator).

The following titrations are indicated:

$$CO_3{}^{2-} + H^+ \rightarrow HCO_3{}^-$$
$$HCO_3{}^- + H^+ \rightarrow H_2O + CO_2$$
$$\text{free } CO_2 + OH^- \rightarrow HCO_3{}^-$$

For the calculations the reactions described by (9.11₁) and (9.11₂) are considered. Equation (9.2) and (9.15) are used together with (9.19).

$$(T.A.) = [HCO_3^-] + 2[CO_3{}^{2-}] + [OH^-] - [H^+] \qquad (9.19)$$

For evaluating the influence of the ionic strength on F_{20} the correction values to be added to F_{20} have been calculated for different ionic strengths and pH values. The (C.A.) is also influenced by the ionic strength at higher pH values. Both corrections are incorporated in table 3.4. This is calculated for units of meq/l, and F_{20} is therefore replaced by δ.

The calculations are based on "Standard composition water" Rodhe (1949), Karlgren (1962), which is the average composition of fresh water, calculated for the whole world. The composition is indicated in table 9.5.

Table 9.5. "Standard composition water"
Data from L. Karlgren. Vattenkemiska Analysmetoder, Limnologiska Institutionen, Uppsala, 1962.

Cations as eq-%				Anions as eq-%		
Ca	Mg	Na	K	HCO$_3$	SO$_4$	Cl
63·5	17·4	15·7	3·4	74·3	15·7	10·0

9.9 POTENTIAL DIFFERENCES

When a rod of a metal (other than a noble metal) is placed in a solution of a salt of the same metal a potential difference will appear between metal and solution. Metal ions tend to go into solution. As the metal ions are positive, the rod becomes electrically negative relative to the solution. This electric potential difference tends to hold back the positive metal ions, which are, moreover, already present in the solution. The rod will almost instantaneously reach equilibrium with the solution when as many metal ions are dissolving as are being deposited per unit of time.

According to Nernst the potential difference E (in volts) depends on the tendency of the metal to dissolve and the concentration of the metal ions in solution, C, as given in equation (9.20). When this concentration exceeds a certain value ("saturation value") the process is reversed.

$$E = \frac{RT}{nF} \ln \frac{K}{C} \qquad (9.20)$$

where R is the molar gas constant, T is the absolute temperature, n is the number of electrons involved, F is the faraday, K is a constant.

A metallic-rod in a solution of its salt is called an *indicator electrode*. It is not possible to measure the potential of one electrode. Two rods must therefore be placed in two solutions with concentrations C_1 and C_2 and connected by a salt bridge. The potential difference between the two rods will be

$$E = E_1 - E_2 = \frac{RT}{nF} \ln \frac{C_2}{C_1} \qquad (9.21)$$

There may also be a potential difference between the two solutions due to a difference in diffusion rate of anions and cations, a so called diffusion potential = junction potential. By using an appropriate salt bridge between the two solutions the size of this potential can be made insignificant.

The potential of an electrode is measured by comparing it with the potential of an arbitrary standard electrode. To obtain this standard potential the metallic rod is placed in a saturated solution of one of its salts. The most commonly used electrode consists of Hg as the metal in a slurry of Hg_2Cl_2 (calomel-electrode) or Hg_2SO_4 in contact with 1 N or saturated KCl (or K_2SO_4).

This type of electrode is called a *reference electrode*. Equation (9.20) holds also for H_2-gas in contact with H^+. The H_2-gas is kept in equilibrium in the solution by bubbling H_2 at one atmosphere pressure over spongy platinum (from which the electrical connection is taken). The potential of this electrode depends only on the H^+ concentration of the solution (and the temperature).

When this electrode is placed in a solution containing 1 N H^+ equation (9.20) becomes

$$E = \frac{RT}{nF} \ln K$$

Measuring this potential relative to a calomel electrode gives

$$E_0 = \frac{RT}{nF} \ln K - E_{\text{cal. electrode}} \tag{9.22}$$

In a second solution, with $[H^+] = C_H$ the potential becomes

$$E_c = \frac{RT}{nF} \ln \frac{K}{C_H} - E_{\text{cal. electrode}} \tag{9.23}$$

Subtracting (9.22) from (9.23) gives

$$E_c = E_0 - \frac{RT}{nF} \ln C_H \tag{9.24}$$

At 18°C $(RT/nF) = 0.0577$ (in which the conversion from ln to $\log_{10}$ is included). Then equation (9.24) becomes

$$- \log C_H = \text{pH} = \frac{E_c - E_0}{0.0577}$$

Thus when $E_c - E_0$ equals 57.7 mV the pH equals 1, when $E_c - E_0 = 2 \times 57.7$ mV, the pH = 2. This hydrogen electrode can therefore be used as an *indicator electrode* for H^+ concentrations, with the same electrode in 1 N $H^+ + 1$ atm H_2 as reference electrode. The combination of the H_2-electrode and calomel electrode can be used for a direct determination of the pH, after calibration in a buffer with a known pH.

It is more convenient to use a simpler H^+ sensitive electrode, the glass electrode. This is a small thin glass bulb (ca. 0.05 mm thick) which is filled with an electrolyte. The potential of this electrode depends on $[H^+]$ in the same way as the normal H_2-electrode. It must be calibrated against a buffer solution with a known pH value.

The pH scale is defined at the present time by the pH of a 0.1 M/l potassium hydrogenphthalate solution at 20°C, and this solution is very useful for calibrating glass electrodes too. The pH of this solution is only slightly temperature dependent. See § 3.2.1 buffer solution B.

The actual numerical value of the potential can be defined in two ways. Either the normal H_2-electrode or the calomel electrode is arbitrarily set equal to zero. The first system is at present more commonly used.

9.10 OXIDATION-REDUCTION POTENTIALS

When a noble metal such as Pt is placed in a solution of, for example, Fe^{3+} ions, the Pt becomes positively charged. The Fe^{3+} ions react with the electrons in the Pt-metal according to

$$Fe^{3+} + e^- \rightleftharpoons Fe^{2+} \tag{9.25}$$

When the Pt-rod is placed in a solution of Fe^{2+} ions the rod will become negatively charged.

The same processes occur when the Pt-rod is placed in solutions of salts which take up or give off electrons, for example Cr^{3+}, $Fe(CN)_6^{4-}$, MnO_4^-, $Cr_2O_7^{2-}$.

These potential differences are called oxidation-reduction potentials ($=$ redox potentials). They depend on the nature and the concentration of the ions involved and are therefore fundamentally not different from the potentials described in § 9.9.

When the Pt-rod is placed in a solution containing both Fe^{2+} and Fe^{3+} ions the Pt will become positive or negative, depending on whether ferric or ferrous ions are present in excess. At one ratio of Fe^{3+} to Fe^{2+} the Pt-rod remains neutral. The reaction velocities in reaction (9.25) to the left or to the right are then equal, so that the equilibrium constant

$$K = \frac{[Fe^{2+}]}{[Fe^{3+}]} \tag{9.26}$$

The Pt-rod therefore remains neutral in a solution in which the ratio of Fe^{2+} to Fe^{3+} equals K.

The E.M.F. between two Pt-rods placed in two separate solutions (A and B) in which the concentrations of the oxidized ions are $[Ox_A]$ and $[Ox_B]$ respectively and the concentrations of the reduced ions $[Red_A]$ and $[Red_B]$ (and which solutions are in electrical contact with each other) is

$$E = \frac{RT}{nF} \ln \frac{[Ox_A]}{[Red_A]} - \frac{RT}{nF} \ln \frac{[Ox_B]}{[Red_B]} \tag{9.27}$$

provided that the oxidation-reduction reaction is reversible. For reaction (9.25), equation (9.27) becomes ($n = 1$)

$$E = \frac{RT}{F} \ln \frac{[Fe_A^{3+}]}{[Fe_A^{2+}]} + \frac{RT}{F} \ln \frac{[Fe_B^{2+}]}{[Fe_B^{3+}]} \tag{9.28}$$

When solution B is in equilibrium equation (9.28) becomes:

$$E = \frac{RT}{F} \ln \frac{[Fe_A^{3+}]^i}{[Fe_A^{2+}]} + \frac{RT}{F} \ln K$$

or in general, replacing $RT/F \ln K$ by E_0

$$E = E_0 + \frac{RT}{F} \ln \frac{[Ox]}{[Red]} \tag{9.29}$$

in which $[Ox]$ means the concentration of the oxidized ions and $[Red]$ that of the reduced ions. E_0 is the potential of the Pt electrode in a solution in which $[Ox] = [Red]$, measured against for instance a calomel electrode. The lower the normal oxidation reduction potential, the stronger the reducing capacity of the substance involved. It is customary to set the potential of the normal H_2-electrode equal to zero. A solution having a negative oxidation-reduction potential is called reducing (giving off electrons), a solution with a positive potential is oxidizing (taking up electrons).

9.11 pH DEPENDENT REDOX POTENTIALS

The redox potentials of some organic compounds are sensitive to the pH of the solution. This can be demonstrated for instance with the reaction

$$\underset{\text{quinone}}{C_6H_4O_2} + 2H^+ + 2e^- \rightleftharpoons \underset{\text{hydroquinone}}{C_6H_6O_2}$$

If [quinone] = [hydroquinone] equation (9.29) becomes

$$E = E_0 + \frac{RT}{F} \ln [H^+]$$

or at 18°C

$$E = 0.704 + 0.0577 \log [H^+] \tag{9.30}$$

By using quinhydrone—a slightly soluble compound formed by the combination of one molecule of quinone and one molecule of benzohydroquinone—either the oxidation reduction potential or the hydrogen ion concentration can be measured. Quinhydrone is however usually used only to calibrate Pt-electrodes, because for routine pH determinations the glass electrode is more convenient. When calibrating Pt electrodes quinhydrone is added to a buffer solution of known pH and the potential against the H_2-electrode is calculated with equation (9.30):

$$E = 0.704 - 0.0577 \text{ pH}$$

If a saturated calomel reference electrode is used the calomel electrode will be negative with respect to the quinhydrone electrode and $E = 0.45 - 0.058$ pH.

As hydroquinone is a weak acid ($K \sim 10^{-10}$) the dissociation becomes appreciable above pH = 8.5 and the hydroquinone electrode cannot be used then.

For purposes of comparison the potentials of pH sensitive systems are calculated to E_7, that is the potential the system would have at pH = 7. The calculation is carried out by assuming a rise of one pH unit to be equivalent to a decrease of 58 mV.

In natural waters and muds potential differences between -0.1 V (O_2 free) and $+0.5$ V (O_2 saturated) relative to the calomel reference electrode occur. In theory water saturated with O_2 should have a value of about 0.8 V. The reason for the discrepancy between 0.5 V and 0.8 V lies probably in the fact that the Pt-electrode becomes covered with a film of oxide and is no longer completely reversible.

The negative values are normally reached only in sediments. Waters with a potential lower than 0.1 to 0.2 V are generally called "reducing", although this is a relative description, as it depends also on the system to be reduced.

Mortimer (1942) has given a list of approximate redox potential ranges, within which certain reductions proceeded actively (see table 9.6).

It is important to realise that the decrease of redox potentials in sediments mentioned in table 9.6 is caused by the depletion of O_2 and the release of organic compounds by the mud. The reactions follow the redox potential; the potentials mentioned are not the potentials of the systems in column 1.

Table 9.6. Reduction of some systems and prevalent redox potentials and O_2 concentrations, Mortimer (1942).

reduction reaction	redox potential*	prevalent O_2 concentration
$NO_3^- \rightarrow NO_2^-$	0·45–0·40	4 mg/l
$NO_2^- \rightarrow NH_3$	0·40–0·35	0·4 mg/l
$Fe^{3+} \rightarrow Fe^{2+}$	0·30–0·20	0·1 mg/l
$SO_4^{2-} \rightarrow S^{2-}$	0·10–0·06	0·0 mg/l

* The lower potential is the limit below which Mortimer could not detect the oxidized phase.

9.12 POTENTIOMETRIC TITRATIONS

All potential differences between reference electrodes and indicator electrodes (such as H^+ indicator or Ag^+ indicator and oxidation reduction electrodes) can be used to follow a titration in order to determine the end point.

When the potential is E Volt the addition of a fixed quantity of for instance a Ag^+ solution (V ml) in the case of a Cl^- determination causes a change: ΔE. It can be shown that the $\Delta E/\Delta V$ is maximal and therefore $\Delta^2 E/\Delta V^2 = 0$ at the equivalence point. A graph of E plotted versus ml of reagent added therefore shows a rapid change near the equivalence point, which has a potential characteristic of the reaction. It is, however, more accurate to determine the end point by plotting the rate of change of E against V ($\Delta E/\Delta V$ vs. V) than by using the E of the end point itself, as a small error in E may introduce a large error in the quantity of reagent necessary. When the rate of change of E is used, the actual value of E itself need not be known.

Potentiometric titrations can be used in limnology for the determination of alkalinity, chloride, and for the oxidative or reductive capacity of a water (i.e. oxygen, oxidability, ferrous compounds). Potentiometric titrations can be made specific and can be automated easily.

9.13 DEAD-STOP END POINT TITRATIONS

The detailed mechanism of the dead-stop titration is complicated. It is explained in standard works (for example Lingane, 1958). There follows a very brief outline of the essentials.

The dead-stop end point titration is an amperometric or potentiometric titration with two identical Pt-electrodes. One of these is made the indicator electrode by electrical polarization with a small constant voltage (10–500 mV); the other one serves as a reference electrode.

During the titration the electric current or the voltage is measured. At the end point there is a sharp change in current or voltage.

The configuration of the titration curve depends on whether the titrate, the titrant or both are electroactive, i.e. reducible. When the titrate is not reducible the current remains constant (practically zero) before, but increases beyond the E.P. When the titrant is not reducible there is first a decrease of current, which becomes constant after the E.P. When both titrant and titrate are reducible a V-shaped trace is produced.

A different type of amperometric titration curve will be obtained when the electrodes exchange the roles of "indicator" and "reference" during the titration (when titrate and titrant both establish reversible redox couples).

With choice of different electrodes ("stirring" or "dropping") and changes in the voltage numerous applications are possible. In limnochemistry the main applications are the titrations involving I_2, $Cr_2O_7^{2-}$, Ce^{4+}, MnO_4^-, CrO_4^{2-}, SO_4^{2-} (with Ba^{2+}).

It is possible to make a dead-stop titrator relatively easily. As only low voltages and small currents are necessary the method is suitable for field conditions. The use of a micro burette is advisable.

Accuracy

In macro titrations (e.g. 0·1 N titrant, even when a micro burette is used) it is often possible to obtain an error as small as 0·1%, even without graphing the current readings against volume of titrant. In the case of a micro titration it is necessary to graph current against ml titrant as the trace is always curved at the end point. A linear extrapolation is possible using points sufficiently distant from either side of the end point. The accuracy is in this case not better than with a potentiometric titration, but the apparatus is much more simple.

Note

Dead stop titrators may be bought. A simple circuit diagram for the construction of a cheap one may be obtained from the editor of this Manual.

REFERENCES, MANUFACTURERS ADDRESSES AND PARTICIPANTS

10.1 List of Recommended Handbooks and General Works

Analytical microbiology; ed. by F. Kavanagh. New York, Academic Press, 1963. Chapter 7, pp. 411–565.

BATES R.G. *Determination of pH, Theory and Practice*. New York, London, Wiley, 1964. 435 p. First published 1954: Electromethod pH determination.

BOLLINGER H.R., BREUNER M., GANSHIRT H., MANGOLD H.K., SEIDLER H., STAHL, W.D. and E. In: *Thin-Layer Chromatography; a Laboratory Handbook*; ed. by E. Stahl. New York, Academic Press, 1965.

BRADSTREET R.B. *The Kjeldahl Method for Organic Nitrogen*. New York, London, Academic Press, 1965. 239 p.

ELWELL W.T. and GIDLEY J.A.F. *Atomic Absorption Spectroscopy*; London, Pergamon, 1966.

Flame Photometry; a manual of methods and applications. Princeton, 1957.

FLASCHKA H.A. *EDTA Titrations*; an introduction to theory and practice: 2nd ed. Oxford, etc., 1964. 144 p.

HARNED H.S. and OWEN B.B. *The Physical Chemistry of Electrolytic Solutions*; 3rd ed. New York, Reinhold, 1958. 838 p. Is: (American Chem. Soc. Monogr., nr. 137).

HERRMANN R. und ALKEMADE C.TR.J. *Flammenphotometrie*. Berlin, etc., 1960. 394 p.

HUTCHINSON G.W. *A Treatise on Limnology*; 2 vls. New York etc., 1957. Vol. I: Geography, physics, and chemistry.

JACKSON M.L. *Soil Chemical Analysis*; 2nd ed. Englewood Cliffs, Prentice Hall, 1958, 498 p.

JEFFERY P.G. and KIPPING P.J. *Gas Analysis by Gas Chromatography*. Oxford, Pergamon Press, 1964. 216 p.

JONES A.G. *Analytical Chemistry Some New Techniques*. London, Butterworth Sc. Publ., 1960. 268 p.

KAVANAGH. See: *Analytical microbiology*; ed. by F. Kavanagh.

KOLTHOFF I.M. and SANDELL E.B. *Textbook of Quantitative Inorganic Analysis*; 3rd ed. New York, MacMillan, 1952. 759 p.

KOLTHOFF I.M. and LINGANE J.J. *Polarography*; 2nd compl. rev. augm. ed. 2 vls. New York, London, Interscience Publ., 1952. Vol. 1: Theoretical principles, instrumentation and technique. Vol. 2: Inorganic polarography, organic polarography, biological applications, amperometric titrations.

KOLTHOFF I.M. and BELCHER, R. *Volumetric Analysis*. New York, Interscience Publ., 1957. Vol. 3: Titration methods: Oxydation-reduction reactions.

LEDERER E. and LEDERER M. *Chromatography*; a review of principles and applications; 2nd rev. ed. Amsterdan, New York, Elsevier Publ. Comp., 1957, 711 p.

LINGANE J.J. *Electroanalytical Chemistry*; 2nd rev. ed. New York, Interscience Publ., 1958. 669 p.

MACKERETH F.J.H. *Water Analysis for Limnologists*. Freshwater Biol. Ass. Sc. Publication nr. 21. 1963.

STUMM W. and MORGAN J.J. *Aquatic chemistry*. New York, Wiley Interscience, 1970. 583p.

MULLEN P.W. *Modern Gas Analysis*. New York, Intersc. Publ., 1955.

REYNOLDS R.J. and ALDOUS K. *Atomic Absorption Spectroscopy*. London, Griffin, 1969.

RILEY, J.P. and SKIRROW G. ed. *Chemical Oceanography*. New York, Academic Press, 1965.

SANDELL E.B. *Colorimetric Determination of Traces of Metals*; 3rd ed. London, New York, Interscience Publ., 1959. 1032 p. Is: Vol. 3. Chemical Analysis.

SQUIRREL D.C.M. *Automatic Methods in Volumetric Analysis*; with a preface by J. Haslam. London, Hilger and Watts, 1964. 201 p.

STAHL E. See: *Thin-layer Chromatography; a Laboratory Handbook*, 1965.

Standard Methods for the Examination of Water and Wastewater, including Bottom Sediments and Sludge; 12th ed. New York, Am. Publ. Health Ass., 1965.

M

STRICKLAND J.D.H. and PARSONS T.R. *Bull.* 125 *of the Fish Res. Board of Canada*; 2nd rev. ed. Ottawa, 1965. 203 p.
Thin-layer Chromatography; a Laboratory Handbook; ed. by E. Stahl. New York, Academic Press, 1965.
VOGEL A.I. *A Text-book of Quantitative Inorganic Analysis*; 3rd ed. London, Longmans, Green & Co., 1961.

10.2 REFERENCES

Consult also List of Recommended Handbooks and General Works, p. 153.

ÅBERG B. and RODHE W. 1942 Uber die Milieufaktoren in einigen südschwedischen Seen. *Symb. Bot. Ups.*, 5(3); 1–256.
ALSTERBERG G. 1926 Die Winklersche Bestimmungsmethode für in Wasser gelösten, elementaren Sauerstoff sowie ihre Anwendung bei Anwesenheit oxydierbarer Substanzen. *Biochem. Zeitschr.*, 170; 30–75.
ARMSTRONG F.A.J., WILLIAMS P.M. and STRICKLAND J.D.H. 1966 Photo-oxidation of organic matter in sea water by ultra-violet radiation, analytical and other applications. *Nature*, 211 (5048); 481–483.
BACHMAN R.W. and GOLDMAN C.R. 1964 The determination of microgram quantities of molybdenum in natural waters. *Limnol. Oceanogr.*, 9; 143–146.
BEADLE L.C. 1958 Measurement of dissolved oxygen in swamp waters. Further modification of the Winkler method. *Journ. Exp. Biol.*, 35; 556–566.
BLAŽKA P. 1966a Bestimmung der Proteine in Material aus Binnengewässern. *Limnologica* (Berlin); 4(2): 387–396.
—— 1966b Bestimmung der Kohlenhydrate und Lipide. *Limnologica* (Berlin); 4(2); 403–418.
BREIDENBACH A.W., LICHTENBERG J.J., HENKE C.F., SMITH D.J., EICHELBERGER J.W. and STIERLI H. 1964 The identification and measurement of chlorinated hydrocarbon pesticides in surface water. *U.S. Publ. Health Serv. Publ. no.* 1241, Div. Water Supply and Poll. Control, Washington.
BRIGGS R. and VINEY M. 1964 The design and performance of temperature compensated electrodes for oxygen measurements. *Journ. Sci. Instrum.*, 41(2); 78–83.
BURNS E.R. and MARSHALL C. 1965 Correction for chloride interference in the chemical oxygen demand test. *Water Poll. Contr. Feder. Journ.*, 37(12); 1716–1721.
BUSCH A.W. 1966 Energy, total carbon, and oxygen demand. *Water Resources Res.*, 2; 59–69.
—— 1967 Total carbon analysis in water pollution control. In: Golterman and Clymo, Amsterdam, 1967.
CARLUCCI A.F. and SILBERNAGEL S.B. 1966a Bioassay of sea water. (1) A ^{14}C-uptake method for the determination of vitamin B_{12} in sea water. *Can. Journ. Microbiol.*, 12; 175–183.
—— —— 1966b Bioassay of sea water (2). Methods for the determination of concentrations of dissolved vitamin B_{12} in sea water. *Can. Journ. Microbiol.*, 12; 1079–1089.
—— —— 1967a Bioassay of sea water (4). The determination of dissolved biotin in sea water using ^{14}C-uptake by cells of *Amphidinium carteri*. *Can. Journ. Microbiol*, 3 (8); 979–86.
—— —— 1967b Determination of vitamins in sea water. In: Golterman and Clymo, Amsterdam, 1967
CARPENTER J.H. 1965 The accuracy of the Winkler method for dissolved oxygen analysis. *Limnol. Oceanogr.*, 10(1); 135–140.
—— 1966 New measurements of oxygen solubility in pure and natural water. *Limnol. Oceanogr.*, 11(2); 264–277.
CHAN K.M. and RILEY J.P. 1966 The determination of Vanadium in sea water and natural waters biological materials and silicate sediments and rocks. *Anal. Chim. Acta*, 34; 337–345.
—— 1967 The determination of molybdenum in natural waters, silicates and biological materials. (to be publ. in *Anal. Chim. Acta*).
CHENG K.L., MELSTED S.N. and BRAY, R.H. 1953 Removing interfering metals in the versenate determination of calcium and magnesium. *Soil Sci.*, 75; 37–40.
DAMAS H. 1954 Etude limnologique de quelques lacs ruandais. (2). Etude thermique et chimique. *Mém. Inst. Roy. Col. Belge.* 24, 1–116.
DUSSART B. and FRANCIS-BOEUF C. 1949 Technique du dosage de l'oxygène dissous dans l'eau basé sur la méthode de Winkler. *Circ. Centre Rech. Etudes Océanogr., Instr. Techn.*, no. 1.
DUURSMA E.K. 1961 Dissolved organic carbon nitrogen and phosphorus in the sea. *Neth. Journ. Sea Res.*, 1; 1–148.
—— and ROMMETS J.W. 1961 Interprétation mathématique de la fluorescence des eaux douces, saumâtres et marines. *Neth. Journ. Sea Res.*, 1; 391–405.

EFFENBERGER M. 1962 Konduktometrische Bestimmung des organischen Kohlenstoffs in Gewäs sern. *Sc. Papers Inst. Chem. Technol.*, Prague, *Techn. of water*, **6**(1); 471–493.
—— 1967 A simple flow-cell for the continuous determination of oxidation reduction potential. In: Golterman and Clymo, Amsterdam, 1967.
FABRICAND B.P., SAWYER R.R., UNGAR S.G. and ADLER S. 1962 Trace metal concentrations in the ocean by atomic absorption spectroscopy. *Geochim. et Cosmochim. Acta*, **26**; 1023–1027.
FALES F.W. 1951 The assimilation and degradation of carbohydrates by yeast cells. *Journ. Biol. Chemistry*, **193**; 113–124.
FARKAS T. and HERODEK S. 1964 The effect of environmental temperature on the fatty acid composition of Crustacean plankton. *Journ. Lipid Res.*, **5**; 369–373.
FASSEL V.A. and MOSOTTI V.G. 1965 Evaluation of spectral continua as primary light sources in atomic-absorption spectroscopy. *Coll. Spectr. Internat.* **12**. Exeter, 1965.
FISHMAN M.J. and SKOUGSTAD W.M. 1964 Catalytic determination of Vanadium in water. *Anal. Chem.*, **36**; 1643–1646.
—— 1965 Rapid field and laboratory determination of phosphate in natural water. *U.S. Geol. Surv. Prof. Paper*, 525-B (*Anal. Techn.*); B 167–B 169.
—— and DOWNS S.C. 1966 Methods for analysis of selected metals in water by atomic absorption. *USGS Water Supply Paper*, 1540-C; 23–45.
FØYN E. 1955 "The oxymeter". *Fiskeridir. Skr. Havundersøk.*, **11**(3); 1.
—— 1967 Density and oxygen registration. In: Golterman and Clymo, Amsterdam, 1967.
FOX H.M. and WINGFIELD C.A. 1938 A portable apparatus for the determination of oxygen dissolved in a small volume of water *Journ. Exp. Biol.*, **15**; 437–443.
GLEBOVICH T.A. 1963 Determination of boron in waters with H-resorcinol. See: *Chem. Abstr.*, **61**, nr. 14359b.
GOLDMAN C.R. 1965 Micronutrient limiting factors and their detection in natural phytoplankton populations. *Mem. Ist. Ital. Idrobiol.*, **18** Suppl. 121–135.
GOLTERMAN H.L. 1960 Studies on the cycle of elements in fresh water. *Acta Bot. Neerl.*, **9**; 1–58.
—— 1967 Opening address. In: Golterman and Clymo, Amsterdam, 1967.
—— 1967 Tetraethylsilicate as a "molybdate unreactive" silicon source for diatoms cultures. In: Golterman and Clymo, Amsterdam, 1967.
—— and WURTZ I.M. 1961 A sensitive, rapid determination of inorganic phosphate in presence of labile phosphate esters. *Anal. Chim. Acta*, **25**; 295–298.
—— and CLYMO R.S. 1967 "Chemical Environment in the Aquatic Habitat" Proceedings of an IBP symposium, 10–16 October, 1966. Royal Netherlands Academy of Sciences, Amsterdam, 1967.
GOMORI 1955 In: Methods in enzymology, vol. 1. New York, Academic Press, 1955.
GOODENKAUF A. and ERDEI J. 1964 Identification of chlorinated hydrocarbon pesticides in river water. *Journ. Amer. Water Wks. Ass.*, **56**; 600–606.
GRAAF I.M.DE and GOLTERMAN H.L. 1967 An old colorimetric method for organic carbon. In: Golterman and Clymo, Amsterdam, 1967.
GREENHALGH R. and RILEY J.P. 1962 The development of a reproducible spectrophotometric curcumin method for determining boron, and its application to sea water. *The analyst*, **87**; 970–976.
HAFFTY J. 1960 Residue method for common minor elements. *Water Supply Paper*, 1540-A.
HANES CH.S. 1929 An application of the method of Hagedorn and Jensen to the determination of larger quantities of reducing sugars. *Biochem. Journ.*, **23**; 99–106.
HANSEN A.L. and ROBINSON R.J. 1953 The determination of organic phosphorus in sea water with perchloric acid oxydation. *Journ. Mar. Res.*, **12**; 31–42.
HART I.C. 1967. Nomograms to calculate dissolved-oxygen contents and exchange (mass-transfer) coefficients. Water Research, **1**; 391–395.
HARVEY H.W. 1957 Bioassay of nitrogen. *Journ. Mar. Biol. Ass.*, U.K., **36**; 157.
HARWOOD J.E., VAN STEENDEREN R.A. and KUHN A.L. 1969 A rapid method for orthophosphate analysis at high concentrations in water. *Water Research*, 3; 425–432.
HERRMANN R. 1965 Grundlagen und Anwendung der Atomabsorptionsspektroskopie in Flammen. *Zeitschr. Klin. Chem.*, **31**; 178.
HEWITT B.R. 1958 Spectrophotometric determination of total carbohydrate. *Nature*, **182**(4630); 246–247.
HOBBIE J.E. 1967 Glucose and acetate in freshwater. Concentrations and turnover rates. In: Golterman and Clymo, Amsterdam, 1967.
—— and WRIGHT R.T. 1965 Bioassay with bacterial uptake kinetics: glucose in freshwater. *Limnol. Oceanogr.*, **10**; 471–474.

156   *References*

HOLDEN A.V. and MARSDEN K. 1966 The examination of surface waters and sewage effluents for organochlorine pesticides. *Journ. Inst. Sewage Purif.*, **3**; 295–299.

HOLMES R.W. 1943 Silver staining of nerve axons in paraffin section. *Anat. Record*, **86**(2); 157–186.

HOLM-HANSEN O., LORENZEN C., HOLMES R.W. and STRICKLAND J.D.H. 1965 Fluorimetric determination of chlorophyll. *J. Cons. int. Explor. Mar.* **30**; 3–15.

HULME A.C. and NARAIN R. 1931 The ferricyanide method for the determination of reducing sugars; a modification of the Hagedorn-Jensen-Hanes technique. *Biochem. Journ.*, **25**; 1051–1061.

HUTNER S.H., PROVASOLI L. and BAKER H. 1961 Development of microbiological assays for biochemical, oceanographic, and clinical use. *Microchem. Journ.*, *Symp. Series*, **1**; 95–111.

JÖNSSON E. 1966 The determination of Kjeldahl nitrogen in natural water. *Vattenhygien* **1**; 10–14.

KALLE K. 1955/56 Fluoreszensmessungen in den Niderschlagwässern und in künstlichem Rauhreif. *Ann. der Meteor.*, **7**; 374–385.

KARLGREN L. 1962 Vattenkemiska analysemetoder. Limnol. Institutionen, Uppsala.

KAVANAGH F. ed. *Analytical Microbiology*, New York, Academic Press, 1963. Chapter **7**; pp. 411–565.

KAY H. 1954 Eine Mikromethode zur chemischem Bestimmung des organisch gebundenen Kohlenstoffs im Meerwasser. *Kieler Meeresf.*, **10**; 26–36.

KEELER R.F. 1959 Color reaction for certain amino acids, amines, and proteins. *Science*, **129**; 1617–1618.

KERR J.R.W. 1960 The spectrophotometric determination of microgram amounts of calcium. *Analyst*, **85**; 867–870.

KNOWLES G. and LOWDEN G.F. 1953 Methods for detecting the end point in the titratio of Iodine with Thiosulphate. *Analyst*, **78**; 159.

KOBAYASHI J. 1967 Silica in fresh water and estuaries. In: Golterman and Clymo, Amsterdam, 1967.

KOPP J.F. and KRONER R.C. 1965 A direct-reading spectrochemical procedure for the measurement of nineteen minor elements in natural water. *Appl. Spectroscopy*, **19**; 155–159.

KOVACS M.F. 1963 Thin-layer chromatography for chlorinated pesticide residue analysis. *Journ. Assoc. Offic. Agric. Chem.*, **46**; 884–893.

KREY J. 1951 Quantitative Bestimmung von Eiweiss im Plankton mittels der Biuretreaktion. *Kieler Meeresforschung*, **8**; 16–29.

—— and SZEKIELDA K.-H. 1965 Bestimmung des organisch gebundenen Kohlenstoffs im Meerwasser mit einem neuen Gerät zur Analyse sehr kleiner Mengen CO_2. *Zeitschr. anal. Chem.*, **207**, B.5; 338–346.

KROGH A. and KEYS A. 1934 Methods for the determination of dissolved organic carbon and nitrogen in sea water. *Biol. Bull.*, **67**; 132–144.

LARSON T.E. 1938 Properties and determination of methane in ground waters. *Journ. Am. Water Wks. Ass.*, **30**; 1828.

LEE G.F. 1967 Automatic methods. In: Golterman and Clymo, Amsterdam, 1967.

—— and STUMM W. 1960 Determination of ferrous iron in the presence of ferric iron with bathophenanthroline. *Journ. Amer. Water Wks. Ass.*, **52**; 1567–1574.

LEWIN R.A. 1961 Phytoflagellates and algae. In: Encyclopedia of plant physiology; ed. by W. Ruhland. *Berlin, Springer Verlag*, 1961. Vol. **14**, pp. 407–417.

MACIOLEK J.A. 1962 Limnological organic analyses by quantitative dichromate oxidation. *Res. report nr. 60 of Bur. sport fish and wildlife*, U.S. Fish and Wildlife service.

MACKERETH F.J.H. 1955 Rapid micro-estimation of the major anions of freshwater. *Proc. Soc. Wat. Trtmnt. Exmn.*, **4**; 27–42.

MACKERETH F.J.H. 1964 An improved galvanic cell for determination of oxygen concentrations in fluids. *Journ. Scient. Instrum.*, **41**(2); 38–41.

MACKINNEY G. 1940 Criteria for purity of chlorophyll preparations. *Journ. Biol. Chem.*, **132**; 91–109.

—— 1941 Absorption of light by chlorophyll solutions. *Journ. Biol. Chem.*, **140**; 315–322.

MADGWICK J.C. 1966 Chromatographic determination of chlorophylls in algal cultures and phytoplankton. *Deep-Sea Res.*, **13**(3); 459–466.

MALISSA H. and SCHÖFFMANN E. 1955 Über die Verwendung von substituierten Dithiocarbamaten in der Mikroanalyse. *Mikrochim. Acta* (1955); 187–202.

MATSUKA M., OTSUKA H. and HASE E. 1966 Changes in contents of carbohydrate and fatty acid in the cells of Chlorella prototcoides during the processes of the de- and re-generation of chloroplasts. *Plant Cell Physiol.*, **7**; 651–662.

MEINKE, W. W. 1955 Trace-elements sensitivity; comparison of activation analysis with other methods. *Science*, **121**; 177–184.

MENZEL D.W. and VACCARO R.F. 1964 The measurement of dissolved organic and particulate carbon in sea water. *Limnol. Oceanogr.*, **9**; 138–142.

—— and CORWIN N. 1965 The measurement of total phosphorus in sea water based on the liberation of organically bound fractions by persulfate oxidation. *Limnol. Oceanogr.*, **10**(2); 280–282.

MONTGOMERY H.A.C. and THOM N.S. 1962 The determination of low concentration of organic carbon in water. *Analyst*, **87**(1038); 689–697.

—— and COCKBURN A. 1964 Errors in sampling for dissolved oxygen. *Analyst*, **89**; 679.

—— THOM N.S. and COCKBURN A. 1964 Determination of dissolved oxygen by the Winkler method and the solubility of oxygen in pure water and sea water. *Journ. appl. Chem.*, **14**; 280.

MORGAN J.J. and STUMM W. 1965 Analytical chemistry of aqueous manganese. *Journ. Amer. Water Wks. Ass.*, **47**; 107–119.

MORTIMER C.H. 1942 The exchange of dissolved substances between mud and water in lakes. *Journ. of Ecology*, **30**; 147–201.

MURPHY J. and RILEY J.P. 1958 A single-solution method for the determination of soluble phosphate in sea water. *Journ. Mar. Biol. Ass. U.K.*, **37**; 9.

—— —— 1962 A modified single-solution method for the determination of phosphate in natural waters. *Anal. Chim. Acta*, **27**; 31.

NICOLSON N.J. 1966 The colorimetric determination of iron in water. *Proc. Soc. Water Treatment and Examination*, **15**; 157–8.

O'CONNOR J.T. and RENN C.E. 1963 Evaluation of procedures for the determination of zinc. *Journ. Amer. Water Wks. Ass.*, **55**; 631–638.

—— KOMOLRIT K. and ENGELBRECHT R.S. 1965 Evaluation of the orthophenanthroline method for the ferrous iron determination. *Journ. Amer. Water Wks. Ass.*, **57**; 926–933.

OHLE W. 1953 Die chemische und die elektrochemische Bestimmung des molekular gelösten Sauerstoffs der Binnengewässer. In: *Mitt. Int. Ver. Limnol.*, no. 3; 1–44.

OLSEN S. 1967 Recent trends in the determination of phosphate in the aquatic environment. In: Golterman and Clymo, Amsterdam, 1967.

OTSUKA H. and MORIMURA Y. 1966 Change of fatty acids composition of Chlorella ellipsoidea during its cell cycle. *Plant Cell Physiol.*, **7**; 663–670.

PARK K. 1965 Gas-chromatographic determination of dissolved oxygen, nitrogen, and total carbon dioxide in sea water. *Journ. Oceanogr. Soc.*, Japan, **21**; 28–29.

—— and CATALFOMO M. 1964 Gas-chromatographic determination of dissolved oxygen in seawater using argon as carrier gas. *Deep-Sea Res.*, **11**; 917–920.

PARSONS T.R. and STRICKLAND J.D.H. 1963 Discussion of spectrophotometric determination of marine-plant pigments, with revised equations for ascertaining chlorophylls and carotenoids. *J. Mar. Res.*, **21**; 155–63.

POMEROY R. and KIRSCHMAN H.D. 1945 Determination of dissolved oxygen; proposed modification of the Winkler method. *Industr. Engng. Chem. (Anal.)*; **17**(11); 715–716.

POVOLEDO D. 1967 The determination of organic carbon and nitrogen by wet-dry combustion with gas-chromatographic detection (comment to the paper of A.W. Busch). In: Golterman and Clymo, Amsterdam, 1967.

PROCTOR C.M. and HOOD D.W. 1954 Determination of inorganic phosphate in sea water by an iso-butanol extraction procedure. *Journ. Mar. Res.*, **13**; 122–132.

PROCHÁZKOVÁ L. 1964 Spectrofotometric determination of ammonia as rubazoic acid with bispyrazolone reagent. *Anal. Chem.*, **34**(4); 965–971.

RAINWATER F.H. and THATCHER L.L. 1960 Methods for collection and analysis of water samples. *Geol. Surv. Water-Supply Paper*; 1454.

RAY N.H. 1954 Gas chromatography. II. The separation and analysis of gas mixtures by chromatographic methods. *Journ. appl. Chem.*, **4**; 82–85.

REBSDORF A. 1966 Evaluation of some modifications of the Winkler method for the determination of oxygen in natural water. *Verh. Internat. Ver. Limnol.*, **16**; 459–464.

REPORT of SCOR-Unesco working group 17, 4–6 June, 1964. 1966 Determination of photosynthetic pigments in sea-water. Paris, Unesco, 1966. 69 p.

RICHARDS F.A. and THOMPSON T.G. 1952 The estimation and characterization of plankton populations by pigment analyses. II. A spectrophotometric method for the estimation of plankton pigments. *Journ. Mar. Res.*, **11**; 156–172.

RILEY, J.P. and SINHASENI P. 1958 The determination of copper in sea water, silicate rocks and biological materials. *Analyst*, **83**; 299–304.

158 References

ROBINSON R.J. 1941 Perchloric acid oxidation of organic phosphorus in lake waters. *Industr. Engng. Chem.* (*Anal.*), **13**(7) 465–466.

RODHE W. 1948 Environmental requirements of fresh-water plankton algae. *Symb. Bot. Upsal.*, **10**; 1–49.

—— 1949 The ionic composition of lake waters. *Verh. Internat. Ver. Limnol.*, **10**; 377–386.

ROSKAM R.TH. and LANGEN D.de. 1963 A compleximetric method for the determination of dissolved oxygen in water. *Anal. Chim. Acta.*, **28**; 78–81.

ROSSUM J.R., VILLARRUZ P.A. and WADE J.A.A. 1950 A new method for determining methane in water. *Journ. Am. Water Wks. Ass.*, **42**(7); 413–415.

SCHMITT Cl. 1955 Contribution a l'étude du système cheaux-carbonate de calcium bicarbonate de calcium-acide carbonique-eau. *Ann. de l'école nat. sup. de mécanique*, Nantes.

SHAPIRO J. 1965 On the measurement of ferrous iron in natural waters. *Limnol. Oceanogr.*, **11**; 293–298.

—— 1967 Differences in the composition and behaviour of humic substances from various waters. In: Golterman and Clymo, Amsterdam, 1967.

—— 1967 On the relationship between measured iron and available iron. In: Golterman and Clymo, Amsterdam, 1967.

SILVEY W.D. and BRENNAN R. 1962 Concentration method for the spectrochemical determination of seventeen minor elements in natural water. *Anal. Chem.*, **34**; 784.

SLYKE D.D., DILLON VAN.R.T., MACFADGEN D.A. and HAMILTON P. 1941 Gasometric determination of carboxyl groups in free amino acids. *Journ. Biol. Chem.*, **141**; 627–669.

SMITH C.F. 1953 The wet ashing of organic matter employing hot concentrated perchloric acid. *Anal. Chim. Acta*, **8**; 397–421.

STANGENBERG M. 1959 Der biochemische Sauerstoffbedarf des Seewassers. *Mem. Ist. Ital. Idrobiol.*, **11**; 185–211. *Naturwissenschaften*, **42**; 344.

STEPHENS K. 1963 Determination of low phosphate concentrations in lake and marine waters. *Limnol. Oceanogr.*, **8**(3); 361–362.

STRAŠKRABOVÁ-PROKEŠOVÁ V. 1966 Oxidation of organic substances in the water of the reservoirs Slapy and Klicava. Pages 85–111. In: Hydrobiological studies; ed. by J. Hrbáček. Prague, Acad. Publ. House, 1966, part 1.

SWINNERTON J.W., LINNENBOM V.J. and CHEEK C.H. 1962a Determination of dissolved gases in aqueous solution by gas chromatography. *Anal. chem.*, **34**; 483–485.

—— —— —— 1962b Revised sampling procedure for determination of dissolved gases in solution by gas chromatography. *Anal. Chem.*, **34**; 1509.

—— —— —— 1964 Determination of argon and oxygen by gas chromatography. *Anal. Chem.*, **36**; 1669–1671.

SZEKIELDA K.-H. 1967 Methods for the determination of particulate and dissolved carbon in aquatic solutions. (Lit. review). In: Golterman and Clymo, Amsterdam, 1967.

—— and KREY J. 1965 Die Bestimmung des partikulären organisch gebundenen Kohlenstoffs im Meerwasser mit einer neuen Schnellmethode. *Mikrochim. Acta*, **1**; 149–159.

TALLING J.F. and DRIVER D. 1963 Some problems in the estimation of chlorophyll-a in phytoplankton. Proc. conference on primary productivity measurements, marine and fresh-water; held at Univ. Hawaii, 1961. U.S. Atomic Energy. Comm. TID–7633; 142–146.

TARRAS M. 1948 Photometric determination of magnesium in water with Brilliant Yellow. *Analyt. Chem.*, **20**; 1156–1158.

TEASLEY J.I. and COX W.S. 1963 Determination of pesticides in water by microcoulometric gas chromatography after liquid-liquid extraction. *Journ. Am. Water Wks. Ass.*, **55**; 1093–1096.

TILLMANS J. and HEUBLEIN O. 1912 Uber die Kohlensauren Kalk angreifende Kohlensäure der natürlichen Wässer. *Gesundheits-Ingenieur*, **35**(34): 669–677.

VALLENTYNE J. 1967 Pheromones and related substances. In: Golterman and Clymo, Amsterdam, 1967.

VERNON L.P. 1960 Spectrophotometric determinations of chlorophylls and pheophytins in plant extracts. *Anal. Chem.*, **32**(9); 1144–1150.

WALPOLE G.ST. 1914 Hydrogen potentials of mixtures of acetic acid and sodium acetate. *Journ. Chem. Soc.*, **105**; 2501–2529.

WALSH A. 1965 Some recent advances in atomic-absorption spectroscopy. Coll. Spectr. Internat. XII. Exeter, 1965.

WATT W.D. 1965 A convenient apparatus for in situ primary production studies. *Limnol. Oceanogr.*, **10**(2); 298–300.

WEBER W.J. and STUMM W. 1963 Mechanism of hydrogen ion buffering in natural waters. *Journ. Am. Wat. Wks. Ass.*, **55**; 1553–1578.

WILCOX L.V. 1950 Electrical conductivity. *Journ. Am. Wat. Wks. Ass.*, **42**; 775–776

WILLIS J.B. 1962 Determination of lead and other heavy metals in urine by atomic absorption spectroscopy. *Anal. Chem.*, **34**; 614–617.

WRIGHT R.T. and HOBBIE K.E. 1966 Use of glucose and acetate by bacteria and algae in aquatic ecosystems. *Ecology*, **47**; 447–464.

YEMM E.W. and WILLIS A.J. 1954 The estimation of carbohydrates in plant extracts by anthrone. *Biochem. Journ.*, **57**; 508–514.

YENTSCH C.S. and MENZEL D.W. 1963 A method for the determination of phytoplankton chlorophyll and phaeophytin by fluorescence. *Deep-Sea Res.*, **10**; 221–231.

ZOBELL Cl.E. and BROWN B.FAY 1944 Studies on the chemical preservation of water samples. *Journ. Mar. Res.*, **5**(3); 178–184.

ZSCHEILE F.P. 1934 A quantitative spectro-photoelectric analytical method applied to solutions of chlorophylls a and b. *Journ. Phys. and colloid chem.*, **38**; 95–102.

—— 1934 An improved method for the purification of chlorophylls a and b; the quantitative measurement of their absorption spectra; evidence for the existence of a third component of chlorophyll. *Botan. Gazette*, **95**; 529–562.

—— COMAR C.L. and MACKINNEY G. 1942 Interlaboratory comparison of absorption spectra by the photoelectric spectrophotometric method. Determinations on chlorophyll and Weigert's solutions. *Plant Physiol.*, **17**; 666–670.

10.3 MANUFACTURERS ADDRESSES

Hydrobios Apparatebau GmbH Am Jägersberg 7 23 Kiel—Holtenau Germany	Ruttner flask Kemmerer flask Friedinger flask
Foerst Mechanical Specialities 4711 W. North Ave. Chicago 39, Illinois U.S.A.	Kemmerer flask
Wildlife Supply Co. 2200 South Hamilton Street Saginaw, Michigan U.S.A.	Kemmerer flask
Hans Büchi Marktgasse 53 Bern Switzerland	Friedinger flask
Vålas Otterhall Göteborg Sweden	Water sampler
Millipore Filter Corporation Bedford, Massachusetts U.S.A.	Membrane filters
For Europe:	
Millipore Filter Corporation Steenweg op Leuven 1026 Brussels 14 Belgium	
Membrane Filter Ges. Göttingen Germany	Membrane filters
Gelman Instrument Comp. Ann Arbor, Michigan U.S.A.	Glass fibre filters
Selas Flotronics Box 300 Spring House, Pennsylvania U.S.A.	Silver membrane filters

Carl Zeiss Oberkochen/Württ Germany	Colorimeter with fluorimeter attachment Spectrophotometer with fluorimeter attachment Flame spectrophotometer
Dr. Bruno Lange GmbH Hermannstr. 14–18 Berlin 37 Germany	Field colorimeter
Electronic Switchgear (London) Ltd Letchworth, Herts Great Britain	Field conductivity meter
The Lakes Instrument Co. Oaklands, Windermere Westmorland Great Britain	Dissolved O_2-meter with membrane-covered probe
Electronic Instruments Ltd. Richmond, Surrey Great Britain	Dissolved O_2-meter with membrane-covered probe
Honeywell Inc. Wayne and Windrim Avenues Philadelphia U.S.A.	Dissolved O_2-meter with membrane-covered probe
Yellow Springs Instrument Co. Yellow Springs Ohio U.S.A.	Dissolved O_2-meter with membrane-covered probe
Baker Chemical Company Phillipsburg New Jersey U.S.A.	Reagents
British Drug House Ltd. Poole, Dorset Great Britain	Reagents
Bush Beach and Segner Bayley Marlow House, Lloyd's Avenue London E.C.3 Great Britain	Reagents

162

Hach Chemical Company Ames, Iowa U.S.A.	Reagents
Wacker–Chemie GmbH Postfach 1 München Germany	Reagents

IBP TECHNICAL MEETING: CHEMICAL ENVIRONMENT IN THE AQUATIC HABITAT

List of participants and observers

AHL T. Uppsala Universitet, Limnologiska Institutionen, Uppsala, Sweden.
ARMSTRONG F.A. Fisheries Research Board of Canada, Freshwater Institute, 501 University Crescent, Winnipeg 19, Man., Canada.
BEADLE L.C. Blackhill, Sandhoe, Hexham, Northumberland, England.
BURGESS P. Zoology Department, University of Liverpool, Liverpool 3, England.
BUSCH A.W. Rice University, Department of Chemical Engineering, Houston 1, Texas, U.S.A.
CARLUCCI A.F. University of California, Institute of Marine Resources, La Jolla, California, U.S.A.
CASEY H. Freshwater Biological Association, River Laboratory, East Stoke, Wareham, Dorset, England.
COOPER L.H.N. Marine Biological Association, The Laboratory, Citadel Hill, Plymouth, England.
DUSSART B.H. Centre d'Hydrobiologie du CNRS, Gif sur Yvette (S et O), France.
DUURSMA E.K. Musée Océanographique, Monaco-ville, Monaco.
EFFENBERGER M. Forschungsinstitut für Wasserwirtschaft, Praha 6, Podbabská 30, Czechoslovakia.
FOGG G.E. Westfield College, Department of Botany, London N.W.3, England.
FØYN E. Universitetet i Oslo, Institutt for Marin Biologi, Frederiksgatan 3, Oslo 1, Norway.
GIESKES J. Institut für Meereskunde, Kiel, Germany.
GJESSING E.T. Norwegian Institute for Water Research, Blindern-Oslo, Norway.
GOLDMAN C.R. University of California, Department of Zoology, Davis, California, U.S.A.
GOLTERMAN H.L. Hydrobiologisch Instituut, Nieuwersluis, Netherlands.
GRAAF I.DE. Hydrobiologisch Instituut, Nieuwersluis, Netherlands.
HARTLAND-ROWE R. University of Alberta, Department of Biology, Calgary, Canada.
HERON, J. Freshwater Biological Association, The Ferry House, Far Sawrey, Ambleside, Westmorland, England.
HOBBIE J.E. North Carolina State University, School of Agriculture and Life Science, Department of Zoology, Raleigh, U.S.A.
HOGENDIJK C.J. Hydrobiologisch Instituut, Nieuwersluis, Netherlands.
HOLDEN A.V. Freshwater Fisheries Laboratory, Faskally, Pitlochry, Perthshire, Scotland.
HRBÁČEK J. Czechoslovakian Academy of Sciences, Institute of Biology, Vltavská 17, Praha 5, Czechoslovakia.
KLEIJN H.F.W. Laboratorium voor Instrumentele Analyse, Jaffalaan 9, Delft, Netherlands.
KOBAYASHI, J. Ohara Institute for Agricultural Biology, Okayama University, Kurashiki, Japan.
KRAUSE H. Limnologisches Institut der Universität Freiburg, Falkau, Germany.
MONTGOMERY H.A.C. Water Pollution Research Laboratory, Stevenage, Herts, England.
MOED J. Hydrobiologisch Instituut, Nieuwersluis, Netherlands.
NICOLSON, N.J. Water Research Association, Ferry Lane, Medmenham, Marlow, Buckinghamshire, England.
OHLE W. Hydrobiologische Anstalt, Postfach 89 Plön/Holstein, Germany.
OLSEN, S. University of Washington, Laboratory of Radiation Biology, Fisheries Center, Seattle, Washington, U.S.A.
POSTMA H. Nederlands Instituut voor Onderzoek der Zee, Den Helder, Netherlands.
POVOLEDO D. Fisheries Research Board of Canada, Freshwater Institute, 501 University Crescent, Winnipeg 19, Man., Canada.
PROCHÁZKOVÁ L. Czechoslovakian Academy of Sciences, Institute of Biology, Vltavská 17, Praha 5, Czechoslovakia.
RAYMONT J.E.G. Department of Oceanography, The University, Southampton, England.
REBSDORF A. Ferskvandsbiologisk Laboratorium, Hillerød, Danmark.
RZOSKA J. IBP Central Office, 7 Marylebone Road, London N.W.1, England.
SHAPIRO J. Institute of Technology, School of Earth Sciences, Limnological Research Center, Minneapolis, Minnesota, U.S.A.
STANGENBERG M. Wyzsza Szkoła Rolnicza, Zakład Limnologii i Rybactwa, Wrocław, ul. K. Bartla 6, Poland.
SZEKIELDA K.H. Institut für Meereskunde, Kiel, Germany.

VALLENTYNE J.R. Fisheries Research Board of Canada, Freshwater Institute, 501 University Crescent, Winnipeg 19, Man., Canada.

VEGTER F. Hydrobiologisch Instituut, Delta Onderzoek, Yerseke, Netherlands.

VINER A.B. c/o Dr. Lund, Freshwater Biological Association, The Ferry House, Ambleside, Westmorland, England.

WAGNER G. Staatliches Institut für Seenforschung, Langenargen a.B., Germany.

WEIBEZAHN F.H. Universidad Central de Venezuela, Facultad de Ciencias, Escuela de Biologia, Departamento de Hidrobiologia, Caracas, Venezuela.

WHITE E. Zoology Department, University of Liverpool, Liverpool 3, England.

YENTSCH C.S. Nova University, Physical Oceanographic Laboratory, Fort Lauderdale, Florida, U.S.A.

Warning about the dangers of $HCLO_4$ (perchloric acid)

Perchloric acid and its derivatives, at elevated temperatures in contact with organic matter or strong reducing agents, are inflammable and explosive.

The vapour may condense on porous surfaces.

Perchloric acid at elevated temperatures should only be used in a fume cupboard, and then only if the cupboard and exhaust systems are made of non-porous materials which are not attacked by any of the reagents used in the fume cupboard. There must be a strong exhaust direct to the roof. It should be possible to wash the duct and hood.

Operators must wear safety glasses and protective clothing.

The fume cupboard should not be used alternately for work with perchloric acid and volatile organic chemicals.

INDEX

This index is intended merely to supplement the Table of Contents

Conversion Table of Temperature F° to C°

$$\left(\frac{F-32}{9}=\frac{C}{5}\right)$$

F°	0	1	2	3	4	5	6	7	8	9
30	−1·1	−0·6	0·0	0·6	1·1	1·7	2·2	2·8	3·3	3·9
40	4·4	5·0	5·6	6·1	6·7	7·2	7·8	8·3	8·9	9·4
50	10·0	10·6	11·1	11·7	12·2	12·8	13·3	13·9	14·4	15·0
60	15·6	16·1	16·7	17·2	17·8	18·3	18·9	19·4	20·0	20·6
70	21·1	21·7	22·2	22·8	23·3	23·9	24·4	25·0	25·6	26·1
80	26·7	27·2	27·8	28·3	28·9	29·4	30·0	30·6	31·1	31·7
90	32·2	32·8	33·3	33·9	34·4	35·0	35·6	36·1	36·7	37·2